Ben Jonson and the Art of Secrecy

Secrets accomplish their cultural work by distinguishing the knowable from the (at least temporarily) unknowable, those who know from those who don't. Within these distinctions resides an enormous power that Ben Jonson (1572–1637) both deplored and exploited in his art of making plays.

Conspiracies and intrigues are the driving force of Jonson's dramatic universe. Focusing on *Sejanus, His Fall; Volpone, or the Fox; Epicoene, or the Silent Woman; The Alchemist; Catiline, His Conspiracy,* and *Bartholomew Fair,* William Slights places Jonson within the context of the secrecy-ridden culture of the court of King James I and provides illuminating readings of his best-known plays.

Slights draws on the sociology of secrecy, the history of censorship, and the theory of hermeneutics to investigate secrecy, intrigue, and conspiracy as aspects of Jonsonian dramatic form, contemporary court/city/church politics, and textual interpretation. He argues that the tension between concealment and revelation in the plays affords a model for the poise that sustained Jonson in the intricately linked worlds of royal court and commercial theatre and that made him a pivotal figure in the cultural history of early modern England.

Rejecting equally the position that Jonson was a renegade subverter of the *arcana imperii* and that he was a thoroughgoing court apologist, Slights finds that the playwright redraws the lines between private and public discourse for his own and subsequent ages.

WILLIAM W.E. SLIGHTS is a professor in the Department of English, University of Saskatchewan.

Ben Jonson and the Art of Secrecy

William W.E. Slights

UNIVERSITY OF TORONTO PRESS
Toronto Buffalo London

© University of Toronto Press Incorporated 1994
Toronto Buffalo London
Printed in paperback 2014

ISBN 978-0-8020-0462-8 (cloth)
ISBN 978-1-4426-5502-7 (paper)

Printed on acid-free paper

Canadian Cataloguing in Publication Data

Slights, William W. E.
  Ben Jonson and the art of secrecy

  Includes bibliographical references and index.
  ISBN 978-0-8020-0462-8 (bound)   ISBN 978-1-4426-5502-7 (pbk.)

  1. Jonson, Ben, 1573?-1637 – Criticism and
  interpretation.   I. Title.

PR2638.S55 1994   822'.3   C94-931629-6

University of Toronto Press acknowledges the financial assistance to
its publishing program of the Canada Council and the Ontario Arts
Council.

This book has been published with the help of a grant from the
Canadian Federation for the Humanities, using funds provided by
the Social Sciences and Humanities Research Council of Canada.

Contents

Acknowledgments vii
Note on Texts ix
Introduction 3

1 Secret Places in Renaissance Drama 15
2 Mystifying the Tyrant and Enforcing the Text: Impossible Combinations in *Sejanus* 32
3 The Play of Conspiracies in *Volpone* 57
4 Private Lies, Public Notice: *Epicoene* and Theatrical Deception 78
5 The New Face of Secrecy in *The Alchemist* 105
6 Catiline's Conspiracy and the Problem of Containment 130
7 State-Decipherers and Politique Picklockes: Interpretation as Self-Replication in *Bartholomew Fair* 145

Conclusion 171
Notes 179
Works Cited 213
Index 227

Acknowledgments

Nowhere is the Romantic myth of single authorship more roundly given the lie than in the writing of a scholarly book. During the years that I have worked on Ben Jonson, I have incurred a great many debts to agencies, institutions, and individuals. I would like to thank the National Endowment for the Humanities, the University of Saskatchewan President's Fund, and the Social Sciences and Humanities Research Council of Canada for funding that enabled me to complete this study. A generous award from the University of Saskatchewan Publications Fund helped to defray the costs of publication.

In trying to understand what has proprietarily been called the Age of Jonson, I have read a great many rare books, which have been cheerfully supplied by the staffs of the Henry E. Huntington, Folger, Bodleian, and British Libraries. I am grateful to them for all their assistance and to the *University of Toronto Quarterly*, *Medieval and Renaissance Drama in England*, and *Texas Studies in Literature and Language*, published by the University of Texas Press, for permission to reprint the essays which, in revised versions, have become the first three chapters of the present volume.

My father, Joseph Rowe Slights, took the same care in teaching me to read English and American literature as he did in teaching me to hunt and fish. I was first encouraged to track down some of the secrets of Ben Jonson's texts by C.L. Barber, G.B. Evans, and Robert Ornstein, all of whom tried to teach me to make sense and to eschew nonsense. Where I have not succeeded in this, I alone am responsible.

I have been fortunate to have colleagues in three universities who are models of scholarly integrity and achievement. *Primus inter pares* is Raymond B. Waddington, who, without fanfare, showed me how it's done. Judith Rice Henderson has generously lent me books on the English Renaissance, and Raymond Stephanson helped me to sort out the issue of gender in the *Epicoene* chapter. Anthony J. Harding's dedication to the pursuit of the highest standards of literary scholarship has encouraged me in all my work. A long-time family friend and the most literate of my Boy Scout leaders, Richard N. Boulton, still manages to keep my reading from being too specialized.

I am more grateful than I can say to my daughter, Jessica, for having quietly and joyfully gone about pursuing her own career as a reader, literary critic, and scholar over the years while I closeted myself with various bits of this book. Finally I want to thank my wife, Camille Wells Slights, for reading and discussing everything I have written about Jonson. She is, in Jonson's terms, an understander.

Note on Texts

I have used the still-standard *Ben Jonson*, ed. C.H. Herford and Percy and Evelyn Simpson, 11 vols. (Oxford: Oxford University Press, 1925-52) for all Jonson quotations. In the notes it is abbreviated as HSS. Passages from the plays are cited by act, scene, and line, except in the case of *Sejanus* and *Catiline*, where there are no scene divisions.

In quotations from early modern texts I have retained old spelling but have expanded contractions.

Shakespeare references are to *The Riverside Shakespeare*, ed. G. Blakemore Evans, et al (Boston: Houghton Mifflin, 1974).

Ben Jonson and the Art of Secrecy

Introduction

Secrecy touches our lives more than we generally like to admit. Most of our thoughts do not immediately get uttered. Some are simply forgotten, but others we purposely suppress. These are the secrets – perceptions, gossip, memories, dreams – that we keep back until time and audience are right. Some of these secrets contribute to a positive sense of self and to the harmonious continuation of our communities. Others create debilitating suspicions and uncertainties in self and society. All work by creating distinctions – between the knowable and the (at least temporarily) unknowable, between those who know and those who don't. Within these distinctions resides an enormous power that Renaissance dramatists, notable among them Ben Jonson, tapped in the process of making plays, representing a culture to itself, and contriving a fit audience for their work. This book is less concerned with the transhistorical continuities that one might trace through some universalized urge to secrecy than with the most productive part of one playwright's career. Its argument is that the tension between concealment and revelation affords a model for the poise that sustained Ben Jonson in the intricately linked worlds of royal court and commercial theatre during the middle years of his career and that made him such a pivotal figure in the cultural history of early modern England.

The utility of choosing secrecy as a topic or place to begin reading Jonson's middle plays is suggested by three distinct but connected circumstances. First, secrecy is invariably an element in the plots that Jonson, an inveterate collector and renovator of classical intrigue comedy forms, employed in all the plays he wrote between 1603 and 1614. Second, secrecy figures prominently not only in the political dynamics of late Elizabethan and early Jacobean society but also in the way that Jonson constructs this experience in his dramatic entertainments. Third, secrecy is frequently an issue in acts of literary interpretation, in our own day as in Jonson's. Indeed, ante- or anti-poststructuralist criticism (surely a phrase to fuel Jonson's satiric engine) generally insists on finding a submerged or arcane principle of coherence or pattern of reference in texts, however resistant they may be to such an approach. But resisting interpretation is one of the things Jonson's middle plays do best. Thus, the form, ideology, and interpretation of these plays are interdependent within the discourse of secrecy.

The form of Jonson's intrigue plots, like the keeping and communicating of secrets, depends crucially on timing and audience. Without trying to argue that Jonson's plots are all the same – they aren't – we can perhaps make some useful generalizations about their shape as a function of withholding and imparting information at carefully arranged moments. *When* things are known is often as important as *what* is known. Here, then, is a common pattern in the plays but not an invariable one. First, a small band of conspirators – usually two (Sejanus and Livia, Volpone and Mosca), sometimes three (Clerimont, Dauphine, and Truewit; Subtle, Face, and Doll), occasionally more (Catiline and his co-conspirators) – sets the terms of its deception in private. Next, the gulls are initiated into another, diversionary conspiracy that is supposed to gain them some advantage over their rivals. Corbaccio's arrangement with Mosca to buy Volpone's patrimony cheap is a case in point. People are then summoned and sent away at carefully timed intervals so that secrets, while being shared, are also kept. Finally, accident overtakes purpose, revelation displaces concealment, and characters who were initially excluded from the secret sources of power stumble into or are told what the theatre audience would like to think it has known all along (Dauphine's trick in *Epicoene* being the major exception). It is typical of Jonson's plays that few characters benefit in any way from the process of either concealment or revelation. What creates meaning out of this whole procedure is the intersection of purposeful suppression and accidental discovery.

The same point of intersection, necessarily less susceptible to the playwright's deliberate plotting than is the process of dramatic construction that I have just outlined, generates the field of political meanings in Jonson's plays. In his two tragedies of intrigue and conspiracy, Jonson pretends not to be glancing at contemporary struggles, but his demurs do not persuade. No amount of insistence that he is neutrally reproducing a chapter from Roman history can obscure the analogy between Tiberius's debaucheries and his government-by-remote-control and the fears of some Englishmen in 1603-4 that King James would operate in precisely the same way. The highly ambivalent celebration of Rome's preservation by counter-intelligence also closely shadows what we know of Jonson's distaste for state-spying in his own time.

Of course, spying at the highest levels in England did not wait for the accession of James. Although G.R. Elton maintains staunchly that there is only one instance of Thomas Cromwell employing spies in the 1530s, he shows that Cromwell 'spent much time himself on ... police duty,' and under Elizabeth, Sir Francis Walsingham organized one of the most extensive and effective spy networks in Europe.[1] Innumerable secret plots were devised and discovered during the closing decades of the sixteenth century. The Ridolfi Plot, the Guise Plan, and the Babington Conspiracy were some of the more notorious covert forays in the Reformation/Counter-Reformation struggle. In the last years of Elizabeth's reign, Jonson himself was interrogated by Richard Topcliffe, the Protestant equivalent in England of the Grand Inquisitor, and subsequently he fell under further ecclesiastical scrutiny when he converted to Roman Catholicism while in prison for manslaughter. Two years later, in 1600, Jonson would doubtless have heard the fantastic tale of the miraculous deliverance of Scotland's King James VI from the Gowrie conspirators. And in 1606, having himself been caught up in the intense response to the Gunpowder Plot of the preceding year, Jonson travestied the wave of English counterspying paranoia in *Volpone*.[2] Not surprisingly, a good deal of the action and rhetoric of political intrigue was either transferred into or constructed by the popular literature of the period.

The theological politics of the plays are no less intriguing than their court politics. Obviously Jonson makes fun of Tribulation Wholesome and Zeal-of-the-Land Busy for their puritan names and their disturbing combination of religious confidence and shrewd calculation. Still, he seems at times to applaud their principled resistance to the depredations of urban gallantry, self-righteous officialdom, and coarse cheaters. He shared some of their distrust and distaste for popular entertainments that lacked the moral integrity of his own. He was particularly critical of the proliferation of such entertainments as wrestling matches and puppet shows.³ A sometime Catholic, Jonson was also a kind of puritan.⁴

It is a commonplace of criticism that Renaissance religious and political struggles frequently appear in concentrated and heightened form on the stage. While it has long been argued that the theatre was a platform from which authorized views of order and Divine Right were preached, an equally strong case has been made for the theatre as a place of subversion.⁵ That neither of these functions of the theatre ever existed in a pure and exclusive form is suggested by the fact that censored plays were, on occasion, subsequently performed at court, while licensed plays often had one or two speeches excised. Certainly the drama became a focal point for official scrutiny as well as patronage, and playwrights – Jonson included – suffered very real penalties for offending courtly, ecclesiastical, and popular sensibilities.⁶ At least from the period of Christopher Marlowe's involvement with the Elizabethan spy community, whether as agent or double-agent, the theatre played a prominent part in shaping the way English men and women viewed secret conspiracies. One of the circumstances that made the theatre such an attractive site for the agent of subversion, the power-consolidating voice of the establishment, and a broad spectrum of intermediate views was that theatrical texts were remarkably unstable and subject to change by a variety of intervening hands. It is not unusual, for example, for Jonson to have had a collaborator (probably George Chapman) in preparing the acting version of *Sejanus*. What is curious – and more than a bit suspicious – is his insistence in the first published version of the play that he has excised all the contributions of the 'second Pen.'⁷ Words that were spoken on stage and subsequently expunged from the printed text could foster immediate political instability as well as long-term editorial speculation. For all of Jonson's intense desire to control the presentation and reception of his work, the poems, masques, and especially the plays have had a life of their own.

Even less manageable than the religious and socio-political ideas released by Jonson's representations of Jacobean culture is the interpretive capital made from the plays by vulgar, prying, and just plain unforeseen interpreters. Jonson always felt that his work had a better chance of being properly understood by a reading audience than by a theatre audience.⁸ Publishing his *Works* in 1616 measurably increased his chances of being taken seriously as a dramatic poet.

Introduction

But even the printed text was subject to foolish or vicious misconstruction (or so Jonson would have us believe) by those who regarded written discourse as a secret code to be cracked. As he says in the Epistle to *Volpone* about a breed of false interpreters, '*Application, is now, growne a trade with many; and there are, that professe to haue a key for the decyphering euery thing: but let wise and noble persons take heed how they be too credulous, or giue leaue to these inuading interpreters*' (lines 65–8). This theory of interpretation was anathema to Jonson, and he often satirized it. It is worth reviewing the roots of the persistent assumption that the most significant texts contain secrets that the initiate must decipher.

The three main sources of such texts and readings in Jonson's experience were the religious, political, and 'natural' or protoscientific writings of the ancients. The mysteries cloaked by these kinds of writing were called, respectively, the *arcana Dei, arcana imperii,* and *arcana naturae*.[9] Each of these well-known Renaissance categories of secrets came to be represented in Jonson's plays.

Both pagan and Christian religious texts relied on mysterious, metaphorical identifications to transcend the toils of the flesh. While Jonson was no atheist, his scepticism about an art of transcendence is especially evident in his comedies, which consistently represent people's absurd yet powerfully disturbing encounters with the flesh, rather than the mystic transformations that figure more prominently in Shakespeare's Ovid-based comedies. The *arcana Dei* appear frequently in Jonsonian drama as the refuge of scoundrels, and examining these holy mysteries must have raised perplexing questions for the conscientious believer. Likewise, Jonson's political tragedies go a great way toward satirically demystifying the secret origins of political power, the *arcana imperii* of the Roman emperors, but at the same time they insist on holding that profoundly flawed power structure in place. Taking his reader behind the scenes of conspiracy and counter-conspiracy, Jonson strips away the imperial pretence and reveals the often banal basis of power. Still, aggressive, male political control emerges from the plays as the best hope for the kind of traditionalist society that Jonson favoured. Finally, Jonson's attacks on the far-fetched secrets of hermetic science, or natural philosophy, for instance in *Mercury Vindicated from the Alchemists at Court, Volpone,* and *The Alchemist,* leave little doubt about his attitude toward the corpus of occult texts that were revered and earnestly deciphered by certain contemporary men of letters. Yet even as hermetic terminology is pressed into service as the discourse of charlatans, it retains its vitality and powerful fascination for the playwright.

Jonson was not alone in his suspicious fascination with viewing texts – religious, political, scientific, or literary – as treasure troves of intended or unintended secrets. Objections to tortured interpretations came from a broad spectrum of readers, ranging from the highest authority in the land, seeking to protect the secret sources of his own political power, to a plain-speaking writer, trying to wrest a bit of power away from another whom he saw as intellectually pretentious. The views of King James and Thomas Dekker can serve as convenient polarities in this debate. In *Basilikon Doron* James strongly condemns over-readings of the Bible, whether the excesses be Catholic or puritan: 'The Scripture is euer the best interpreter of it selfe; but prease not curiously to seeke out farther then is contained therein; for that were ouer vnmannerly a presumption, to striue to bee further vpon Gods secrets, then he hath will ye be.'[10] Inquiring too closely into one kind of secret might lead to presumptuous challenges of another kind, and James had no desire to have his political methods and prerogatives scrutinized.[11]

When Thomas Dekker celebrated the power of his new monarch in *The Magnificent Entertainment Given to King James* (1604), he noted that the figure he had created to represent *Genius Loci* was a character easily accessible to the common multitude who would witness the spectacle and not a scholarly pastiche such as his rival Ben Jonson produced:

> To make a false flourish here with the borrowed weapons of all the old Maisters of the noble Science of Poesie, and to keepe a tyrannicall coyle, in Anatomizing *Genius*, from head to foote, (only to shew how nimbly we can carue vp the whole messe of the Poets) were to play the Executioner, and to lay our Cities housheld God on the rack, to make him confesse, how many paire of Latin sheets, we haue shaken and cut into shreds to make him a garment. Such feates of Actiuitie are stale, and common among Schollers, (before whome it is protested we come not now (in a Pageant) to Play a Maisters prize) ... .
>
> The multitude is now to be our Audience, whose heads would miserably runne a wooll-gathering, if we doo but offer to breake them with hard words.[12]

In Dekker's view, Jonson is one of those pedants who writes hard words, torturing his subjects with historical research, producing dry, stale entertainments which audiences must first anatomize in order to understand. To this extent, Jonson was viewed by others as an advocate of the mysteries of learning and author of his own problems with inadequate interpreters. For his part, Jonson maintains that discovering a direct path to a politically innocent truth is not only impossible but may not even be desirable.

It is primarily in his capacity as masque writer and courtly aspirant that Jonson has been identified as a dealer in secrets by such critics as Stephen Orgel, D.J. Gordon, and Jonathan Goldberg.[13] Their readings have been aimed at unravelling the skein of mystical identifications with which Jonson tied himself to his royal patron. I propose to trace a different, but connected, thread in Jonson's career as a playwright, his fascination with secrecy, which, while it is not necessarily the same as a fascination for power, often takes the form of hostility to those who would misuse secrets as an avenue to illegitimate control. This involves the dramatist in censure of rogues, civic officials, and rival dramatists but also in a high degree of self-reflexive criticism as he compounds intrigues within his own plots and then berates his audiences for their over-curious interest in such intrigues. Jonson knew the duplicity that often marched under the banner of 'natural' plain-speaking of the kind we have just seen Dekker recommending. Dekker was trying to score a point in his contest with Jonson, just as Silius is in *Sejanus* when he makes his plea for a plain, unadorned application of the law to his case:

> might I inioy it naturall,
> Not taught to speake vnto your present ends,
> Free from thine, his, and all your vnkind handling,
> Furious enforcing, most vniust presuming,
> Malicious, and manifold applying,
> Foule wresting, and impossible construction. (*Sejanus*, III.224-9)

The speaker's attack on a variety of ingenious acts of misinterpretation – enforcing, presuming, applying, wresting – is directed squarely at Tiberean courtly dissimulation and the habit of turning a man's words against him at the moment of political purge. There is more than a bit of Jonson's own life in all this, as he repeatedly dealt in *arcana imperii* (for instance in his masques at court) as well as in frank denunciations of politic picklocks of his texts.

The most fully documented cases of searching plays for offensive and subversive material are those that involve licensing performances and printed scripts. Annabel Patterson's *Censorship and Inter-*

pretation: The Conditions of Writing and Reading in Early Modern England, which touches on Jonson's connections with secrets, both official and unofficial, has helped to instigate a wide-ranging discussion of the history of censorship in and beyond the theatre. Patterson views censorship primarily as a coercive tool of the royal court and as a pre-condition of the printed word that made secret encoding a regular feature of writing and reading in the period. Lois Potter's *Secret Rites and Secret Writing: Royalist Literature, 1641–1660*, while it deals with the period following Jonson's death, relates his plays to the maze of secretly encoded intertextuality constructed during the Interregnum. Potter distinguishes her own study from Patterson's by saying, 'Whereas Patterson sees censorship as *creating* a psychology of secrecy, my concentration on the royalists has led me to see the threat of censorship as only part of a psychological *need* for secrecy.'[14] For Jonson, the officially sanctioned habit of secrecy, threatening enough on its own, appeared to have translated itself into the minds of his private and public theatre audiences. He was well aware that his sustenance came from the powerful at court as well as the apparently powerless in the city, and his quarrel on the subject of secrecy was with both. He knew the full force of the 'psychology of secrecy,' and he represented it on stage in its most enticing and destructive guises. More than any other writer of the period, he implicates his audience in his exploration of secrecy.

Jonson understood that the contest to control secret information and its sources embraces far more than the work of official censors. The very nature of critical response itself offers the consumer of dramatic art something rather like the censor's prerogative to approve or to forbid. Audiences hostile to *Sejanus*, *Epicoene*, and *Catiline* shut down the circulation of these plays in the London theatres as effectively as the censor interfered with the free expression of ideas in *Cynthia's Revels* or *Eastward Ho*.[15] Richard Burt argues in *Licensed by Authority: Ben Jonson and the Discourses of Censorship* that it is impossible to separate court censorship from marketplace censureship. This is not to say that all literary criticism is identical with repressive, pre-publication censorship, but rather that the two activities frequently coexist and may fruitfully be placed on the same continuum of efforts to legitimate some forms of discourse while delegitimating others. In Burt's broad, 'genealogically' derived sense of the term, censorship never ceases.[16] In what amounts to an exercise in critical clear-cutting, Burt discredits the 'liberal humanist oppositional perspective' of Annabel Patterson and the 'moderate

Introduction   11

revisionist perspective' of Richard Dutton (169n1), neither of which, in his view, adequately historicizes the issues surrounding regulation of the verbal arts. He is equally dissatisfied with Marxist critics, who, he claims, deny the possibility of censorship in post-Enlightenment societies as a result of their privileging producers over consumers (70). Burt is especially critical of 'traditional moralistic discourse about censorship,' though he admits that his own approach 'does not (indeed, cannot) entirely escape moral critical terrain' (xi).

My own concerns with Jonson's plays as explorations of the linked discourses of secrecy and revelation reside in distinctly moral critical terrain, more precisely in the province immediately adjoining the land of censorship. In fact, the demesnes of secrecy and censorship overlap in significant places. What is suppressed in the process of censoring a text or performance is being treated as knowledge best left unconveyed; what is censured but continues to circulate becomes the open secret of scandal or sedition; what is approved by the censor or critic has the force of authorized, intensified revelation. In the course of his career Jonson felt both the rebuke and the empowerment that could come from censors and critics. He took heart from his successes at court and in the commercial theatre, and, as he makes clear, for instance in the 'Apologeticall Dialogue' (which the censor excised from *Poetaster*), he lost heart for certain forms and projects when his work was ill received. He tended to blame the poor reception of his work on everybody but himself, but he nonetheless developed a critical turn of mind and style of writing that went well beyond sour grapes and taunts at his detractors. Indeed, Jonson did as much as anyone in his age to publish guidelines, however internally inconsistent, for a critical practice that might shape a more informed reading and play-going audience. Far from opposing censorship and censureship in all its forms, Jonson himself practised both, calling for the boycotting, indeed the burning, of his contemporaries' plays and their authors' mutilation on the grounds that the plays were not worth viewing. Supremely confident of his critical judgments, he never expressed misgivings in his plays, prefaces, or the *Conversations* with Drummond about his way of reading a Dekker comedy, a Chapman tragedy, or a Shakespeare romance, or, for that matter, about the way his own plays should be read.[17]

The Jonson that emerges from the middle plays is less concerned about individual misreadings of his own work than about the erroneous constructions generated in concert by ignorant or malicious audiences of courtiers, city fathers, or just plain citizens. His plots variously deal with conspiracies to commit fraud, murder, and treason, but all his conspirators trade in a single commodity: misinterpretation, that is, failures of the critical faculty. When theatre audiences, puritan exegetes, state spies, or charlatans band together to premeditate an attack on truth and decency, Jonson finds his moral ground, summons his critical defences, and launches his satiric attacks. The pattern is evident in all the plays from his middle period.

The six plays that Jonson wrote in the first half of James's reign in England – *Sejanus His Fall* (1603), *Volpone, or the Fox* (1606), *Epicoene, or the Silent Woman* (1609), *The Alchemist* (1610), *Catiline His Conspiracy* (1611), and *Bartholomew Fair* (1614) – reveal a common concern with the dark side of intrigue.[18] Their typical configuration of characters is the conspiratorial huddle, and their pre-eminent linguistic pattern initially conceals, then reveals, secrets. The plays in this group are not, however, uniform in kind or quality. They differ from one another generically, and the group comprises the best known as well as the least loved of Jonson's plays. Still, there is a kind of integrity to this part of Jonson's career. The interpretive difficulties that bedevil and enrich these six plays are different from those that have troubled critics of the earlier five extant plays (the 'humour plays' or comical satires) and the later five (the so-called 'dotages'). Anne Barton, for example, sees such early plays as *Every Man Out of His Humour* (1599) and *Poetaster* (1601) as plotless satires, conforming to a dangerously undramatic and limiting formula, and the post-*Bartholomew Fair* plays as reversions to the dramatic forms and social values of the great age of Elizabeth. Barton is echoing many Jonson scholars when she argues that the first of Jonson's 'middle' plays is a significant watershed in Jonson's career: '*Sejanus* was for him a crucially important play, the tragic glass into which he needed to look if he was ever to escape from the impasse of the comical satires into the new, and liberating, comic form of *Volpone, Epicoene, The Alchemist* and *Bartholomew Fair*.'[19] While I agree that what Barton refers to as Jonson's liberation during his middle period was partly a matter of certain realignments of literary form, I would also maintain that it resulted from a vigorous response to social, political, and intellectual changes. These changes affected town, country, city, and court, all of them constituencies that Jonson addressed at one

Introduction

time or another. Changing conditions produced new ideas and practices in generating income, regulating society, transmitting texts, mounting entertainments, preserving and spreading religious faith, and asserting individual desires. Some of the changes were welcomed by Jonson; others he mocked and reviled. The ones he found most conducive to creating spectacle in the theatre often were those being promulgated under a cloak of secrecy. Attempts to drape the time's deformity and its simple beauties in fancy gear never failed to stimulate his skills as a playwright and cultural commentator. As I have struggled with the interpretive problems of Jonson's middle plays over the years, I have become convinced that the driving social force, distinctive dramatic techniques, and persistent interpretive puzzles in these plays are related in one way or another to the topic of secrecy.

Jonson was not alone among the dramatists of the Jacobean period in his fascination with secret selves, secret plots, and secret meanings, but his notable successes, and even his spectacular flops, showed other playwrights like Webster and Middleton the dramatic possibilities of secrecy. Shakespeare he both learned from and taught, but his major contribution was to the second rank of dramatists, men such as Chapman and Marston. Jonson's developing of the art of secrecy in drama had an enormous influence: for example, the figure of the intelligencer – the state-employed spy – who emerges, substantial if not prosperous, from *Sejanus*, *Volpone*, and *Catiline*, becomes a vital part of the Italianate revenge plays of the later Jacobean period. As we will see in chapter 1, the wealth of ideas about the self and the state contained in Jacobean plays owes a great deal to a troubled and ambivalent contemporary set of attitudes toward the making, keeping, and sharing of secrets. The attractions of privacy and the revulsion from conspiracy mark the extremes of a broad continuum of possible responses to secrecy. As the Cardinal's mistress in *The Duchess of Malfi* (1613) observes, 'It is an equal fault, / To tell one's secret unto all, or none,' a paradoxical truth with which Jonson had been concerned for some years previous.[20] Secrecy, he had discovered, is a powerful form of communication, one that only incidentally and temporarily entails silence. Secrets are revealed in the plays through eavesdropping scenes, conversations with confidants, soliloquies, and myriad other means. Like Joseph Conrad's secret sharer, Jonson's characters live in dread of being discovered in company with their socially unacceptable alter egos. Unlike Conrad's sea captain, however, they gain little knowledge or power in the process of keeping and sharing their secrets.

Michel Foucault remarks that, looking behind the mask of things, one finds not a 'timeless essential secret, but the secret that they have no essence or that their essence was fabricated in a piecemeal fashion from alien forms.'[21] What has been hidden or masked in Jacobean drama seldom, upon discovery, proves satisfyingly complete. It is certainly the case that instead of an integral alternate self or an eternal essence behind the theatrical mask, Jonson and his fellow playwrights were far more likely to uncover, at worst, a cobbled-together charlatan, poised to flee all social and intellectual responsibilities, at best, a bumbling and baffled would-be adjudicator of madly inconsistent human behaviours.

As a necessary prelude to considering Jonson's artful conspirators and his own art of revealing the complicated workings of secrecy in his middle plays, I will look at the uses to which various forms of secrecy were being put in early modern England. Tracing the translation of what amounts to a cultural fetish of secrecy to the stage inevitably entails an assessment of how Shakespeare, as well as his less influential rivals, treats stage space, historical and fictional narratives of secrecy, and, most important, the emerging sense of the private self, its impenetrable 'inner' secrets and its enormously vulnerable outer body. This is the business of chapter 1.

CHAPTER ONE

Secret Places in Renaissance Drama

'The critic will certainly be an interpreter, but he will not treat Art as a riddling Sphinx, whose shallow secret may be guessed and revealed by one whose feet are wounded and who knows not his name.'

OSCAR WILDE, 'The Critic as Artist'

In 1584 Reginald Scot published his contribution to the minor genre of discovery literature. What he discovered – that is, revealed – to the world was not the mysteries of remote places or the tricks of cardsharps, but the much-feared secrets of witchcraft. He gave over the entire fourth book of his *Discoverie of Witchcraft* to the sexual interventions of witches, including the story of a young man who, under a witch's spell, was made 'to leave his instruments of venerie behind him.' The unfortunate young man had, then, to resort to a second witch

> for restitution thereof who brought him to a tree, where she shewed him a nest, and bad him clime vp and take it. And being in the top of the tree, he tooke out a mightie great one, and shewed the same to hir, asking hir if he might not haue the same. Naie (quoth she) that is our parish preests toole, but take anie other which thou wilt.[1]

The text obviously concerns itself with power – the power of some women to dismember and re-member men at will. In a brilliant piece of ironic deconstruction through reinscription (a version of the story had appeared in the *Malleus maleficarum* of 1486), Scot mocks the scare-tactics of Roman Catholic witch hunters.[2] Clearly, Scot is having fun at the expense of the writers and gullible readers of the *Malleus*: a nest bulging with twenty or thirty penises munching on 'provender, as it were at the rack and manger' (78) is rather silly stuff, even as male fantasies go. In Scot's text, the story has the force of an anticlerical fabliau, albeit one that had in former times been passed off by papists as a pious, cautionary tale. Its secrets are sham.

The impotence/secrecy/women configuration of prejudice was by no means silenced in Renaissance England by Scot's discoveries. Indeed, as Keith Thomas points out, 'The mythology of witchcraft was at its height at a time when women were generally believed to be more sexually voracious than men.'[3] The allure with which women seduced men could easily be conflated with the secret charms used by 'witches' to undo men by rendering them impotent.[4] Accounts of such activities were discreetly set apart from ordinary discourse and hence carried the aura of the Latin *secretum*, separate or set apart. Whether recommending transgression or procreation, the voice that revealed sexual secrets came from beyond the margins of the publicly shared text, whispering an always alternate, sometimes subversive, and usually indeterminate version of the received 'truth' about sex. Considerable power inheres in the indeterminacy of such secrets, and our own age, in which pornography proliferates and the term 'intelligence' is regularly prefaced by the modifier 'secret,' is well situated to assess the workings of such secret power on the Renaissance stage. Secrecy, in our age or Scot's, implicates the privy councils of state along with the privy parts of the body.

In her study entitled *Secrets: On the Ethics of Concealment and Revelation*, Sissela Bok remarks that

> The power of ... secrecy can be immense. Because it bypasses inspection and eludes interference, secrecy is central to the planning of every form of injury to human beings. It cloaks the execution of these plans and wipes out all traces afterward. It enters into all prying and intrusion that cannot be carried out openly. While not all that is secret is meant to deceive ... all deceit does rely on keeping something secret.[5]

The same kind of power that Bok writes about in terms of investigative reporting, espionage, political cover-ups, and other activities that characterize our own culture is echoed repeatedly in Renaissance texts.

But beside this sinister sort of occlusion, there is another, more benign motive for what the anthropologist James Fernandez calls 'the doing of secrets.' In the foreword to a study of West African Poro secret societies entitled *The Language of Secrecy*, Fernandez links secret talk with the creation of 'alternative realities' that are shielded from the enervating banality of ordinary discourse.[6] The promise of these alternative realities stimulates human curiosity and contributes to a social construction of reality far beyond the limits of any informational content the secrets might hold. Renaissance hermeticism, for example, had few earth-shattering revelations to make, and yet there was a surprisingly widespread interest in the work of men like Giordano Bruno and John Dee. Simply the process of writing what could not be written, or reading what could be confided only within strict limits, has held a strong fascination.

An epistemology of secrecy would seem, almost by definition, to be beyond reach, but some working hypotheses may provide at least limited access to the secrets embedded in Renaissance dramatic texts. In recent years, some scientists, not wishing to privilege specific forms of research with the term 'pure,' have come to create a category of projects designated as 'curiosity-driven.' One implication of such a term is that, desiring to know more about the 'secrets of the universe,' these scientists will use their wits and research funds to uncover knowledge that lies beyond our present reach, whether it be in the heart of the atom or the most remote corners of the universe. But that wished-for repository of truths, shrouded in secrecy, is always elsewhere. Through a perennial process of deferral, those totally lucid understandings always elude us. Unlike things you've lost, these meanings are never in the last place you look – or the next place either, though hope springs eternal. Given the contingent nature of language, both concealment and revelation are bound to be partial. However, knowledge that is by definition inaccessible to us is not ordinarily conceived of as secret. Rather, the term 'secret' normally entails an intention to conceal.

Institutions, texts, and speaking subjects can all generate secrets. Institutions such as fraternal orders, armies, and a variety of governmental agencies maintain secret files for the good of those they serve and/or for the perpetuation of their own powers. Texts, be they financial statements of corporations or lyric poems, can contain what my literature students call 'hidden meanings,' that is, unauthored, spontaneously self-generated mysteries accessible only to the fully initiated reader. 'Hidden' has a passive force in this usage, but authors also deliberately conceal meanings, at least for a while, in riddles, codes, and deliberate misstatements. Finally, individual speaking subjects use texts and institutions in a gender-relational way to create or to inquire into secrets. Women not only have secrets, they are often conceived of as actually *being* secrets. But they are also thought to be 'leaky vessels' that cannot for long contain secrets.[7] Men set about to discover the secrets of women while at the same time guarding their own. The real issue is power.

Imparting as well as keeping secrets about economic, political, and sexual matters serves to establish what Fernandez calls 'the various orders and domains of social reality.'[8] Just the fact of possessing secret knowledge confers power, and divulging that special knowledge creates a bond or feeling of intimacy between confider and confidant(e). As a case in point, alchemical writers of the Renaissance were able to establish a dedicated following by titillating their readers with the paradox of publicizing arcane scientific secrets.[9] They recorded in black and white, for even the uninitiated to read, what the African Poro refer to as 'deep talk.'

We should not be surprised that dramatic plots, relying as they do on concealment and revelation for the element of suspense and surprise, should take up secrecy as a prime topos. Not only do plays often thematize their own techniques for withholding and imparting information – asides, fortuitous or surreptitious entrances and exits, eavesdropping, and so forth – they also trade in social, religious, and political secrets – such as sexual excess, clerical fraud, intrigues at court, etc. – whose appearance in plays is the result of inconsistent, financially expedient, or simply indifferent work by the censoring officials. While several studies of censorship have appeared recently, there has been no substantial study of secrecy in relation to Elizabethan and Jacobean drama.[10]

From the time of these plays' first performances, critics have felt powerful impulses to hunt down allusions to particular people, thus treating the texts as cryptograms. Like ancient sarcophagi, the plays are sometimes thought to hold a variety of secret information, partially hidden from view by subtle writers and further obscured by the passage of time. (These bits of information on occasion appear to be something like the 'shallow secrets' so despised by Wilde in the lines I have chosen as epigraph for this chapter.) Instead, I will argue that Renaissance dramatic texts represent both the high value that the culture invested in secrets and also the anxieties that arose from relying so heavily on secret sources of power. These secrets should not, however, be imagined to exist only in some remote past, but rather to be a continually intriguing part of the process by which the play-texts are constituted in the act of reading or staging them.

The drama of the English Renaissance often generates an aura of secrecy around actions involving political conspiracy and sexual intimacy. Playwrights devised special languages to signal the importance of secret information and learned to handle essentially open theatrical space in ways that represented intimate politics and nearly as intimate sex. Let us first consider the languages of secrecy and then the matter of the theatrical space required to stage it.

Letters filled with real confidences and supposed cryptic messages are regularly intercepted and decoded for their adulterous and treacherous intents in this drama. The aside becomes an entirely new form of literary discourse based on the assumption of a reluctant speaker with something to hide, an unfit audience on stage, and an off-stage audience eager to overhear every secret utterance. Not only riddling language and prophecy but also bawdy language becomes a way of speaking the unspeakable, as in the case of Livia's highly eroticized conspiracy to murder her husband in Jonson's *Sejanus*. She hatches the plot in the enclosed garden of her physician, Eudemus, who gloats over her lust for Sejanus as he paints her face:

> Seianvs, for your loue! his very name
> Commandeth aboue Cvpid, or his shafts –
> (LIV. Nay, now yo'haue made it worse. EVD. I'le helpe it straight.)
> And, but pronounc'd, is a sufficient charme
> Against all rumour; and of absolute power
> To satisfie for any ladies honour.
> (LIV. What doe you now, Evdemvs? EVD. Make a light *fucus*,
> To touch you ore withall.) (*Sejanus*, II.65–72)

The passage is replete with *double entendres* that link the deceptions of face-painting with those of illicit sex and eventually with murderous intrigue. By reinscribing the association of sexual with political secrets, an association that is especially prominent in his chief sources, Tacitus and Suetonius, Jonson casts a cloak of classical authority over some extremely prurient material.

Despite the elaborate pretence of unspeakability surrounding sexual experience, no secret knowledge is so openly admitted in Renaissance drama as the imagined insatiability of sexually experienced women. Philip Massinger is being deliberately ironic when he gives the bawd in *The City Madam* (1632) the name of Secret. Displaying none of the discretion that men would like to think characterizes one of her trade, Massinger's Secret betrays the confidences of those most secretive of visitors to London, the foreign diplomats.

> SECRET   I am told
> Two ambassadors are come over: a French monsieur,
> And a Venetian, one of the clarissimi,
> A hot-rein'd marmoset. Their followers,
> For their countries' honor, after a long vacation,
> Will make a full term with us. (*The City Madam*, III.i.24–9)

Conquering London's prostitutes is presented as a point of national honour among these sexual politicians. No secret can stay hidden for long in a play of conspiracies such as *The City Madam, Richard III, Catiline,* or *The White Devil*.

Indeed, it would seem that by its very dialogic nature, the drama in general works against silence and secrecy. Not only do characters divulge secrets to other characters in dialogue, but they reveal a great deal to the audience about themselves, their motives and plans for action through the process of internal dialogue that we know as soliloquy. On a very different level, the original actors revealed the details of the playscript to any audience member engaged in the form of industrial espionage that textual scholars have since dignified by the name of memorial reconstruction. A text that may have existed only as a holograph and perhaps a scribal copy, closely guarded by the principal stockholders of the company, was broadcast into the public domain in every performance. Anyone with a prodigious memory wishing to pirate a play before its publication would have been able to so.

Thus far we have been considering only the verbal aspects of secrecy in Renaissance drama. Each secret assignation requires a theatrical space as well as a special linguistic code. Frequently this space represents a lady's private chambers, as it does in the scene in act III of *The Duchess of Malfi* when Antonio, his secret bride, and her lady-in-waiting find a safe refuge from the prying eyes of the Duchess's brothers. The momentary escape from public scrutiny provides the enabling conditions for an open, affectionate banter about sprawling bedfellows and tousled hair. As Frank Whigham observes, 'The private company of women often seems to constitute a secret place in the midst of male society, a haven where the normal modes of subjection are canceled.'[11] Partly because of the conception of domestic and theatrical space, such sororial enclaves would not have been possible, for example, in early medieval drama. The staging arrangements of a large, undifferentiated acting area (the *platea*) with a few biblically sanctioned architectural places (or *loci*) left Rachel mourning the slaughtered innocents in the open street and Noah's wife spinning with her gossips on a hillside.[12] But with the increasingly private use of space in domestic dwellings of the later Middle Ages and the Renaissance, the number of places for concealment, especially for sexual intimacies, rose sharply. The castle setting described in *The Changeling*, for instance, is a warren of potential places of assignation. An intimate sense of interior space was available in the Jacobean private theatres such as the Phoenix and the Salisbury Court in Whitefriars, where *The Changeling* was performed for a number of years;[13] and even the Elizabethan theatre had its 'discovery space' for scenes of stunning revelation and an elaborate system of doors and traps through which characters could disappear in the nick of time to keep their whereabouts hidden from a searching twin, a pining lover, or a would-be assassin.[14]

The disappearing act is seldom perfect in Renaissance drama; someone always seems to be watching. Spying becomes a familiar technique of the multi-perspectivism of Jacobean and Caroline drama. In eavesdropping scenes, skulking characters gain knowledge, often sexual or political or sometimes both, in full view of an audience but unobserved by anyone else on the stage with them. Jonson puts his eavesdroppers in closets, in rafters, up in trees. Middleton's conceal themselves in lofts and coffins. Shakespeare's pop into the cellarage, behind arrases, into bedroom trunks. With the avidity of an undercover agent, Jachimo records the secret places he observes when he emerges from his place of concealment. His knowledge of Imogen, though not actively carnal, creates havoc in the mind of Posthumus, who is already under attack from the contending political forces in *Cymbeline*. In *The Merry Wives of Windsor*, poor old Falstaff gets caught with his pants down and is unceremoniously shoved into a hamper of what were once called unmentionables, to be hung out with the dirty linen. Each of these theatrical places frames a secret and helps to set this form of discourse physically as well as linguistically apart from all others.

Closer consideration of several dramatic texts of the period may help to establish what their attention to verbal and visual secrecy reveals about the culture that spawned and applauded it, but also feared it. A play such as *The Alchemist* repeatedly makes public things that had been labelled coarse, criminal, subversive, and, hence, unmentionable. Dol Common's foul tongue blurts out the hidden anxieties of a male-dominated criminal subculture that in significant ways mirrors the culture at large. Subtle and Face are nervous about their own secrets slipping out. Being keenly aware that language always says more than the casual speaker imagines, they skilfully exploit those secret places in the text of their victims' speech that Jacques Derrida identifies by the term 'invagination,' that is, the enfolding of signifiers in textual crevices as exciting, intriguing, and in some cases terrifying to a reader as a woman's privy parts to a curious heterosexual man.[15] Jonson's cozeners often capitalize on this male fantasy of sexually enfolded secrets.

Dol Common is encouraged to 'milke [Surly's] *Epididimis*' and to 'Firke, like a flounder; kisse, like a scallop, close: / And tickle him with [her] mother-tongue' (III.iii.22 and 69-70). The mother-tongue speaks the most familiar of languages, but its 'close' or secret caresses can steal everything he has, maybe even his 'instruments of venerie.' In *The Alchemist*, Jonson grotesquely inscribes a male obsession with female lips that secretly embrace the penis, an obsession that Freud powerfully reshaped in the celebrated case of Dora. In so doing, Jonson represents men's fascination with the power of women, a power that he systematically marginalized and stifled in most of his plays. Dol's anatomical explicitness, Dapper's audience with the Queen of Fairy in 'Fortune's privy lodgings,' Subtle's secret alchemical laboratory, and Jonson's own scrupulous unfolding of the invaginated secret senses of underworld slang reveal the dramatist's concern with the hidden sources of power.

Jonson knew very well that secrets can both constitute and subvert authorized truths, that they are, in Tefft's terms, both 'conformative' and 'alienative.' His activities on the margins of the Gunpowder Plot, which he dramatized in the subplot of *Volpone*, would seem to indicate that as a loyal Englishman he fully co-operated with the elite group charged with guarding state secrets and that as a Catholic recusant he knew the vulnerability of the individual conscience to state-authorized intrusion. As John Sweeney has shown, Jonson tried to court and coerce public approval but at the same time remained a deeply private person.[16] His work demonstrates that in each act of revelation there is fresh concealment and in each effort to conceal, some measure of revelation. Elaborate games of hide-and-seek are a prominent feature of his self-presentations in dramatic prologues and inductions, and although we feel that we know much more about Jonson than Shakespeare, the selves he chooses to reveal are as playfully elusive as those of a Mosca or a Face. Like these self-consciously tricky slaves, clothed in a little brief authority, Jonson was not above exploiting what Hamlet in the vulgar terms of his antic disposition calls 'the secret parts of [the strumpet] Fortune' (*Hamlet*, II.ii.235).

Dame Fortune plays her secret parts still more brazenly in later Jacobean tragedy than she does in *Volpone* or *The Alchemist*. The plot of *The Changeling* (1622), for example, is a series of cover-ups for secret sexual liaisons. Beatrice-Joanna's lovers all share a planned obsolescence, and her plans require one secret assignation after another. This plot of dark corners is barely under way before the authors bathe it in the oblique light of parody during an exchange between the jealous old doctor, Alibius, and his madhouse man, Lollio:

> Lollio, I must trust thee with a secret,
> But thou must keep it.
> LOLLIO I was ever close to a secret, sir.
> ALIBIUS ... Lollio, I have a wife.
> LOLLIO Fie, sir, 'tis too late to keep her secret; she's known to be
> married all the town and country over.
> ALIBIUS Thou goest too fast, my Lollio, that knowledge
> I allow no man can be barr'd it;
> But there is a knowledge which is nearer,
> Deeper and sweeter, Lollio.
> LOLLIO Well, sir, let us handle that between you and I.
> ALIBIUS 'Tis that I go about, man; Lollio,
> My wife is young.
> LOLLIO So much the worse to be kept secret, sir.
> ALIBIUS Why, now thou meet'st the substance of the point;
> I am old, Lollio.
> LOLLIO No, sir, 'tis I am old Lollio. (*The Changeling*, I.ii.1-20)

And so the old husband's secret fears open out into a crudely encoded discourse studded with puns about a nearer, deeper, sweeter carnal knowledge that must never be explicitly acknowledged. The sexual violation implicit in their speech acts would seem to sanction the very assaults on his wife's chastity that Alibius seeks to prevent. He complains,

> I would wear my ring on my own finger;
> Whilst it is borrowed it is none of mine
> But his that useth it.

And Lollio replies,

> You must keep it on still then; if it but lie by, one or other will be thrusting into't. (I.ii.27–31)

This articulation of the secrecy topos is the necessary prologue to the moment of revelation when each inner sanctum will be violated.

Alsemero's covert attempt to discover whether his wife has been violated is anticipated by Beatrice-Joanna. In her husband's chamber she finds a manuscript copy of Antonius Mizaldus's *Secrets in Nature* (*De Arcanis Naturae*) and reads about the scientific test for determining 'whether a woman be with child or not' and 'whether a woman be a maid or not' (*The Changeling*, IV.i.24–52). She then sets out to subvert the process by which the arcana were supposed to reveal to men the true state of women's secret places, the maidenhead and the womb. But Beatrice-Joanna is no match for De Flores in ferreting out secrets. His curiosity is penetrating and highly sexual. In the opening scene of the play he proposes to 'Thrust [his] fingers into her sockets' (I.i.230), a phrase echoed and reinforced by Lollio's lines quoted above. One recent critic argues that the puns modulate into a grotesque gesture that he calls 'giving the finger' when De Flores thrusts Alonzo's severed ring finger into Beatrice-Joanna's face.[17] The effect on the audience surely is to add horror to humour in Middleton and Rowley's anatomy of secrecy. Nothing remains hidden. *All* the dirty linen of a self-indulgent society gets hung out to view. As Hamlet remarked twenty years before, 'The players cannot keep counsel, they'll tell all' (III.ii.141–2).

Not all secret motives and plots need to wait for the moment of dramatic climax to be revealed. Each play establishes its own rhythm of concealment and revelation. Some secrets are leaked to the audience along the way in the form of soliloquy and aside for expository or anticipatory purposes. Other crucial bits of information are concealed in order to generate suspense. Scenes of public show alternate with scenes of private conference, both romantic and political, in a reassuring rhythm of concealment and revelation. Although some truths are deliberately obfuscated, others escape suppression and offer the promise of eventual closure through disclosure.

No one knew better how to handle the alternation of withholding and imparting secrets than Shakespeare. He skilfully played off scenes of public ceremony against scenes of private conference in the histories and tragedies.[18] But he also knew how to generate a disturbing sense of threat by collapsing this comfortable rhythm. 'Th' equivocation of the fiend / That lies like truth' in *Macbeth* (V.v.42-3) works through a process of simultaneous revelation and concealment that has since come to be called 'disinformation.' The false sense of security that Macbeth derives from the witches' equivocal speaking helps to build, then to destroy, his tyrannical self-confidence.

The destructive power of lies and evasion is equally evident in *Julius Caesar*, a play that explicitly interrogates the wisdom of politic secrets. The particular issue at hand is political conspiracy and its conflict with private conscience and marital intimacy. Brutus's midnight meeting with the conspirators in act II, scene i, is flanked on either side with touchingly domestic conversations. These private expressions are in turn tainted with the covert political 'figures' and 'fantasies' that torture Brutus's mind. Lucius has found a disturbing note secretly tossed into the window just before the conspirators arrive, and as soon as they leave, Portia challenges the conspiracy with a devastating attack on secrecy in marriage.

Shakespeare retained and highlighted two important details from Plutarch's account of the night's activities in the *Life of Marcus Brutus*: first, that no oath was sworn by the conspirators; second, that Portia invoked her marriage vows as the basis of her claim to be made privy to her husband's intentions. When Shakespeare's Brutus asks his fellow conspirators rhetorically, 'what other bond / Than secret Romans' (II.i.124-5) will be required to safeguard the conspiracy, he is equating secrecy with discretion. Under the circumstances, however, 'discretion' is itself transgressive, alienative, and it is challenged by Portia, not on the public but the personal level. She asks,

> Within the bond of marriage, tell me, Brutus,
> Is it excepted I should know no secrets
> That appertain to you? (*Julius Caesar*, II.i.280-2)

Her language of bond and exceptions and appertaining is legalistic and drives home the point that Brutus has neither the letter nor the spirit of the law on his side.[19] In order to demonstrate that she can suffer any secret knowledge patiently in silence (lines 301-2), Portia wounds herself in the thigh, one of the secret places reserved for Brutus's eyes only. Upon this demonstration, Brutus gives in and promises to share all confidences with his long-suffering spouse.

>   thy bosom shall partake
> The secrets of my breast.
> All my engagements I will construe to thee,
> All the charactery of my sad brows. (305-8)

In these lines the face is figured as an arcane text whose 'charactery' requires construction or close reading, but Brutus continues to regard Portia as a simple woman who lacks skill to read the mind's construction, whether in the face or anywhere else. As his secrets grow more tangled, Brutus becomes increasingly estranged from Portia, eventually losing her as completely as he does his audience at the Forum or the battle at Philippi.

In the character of Portia, Shakespeare has reversed the dramatic representation of women as the subversive, secretive Other. As Jonathan Goldberg points out, Portia successfully contends her exclusion from 'the world where men destroy themselves and each other.'[20] She deals openly with a man she loves, and the secret he eventually shares with her proves fatal to them both. But regardless of what attitude female characters adopt toward men, what appears to be at stake is always male fear. Both Volpone and Corvino fear Celia's honesty; the puritanical Malhereux is terrified of the libertine Franceschina, Marston's Dutch courtesan; and, according to Madelon Gohlke's provocative analysis, referred to above, all of Shakespeare's tragic heroes fear effeminization at the hands of the women in their lives.

In a preponderance of Renaissance plays, the dramatic climax – whether tragic or comic – follows upon the revelation of secret plots or identities. Secrets being too good not to be shared, suspenseful concealment is regularly followed by exciting revelation, however incomplete. Time and again these plays demonstrate the truth of the ancient proverb that two may keep counsel *only* when one is away – that is, done away with, dead.[21] Juliet's nurse – that fountainhead of proverbs – finds occasion to invoke this particular one about secrecy when challenging the trustworthiness of Romeo's servant:

'Two may keep counsel, putting one away' (II.iv.197). On the contrary, however, the catastrophe of *Romeo and Juliet* results most directly not from unwisely revealing a secret, but from withholding one, the clandestine marriage of a Capulet to a Montague. Trustworthiness is not at issue in this play, which treats revelation as an afterthought, simply a part of the dénouement. Everyone keeps counsel honourably – Romeo's servant, Friar Lawrence, the Nurse, Romeo, Juliet. But Juliet takes with her to the grave the secret that she is actually alive, the secret that Friar John was barred from conveying to Romeo. As the lovers serially commit suicide, they each project their relationship into that undiscovered (that is, unrevealed) country beyond life. The two primary secret sharers being dead, Friar Lawrence can publicize the confidential information required for dramatic closure, but it will likely affect the building of monuments more than the conduct of lives.

Secrets have integrative as well as disintegrative functions. In Shakespeare's plays, for example, secrets both tear apart and bind together the institutions of society. These plays explore the common compulsion to share even deadly secrets, a compulsion based on the desire for approval and intimacy. This is true of characters who hold secret information and of those who seek it. Parolles, in *All's Well*, will gladly disclose or even make up military secrets to ingratiate himself with his captors. Portia, as we have just seen, will risk anything to be taken into Brutus's confidence. While women are represented as both passively containing secrets and aggressively probing men's, the men generally flee from intimacy the moment that women ask to know their secrets. They do not want to share their knowledge or their power. Even a basically open character like Othello is terrified to the point of paroxysm that his secret, once out, will ruin his authority in the Cypriot outpost: that is, the secret that he is not, in his cuckoldry fantasy, man enough to satisfy his wife in bed and, furthermore, that a terrifyingly uncivilized and unprofessional fury is rising within him. Prompted by Iago, he fabricates a secret liaison between Desdemona and Michael Cassio that he can imagine to be worse even than his own secrets. Then, and only then, can he act to reassert his power.

Up to this point I have been arguing that secrets destroy trust and generally lead to misunderstandings, both tragic and comic, in Renaissance drama. But secrets also function in positive ways as well. *Much Ado about Nothing* affords an example of the mixed nature of our responses to secrecy in this drama. In order to combat Borachio's secret treachery, Hero's loyal supporters have recourse to a secret of their own, namely that she did not die upon being rejected at the altar. One set of supposes supplants another, and the truth, once discovered by the watch, seems almost incidental and certainly accidental. Still, most secrets come to light one way or another. In the history plays, official accounts of the state of the realm are regularly displaced by commoners whose chief strength is that they will not be bound by official secrets. From Jack Cade's rebellion onward, these 'rude' characters present the plausible alternative view that the emperor may not be wearing any clothes at all. Just such a voice is the Gardener's in *Richard II*. Although he initially casts his political commentary in metaphors of his trade – pruning, weeding, annual sap-letting – and chides his assistant for making explicit the analogy with Richard's rule, he soon falls to revealing the dark intelligence contained in a night-letter to a friend of the Duke of York. This is all news to Richard's eavesdropping queen, who, 'press'd to death through want of speaking' (*Richard II*, III.iv.72), emerges from her place of concealment to say what is hidden in her most secret heart.[22] When she accuses the Gardener of something akin to original sin for contradicting the official version of governmental stability, he protests that he 'speak[s] no more than every one doth know' (III.iv.91). The secret is out: the balance of power has shifted from Richard to Bullingbrook. The corollary to this 'open' secret is the universally acknowledged truth that a king in possession of a great country must be in want of an heir. All that Richard can produce in Pomfret Castle is 'a generation of still-breeding thoughts' (V.v.8). The still-breeding thoughts never have the chance to become part of the body politic; they are, in fact, still-born.[23]

Similar concerns about generation underlie the conspiratorial conflicts of power, romantic as well as political, that flourish among the variously incarcerated characters in *The Tempest*. In this play, secrets are viewed, by turns, with contempt and mystifying appreciation. Antonio's clandestine conspiracy with the King of Naples bears the taint of the primal eldest curse – a brother's betrayal; yet in his account of the past, Prospero speaks in ameliorating awe of the 'secret studies' (*The Tempest*, I.ii.77) that formerly caused his own mind to stray from matters of state in Milan. The signals concerning secrecy in this play are extraordinarily mixed. Sebastian and Antonio's hushed plotting over the sleeping King of Naples, for example, is countered by Prospero and Ariel's eavesdropping. Underlying each clandestine manoeuvre, right down to the clowns' attempted *coup d'état*, is a basic anxiety concerning the patrilineal flow of power. One suspects that such anxieties are part of what made the intimacy of sexual secrets so terrifying to the culture that Shakespeare represented to itself on the stage of the Globe Theatre.

Our sense that the Renaissance stage represented wonderful complexities of character, some of them barely glimpsed, grows partly out of the characters' allusions to a self or selves that exist apart from dialogue and action. The most obvious instance of a character alluding cryptically to a secret self involves the stage convention of disguising. For example, the part or role of Cesario conceals another part of Viola's life that is 'as secret as maidenhead' (*Twelfth Night*, I.v.216), that in fact *is* maidenhead. Her 'woman's part' and her woman's name remain theatrically and sexually impenetrable until the final revelations of identity occur. Likewise Volpone's multiple disguises keep Jonson's protean shape-shifter hidden from all except Mosca, whose knowledge of the 'true' Volpone necessitates the final act of double exposure.

Often the proliferation of possible selves is a function of the text's having at least two distinct audiences who construct quite different realities based on what they have heard a character say. Viola/Cesario's innocuous equivocation, 'My father had a daughter lov'd a man' (II.iv.107), permits her to keep alive one set of fantasies while communicating a very different set of possible meanings to Orsino. Volpone and Mosca, like the three tricksters in *The Alchemist*, have a terrible time keeping their on-stage audiences co-ordinated with the identities they themselves are currently assuming. The audience off stage is generally let in on all the possibilities, and occasionally the 'wrong' character on stage suspects that fake identities are in play. Surly spots the charlatan under the alchemist's ruse, and it may be that Orsino has heard as well as glimpsed the secret sharer of Cesario's personality, the female twin inside him that sparks the Duke's admiration and love.

But there is more at stake in all this than just the Renaissance convention of comic disguising. Paradoxically, the same text is used for the purpose of self-revelation as for self-concealment. Every gesture of self-display is accompanied by a corresponding act of self-disguise that withholds the most precious self from public scrutiny. As Cesario is thrust into the public eye, Viola tries defensively to shrink from view. Characters as diverse as Romeo, Timon, and Prospero appear, particularly at moments of intense stress, to intuit and to speak about aspects of themselves, indeed whole identities, that we had not previously known of. In their moments of self-referentiality, they assert, at least implicitly, that they can construct for themselves identities that are under their control and immune from what Hamlet calls the 'form and pressure' of the times (III.ii.24). As David Miller puts it in his study of Dickens, 'Secrecy would seem to be a mode whose ultimate meaning lies in the subject's formal insistence that he is radically inaccessible to the culture that would otherwise entirely determine him.'[24] There is something reassuring, almost therapeutic about the sense of privacy and inviolability created through this strategy. It postulates an elusive series of potential selves that open out endlessly and provide an alternative to the crushing limitations of what is often perceived as an intrusive, monolithic 'reality.' From the perspective of the theatre audience, each fresh revelation that indicates the inadequacy of our former state of knowledge about a character also creates uncertainty about our present perceptions. Shakespeare's comedies often ask us to enjoy the liberating possibilities of alterity; Jonson's display the disintegrative effect of other selves. In each case the fiction of multiple or layered selves is both exhilarating and unsettling.

The secret or hidden other self as it is represented in Renaissance drama is at best a temporary stay against co-optation, at worst the progressive fragmentation of a Volpone or the malicious reinvention of an Iago. Any sense of self that relies heavily on secrecy suggests unresolved anxieties in the culture which produces that self. Writing about the Ben Jonson corpus, Thomas M. Greene speaks of 'the centered self,' the fixed foot, so to speak, that makes our circle just. Greene may be right that the dramatic satirists of the English Renaissance believe in an ideal, integral self, but what they represent on stage is the disintegration of self in such practisers as Volpone, Jeremy/Face, Ephestian Quomodo, Nymphodoro, and Luke Frugal. Even characters who retain a degree of moral integrity find themselves desperately trying to hold on to a safe, secret self that can transcend the 'pacts and sects of great ones, / That ebb and flow with th' moon.' A powerless and humiliated woman whose name we never learn declares defiantly, 'I am Duchess of Malfi still,' and a dying prince, having nominated his successor, invites yet forestalls further inquiry into the mysteries of his tragedy with the enigmatic line, 'the rest is silence.' The secrets of that silence, like

Viola's sex-combining disguise and the Duchess's enduring stillness, beg to be brought to light through an act of interpretation that allows a wide margin for divination.

Near the end of *The Genesis of Secrecy*, Frank Kermode asks, 'What is the interpreter to make of secrecy considered as a property of all narrative, provided it is suitably attended to?' By way of response, while issuing stern warnings, Kermode promises small, yet rich, gifts.

> Outsiders see but do not perceive. Insiders read and perceive, but always in a different sense. We glimpse the secrecy through the meshes of a text; this is divination, but what is divined is what is visible from our angle. It is a momentary radiance.[25]

Dealing largely with scriptural interpretation as the basis for his model of how we read, Kermode wants the religious resonances of the term 'divination,' the sense of holy mysteries available to the devout reader. But even such aggressively secular texts as some of those I have been considering invite their readers to peer into their interstices, into Kermode's meshes of the (intra)text. Even (and perhaps particularly) in cases where divine revelation is not vouchsafed, we persist in overt acts of textual espionage.

I have been trying to suggest that secrecy was a stock-in-trade of Renaissance dramaturgy and also that it met with severe criticism on the stage. While secrets could be used to hint at the existence of a better world beyond the ordinary one and a self that could be kept safe from intrusion, secrecy was generally represented as 'central to the planning of every form of injury to human beings,' in Sissela Bok's phrase. It was encoded in the dramatic language of riddles, *double entendres*, asides, and soliloquies. It required elaborate strategies for blocking out theatrical space and for defining vantage points that excluded certain audiences from certain knowledge at certain moments. It left its distinctive mark on dramatic design and cut across generic boundaries. It was a cause of censorship in the drama and an artistic response to censorship. It became firmly established as a means for representing and criticizing various structures of authority. Finally, it has become the spur that pricks the sides of our critical intent. Without secrecy, the engaging rhythm of concealment and revelation would vanish from our reading experience. The challenge we take up next is to spy into the secrets of Ben Jonson's texts, there to see just how wounded and how ignorant we are.

CHAPTER TWO

Mystifying the Tyrant and Enforcing the Text: Impossible Combinations in *Sejanus*

The account in Tacitus of Sejanus's fatal loss of favour during the reign of the Emperor Tiberius afforded Jonson a tragic narrative set in a once-vital culture that has taken to shrouding its noble traditions of governance in acts of tyrannical conspiracy. An elaborate maze of official secrets leads eventually to the climactic scene of revelation – the judgment of Sejanus and his dismemberment. While the pattern of concealment and revelation, of secret and discovery, that was to work with such powerful theatrical and satiric force in the great plays of Jonson's middle period is established here, it is not quite brought to life on the stage. As noted earlier, Anne Barton has argued that *Sejanus*, though not in itself a stage success, signals a new departure in Jonson's dramatic art,[1] and I would add that it maps the territory of Jonson's interrogation of institutional as well as personal secrecy.

Silius is the first man to fall victim publicly to the malice that drives the Roman judicial system under Tiberius and his lieutenant, Sejanus. In a futile attempt to expose the senate proceedings against him as a state-inspired conspiracy, Silius calls on his enemies, the consuls, to

> Reueale your selues.
> Alas, I s[c]ent not your confed'racies?
> Your plots, and combinations? I not know
> Minion Seianvs hates me; and that all
> This boast of law, and law, is but a forme,
> A net of Vulcanes filing, a meere ingine,
> To take that life by a pretext of iustice,
> Which you pursue in malice? (III.240–7)

Ordinarily the terms 'confederacy' and 'combination' denote a rebellion against established authority, but Jonson applies them as well to the powers that be, acting in concert to silence a dissident subject. The now-archaic but then more significant term 'combination' had considerable currency in political and ecclesiastical debates of Jonson's day. For example, Archbishop Richard Bancroft applies the term in Jonson's sense to 'our pretended refourmers, the Consistorian Puritanes' in his 1593 work entitled *Daungerous Positions and Proceedings*: 'by reason of their said combination and secretenesse vsed, many thinges lie hidde from those in authority.'[2] The basic idea of an illegal gathering whose proceedings are hidden from the authorities takes on quite a different twist when Jonson applies the term to the convened Roman senate itself. The threat to imperial rule comes from within, from a palace conspiracy engineered by Sejanus for his own advancement, and the threat is countered by another conspiracy between Tiberius and Macro. Although secrets, finally, are more apt to make than to break governments, the celebration of the triumph of imperial stability is at best queasy in *Sejanus*.

Not content to leave his anatomy of power at the safe distance of Roman antiquity, in his address 'To the Readers' in the 1605 quarto of *Sejanus*, Jonson introduces the image of state spies rooting about in 'the *Muses* Gardens, ... their whole Bodies, like Moles, as blindly working vnder Earth to cast any, the least, hilles vpon *Vertue*' (lines 31-3). As a tireless labourer in the Muses' garden, Jonson felt his handiwork as much at risk from the depredations of the government's underground men as do the orators and historians in his play. The parallels between Rome and London evidently did not go unnoticed by the courts of the day, and Jonson was summoned to defend his work.[3]

Before exploring further the fine art of the historical analogy as practised by Jonson, we first need to understand how his arrangement of events in the play and the oddly negative role that he assigns to language generate the inevitability of Jonson's impossibly complex 'combinations,' the inscrutability of the tyrant Tiberius, and the enforcement of meanings on texts as disparate as Cordus's history of the Germanicans and the dismembered body of the aspiring tyrant, Sejanus.

There is a curious disjunction between action and speech in Jonson's tragedy. On one hand, the play is about instrumentality, that is, the thoughtless and inarticulate actions of Tiberius's spies, puppets, and stooges.⁴ They are instructed not to say but to *do* things – to watch silently, to arrest state enemies without explanation, to accuse cryptically, to carry out the emperor's 'justice' swiftly and without apology. On the other hand, the play consists of massive speeches and very little on-stage action. Oratory overwhelms dialogue, so that even on the level of dramatic language, the impression is one of stasis rather than active interchange that constitutes the struggle for power. From our twentieth-century perspective, this is partly an unfortunate result of Jonson's conception of classical tragedy and partly an effective way to represent the impossibility of change within the Tiberian power structure. The play is awash with events, some of them rather exciting, all of them drawn from Roman historians, but none of them significantly altering the predetermined course of Sejanus's rise and fall.

The play's opening act culminates in the admirable but irascible younger Drusus striking Sejanus, calling him, on one hand, an overweening Colossus and on the other, a 'dull camell' (I.564, 568). Sejanus swallows the insults for the time being, preferring carefully plotted future revenge to rash, immediate retaliation. Indeed, Sejanus's strategy of seducing the elder Drusus's wife, Livia, and enlisting her in a plot to poison her husband is already well under way before the violent outburst takes place. As always in this play, conspiracy antedates and vitiates direct action. In act II even the political action centred at the home of Agrippina is drained of its vitality by the realization that her anti-Tiberius movement is thoroughly infiltrated with state spies. As Silius warns Agrippina,

> euery second ghest your tables take,
> Is a fee'd spie, t'obserue who goes, who comes,
> What conference you haue, with whom, where, when,
> What the discourse is, what the lookes, the thoughts
> Of eu'ry person there, they doe extract,
> And make into a substance. (II.444–9)

The process of transforming observation and speculation into 'substance' halts dissident action before it can take shape.

A general and an author inclining toward the Germanican faction are unjustly tried before the senate in act III, thereby establishing Tiberius's tyranny over proponents of both direct action and the written word. Silius boasts his military victories and demands defiantly yet despairingly,

> O, you equall gods,
> Whose iustice not a world of wolfe-turn'd men
> Shall make me to accuse (how ere prouokd)
> Haue I for this so oft engag'd my selfe? (III.250-3)

Silius commits suicide shortly after, permitting the show trials to proceed with the case of the historian Cremutius Cordus, whose annals have been scrutinized by the kind of torturers of the written word whom Jonson denounced so roundly in his own voice ('To the Readers,' lines 29-30). Cordus's accuser and Sejanus's flunky, Satrius Secundus, brands the writer

> a man factious, and dangerous,
> A sower of sedition in the state,
> A turbulent, and discontented spirit,
> Which I will proue from thine owne writings, here,
> The Annal's thou hast publish'd; where thou bit'st
> The present age, and with a vipers tooth,
> Being a member of it, dar'st that ill
> Which neuer yet degenerous bastard did
> Vpon his parent. (III.380-8)

Like William Kinsayder, the venomous persona of John Marston's biting satires on late Elizabethan England, Cordus is said to be poisoning the political body that gave him life. In a massive speech that Jonson boasted to Drummond of having lifted directly from Tacitus,[5] Cordus denies any such construction of his text, beginning, 'So innocent I am of fact, my lords, / As but my words are argu'd' (III.407-8). Despite being able to ridicule the accusing authorities (that is, Sejanus and his spies), Cordus manages only to have his case postponed until the next sitting of the senate and to have his books publicly burned, much as Marston's had been under an order of Council in 1599. Marston's rapid transition from verse satire to stage satire to a church vocation appears fortunate compared to the fate of Cordus, who, Tacitus tells us, killed himself by starvation before his case could be retried.

The remainder of Jonson's third act shows Tiberius and Sejanus conspiring to eliminate certain dissenters while tolerating others, such as Arruntius, who 'only talkes' (II.299). While accepting Sejanus's advice to withdraw from Rome to the Isle of Capri, Tiberius also appoints his next 'instrument,' Macro, to spy on Sejanus in his absence. Act IV is largely given over to establishing Macro as a worthy opponent for Sejanus, indeed as his clone. Tiberius takes the Parasalsian homeopathic line that these two poisons wrestling within the body politic will bring him continued political health.

When the confrontation between the emperor's two poisonous instruments comes in the first half of act V, it reveals a Sejanus as vulnerable to false promises of reconciliation as to superstitious dread. False words and true omens prepare us for the titular hero's final entrapment in the tangles of Tiberius's equivocating letter to the senate establishing his minion's fate. Political decisions and the underlings who play them out are translated into highly vulnerable bodies of text that are first enforced through acts of interpretation and then mutilated beyond recognition. The much-deferred secret in *Sejanus* is how Tiberius will script the fortunes of his second-in-command. The play's characteristic actions of whispering and spying turn the bodies of the emperor's enemies into texts that are forced by the hermeneutic of secrecy to yield up only state-approved meanings and are finally torn to pieces.

Having provided a brief review of what happens in *Sejanus*, I should make some general observations about how these actions are expressed in the play's flood of language. Most notable is the language of secrecy. An extraordinary amount of space is given over to saying what is forbidden to be said and to a characteristic mode of speaking, the whisper. The honest and plain-spoken Agrippina at first protests that she will not alter her behaviour or her speech for all the spies in Rome:

> Were all Tiberivs body stuck with eyes,
> And eu'ry wall, and hanging in my house
> Transparent, as this lawne I weare, or ayre;
> Yea, had Seianvs both his eares as long
> As to my in-most closet: I would hate
> To whisper any thought, or change an act,
> To be made Ivno's riuall. (II.450-6)

Despite her professed distaste for secret speaking, however, her sympathizers have already begun to 'talke in character' (II.334), that is, in secret code, as a way to foil the 'subtill practice' (II.472) being used to infiltrate their gatherings. Arruntius also brands Sejanus and his spies 'subtile whisperers' (III.15).

The subtlety of Sejanus's conversational gambits emerges powerfully as he enlists the aid of Livia's physician, Eudemus, in his efforts to seduce the wife of his arch-enemy, Drusus. Engaging the doctor conspiratorially in man-to-man talk about the secrets of his female patients, Sejanus appears to be whittling away at doctor-patient confidentiality:

> Goe to,
> Yo'are a subtill nation, you Physitians!
> And growne the onely cabinets, in court,
> To ladies priuacies. Faith which of these
> Is the most pleasant lady, in her physicke?
> Come, you are modest now. (I.298-303)[6]

Eudemus coyly refrains from gossip about his patients' excretory and cosmetic habits, but that is not what Sejanus really cares about anyway. Instead, he wishes to use the doctor to convey the message that he is in love with Livia. Having done so, he tells Eudemus, 'I haue put / The secret into thee' (I.347-8), in a way that suggests a kind of surrogate sexual penetration. His entire dalliance with Livia has a surrogate quality, the desired goal being the extraction of secret information from Drusus via his wife, as he explains in a scene-closing soliloquy:

> If Livia will be now corrupted, then
> Thou hast the way, Seianvs, to worke out
> His secrets, who (thou knowest) endures thee not,
> Her husband Drvsvs: and worke against them. (I.369-72)

A man of action, Sejanus is deeply suspicious of political rhetoric. His problem is that he keeps falling into language, allowing his actions and himself to be textualized. He would like to suppress deliberative language altogether. For example, when Tiberius proposes that they consult about how to deal with their political enemies, Sejanus warns,

> Wee shall mispend
> The time of action. Counsels are vnfit
> In businesse, where all rest is more pernicious
> Then rashnesse can be. Acts of this close kind
> Thriue more by execution, then aduice.
> There is no lingring in that worke begun,
> Which cannot praised be, vntill through done. (II.321-7)

His attempt to collapse the space between his scheme and its execution by eliminating all discussion grows out of his conception of power, which in turn keeps him dependent on the language of others. To him, power is identical with praise for deeds accomplished, the kind of words that Tiberius has lavished upon him. But 'close' acts, of the kind they are contemplating against Silius and Cordus, must remain enclosed within a shell of secrecy. They cannot be boasted of or even acknowledged until completed. Even as he gloats over his supposed superiority in secret information, Sejanus hangs on his master's every word. He rushes toward closure, toward the end of his political usefulness and his life, while Tiberius seems to dawdle along through the play, chatting with his intimates, indulging his pleasures, taking an extended vacation from the business of power.

Not that Tiberius is incapable of swift and decisive action when it is called for. Indeed, as he prepares to displace Sejanus with a less independent subordinate, he tells his chosen candidate, Macro, 'We will not take thy answere, but in act' (III.708). Only actions, reported after the fact by 'trusted messengers,' interest Tiberius in this mood. Being Caesar, he finally rejects the equality with another that is implied by the conspiratorial situation that Sejanus has been constructing.

Although he appears to be agreeing with Sejanus about the superfluity of language in the passage from act II that we considered above, Tiberius actually counts on volubility and semiotic indeterminacy to destroy his lieutenant-turned-rival. His nearly one-hundred-line-long letter, read aloud before the senate in act V (and further distinguished by being the only prose lines in Jonson's play), is a tissue of equivocations, ambiguities, and deferrals.[7] Having detailed his manifold gifts to Sejanus at considerable length, he moves toward a tentative conclusion that proves to be no conclusion at all: *'we must thinke, we haue plac'd our benefits ill: and conclude, that, in our choise, either we were wanting to the gods, or the gods to vs'* (V.606-8). The emperor's present view that his benefits were misplaced in Sejanus dissolves into his speculation about whether in making this choice he let down the gods or the gods him. He proceeds immediately to protest that he did not want to change his mind about his favourite but that considerations of state have forced him to. The handwriting on the wall is clear enough that, as the stage direction puts it, '*The Senators shift their places*' away from the formerly magnetic and self-assured Sejanus. Only one senator, Haterius, remains by Sejanus's side, not out of loyalty but because his gouty legs will not permit him to shift as quickly as the winds of politics require. When Tiberius assures the senate that *'it is not our power that shall limit your authoritie, or our fauour, that must corrupt your iustice'*

Tyrant and Text in *Sejanus*

(V.633-5), he means that it *is* his power that will limit their authority and his favour that will corrupt their justice. Such contrary-to-fact disclaimers effectively transfer responsibility for reinterpretation (in this case, complete negation) to the reader of the letter. As in any act of literary deconstruction, the agency of the author is obliterated and responsibility for the text and its consequences devolve upon the interpreter. Tiberius's evasion is complete. He need not even be present for his will to be done.

The matter of interpretation, or 'construction,' as Jonson tends to call it in *Sejanus*, has been admirably analysed by George Rowe, who says in part, 'The ability to deny Romans the intended meanings of their words and actions, to destroy the importance of context and of difference in order to impose a preordained (and usually malicious) significance on what is said and done, is what makes Sejanus and Tiberius so powerful and destructive.'[8] Silius, struggling under the burden of false meanings wrested from his actions, begs to be

> Free from ... all your vnkind handling,
> Furious enforcing, most vniust presuming,
> Malicious, and manifold applying,
> Foule wresting, and impossible construction. (III.226-9)

Such impossible constructions are the work of the impossible combinations of this chapter's title, those unholy and unstable conspiracies of the powerful and the ambitious. Sabinus singles out the ambitious, the 'enuious instruments' of the anti-Germanicans, in his denunciation of the wilful misconstruction of texts. What, he wonders, will become of us:

> when our writings are,
> By any enuious instruments (that dare
> Apply them to the guiltie) made to speake
> What they will haue, to fit their tyrannous wreake?
> When ignorance is scarcely innocence:
> And knowledge made a capitall offence? (IV.132-7)

The offence of knowing what is being said was, as we shall see, a signal crime under the rule of Tiberius, and all professions of innocence were studiously ignored. Intention is not so much obliterated as reconstructed according to the dominant authority. Written texts are transformed into a human body to be twisted into the shape desired by the state censors, 'those common Torturers, that bring all wit to the Rack' ('To the Readers,' lines 29-30). In a stunning reversal of tenor and vehicle within this text/body metaphor, Tiberius reduces men to the level of written words and puts them through the prototypical shredder.

The only person to escape such a fate is Tiberius, and he does so by a deliberate program of obfuscation. His inaccessibility to both 'construction' and 'combination' is represented metaphorically by the enormous empty space between Tiberius's breast (his secret intention) and his lips (the source of his public pronouncements). The occasion of the metaphor is Arruntius's scepticism about a *'forme of speaking'* (Jonson's marginal note at III.93) by which Tiberius has the senators ratify his hypocritical hopes for the prosperity of the line of Germanicus.

> TIB Let fortune giue them nothing; but attend
> Vpon their vertue: and that still come forth
> Greater then hope, and better then their fame.
> Relieue me, Fathers, with your generall voyce.
> SEN *May all the gods consent to* Caesar's *wish,*
> *And adde to any honours, that may crowne*
> *The hopefull issue of* Germanicvs.
> TIB We thanke you, reuerend Fathers, in their right.
> ARR If this were true now! but the space, the space
> Betweene the brest, and lips – Tiberivs heart
> Lyes a thought farder, then another mans. (III.88-98)

That void between breast and lips is the interpretive space in which the other characters vainly attempt to locate, to anticipate, and hence to control the emperor's true desires. Tiberius's secrets remain beyond interpretation by the measure of an unarticulated thought.

The tyranny of self-mystification that is a prominent feature of Jonson's representation of Tiberius derives partly from a remark in Dio Cassius's history. Dio, who often favours psychological analysis over chronological recitation, says that Tiberius 'became angry if anyone gave evidence of understanding him, and he put many to death for no other offense than that of having comprehended him.'[9] Here is a ruler for whom inscrutability is a matter of life or death. To be understood was, for him, to be rendered as powerless as a text before its interpreters. To avoid this fate, he develops an aggressively indeterminate style of expression, one characterized by contradiction and ambiguity, according to the analysis offered by Lepidus:

>   These crosse points
> Of varying letters, and opposing *Consuls*,
> Mingling his honours, and his punishments,
> Fayning now ill, now well, raysing Seianvs,
> And then depressing him, (as now of late
> In all reports we haue it) cannot be
> Emptie of practice: 'Tis Tiberivs arte.
> ...
> His subtilty hath chose this doubling line,
> To hold him euen in. (IV.447-66)

Tiberius has developed into a high art form the rhetoric of the political double-cross. His elaborate riddles (IV.504) keep his would-be interpreters Laco, Pomponius, Minutius, and Terentius grasping at straws as they peruse his letters:

>   TER. I haue here
> His last, and present letters, where he writes him
> The *Partner of his cares*, and *his* Seianvs –
> LAC. But is that true, it is prohibited,
> To sacrifice vnto him? TER. Some such thing
> Caesar makes scruple of, but forbids it not;
> No more then to himselfe: sayes, he could wish
> It were forborne to all. LAC. Is it no other?
> TER. No other, on my trust. For your more surety,
> Here is that letter too. (IV.482-91)

Laco notes a lacuna in the text: Tiberius has omitted Sejanus's titles. Mere haste, responds Pomponius. But is it the emperor's own handwriting, Minutius wants to know. And so the random, inconclusive deconstruction of Tiberius stumbles along, never reaching to that further thought of his than other men's. The *arcana imperii* remain tantalizingly beyond the reach of ordinary mortals. As Jonson's own ruler, the recently installed King James, well knew, state secrets lie at the root of official power and must be carefully guarded.

Michel Foucault argues in *Discipline and Punish* that the public display of subjects' bodies being tortured for threatening the seat of power is the presentational counterpart of what is hidden under the veil of state secrecy.[10] While Foucault's analysis can help us to unpack a great deal of the violence in Jacobean tragedy, it is less useful in the case of *Sejanus* than other plays of the period. Jonson certainly

concerns himself with the instructive spectacle of the body in pain
– sexually violated, sinew-cracked, dismembered – but he understands Tiberius's peculiar genius for keeping his violent physical excesses off the public scaffold.

Jonson constructs the flesh of what Francis Barker calls the tremulous private body[11] on two basic patterns: the obscenely soft, fawning body and the mutilated body. To possess a human form, then, is either disgusting or fearful. Of the first kind are the gooey, overfed bodies of those who have glutted themselves on others' power, those men with 'soft, and glutinous bodies, that can sticke, / Like snailes, on painted walls' (I.8-9). Sejanus himself is thought to be such a one, having attached himself sexually to an obese man at the start of his climb up the painted palace walls. 'I knew him,' declares Arruntius,

> at Caivs trencher, when for hyre,
> He prostituted his abused body
> To that great gourmond, fat Apicivs;
> And was the noted *pathick* of the time. (I.213-16)

In Arruntius's eyes Sejanus has taken on the impress of the degenerate men with whom he associated on his rise to second-rate power. At the apex of his career, Sejanus's body is torn to bits by the angry multitude in a climax that is anticipated by a series of allusions to bodily mutilation.

As a repository for secrets, the human breast is particularly vulnerable to acts of violent intrusion. Such riches are irresistible to those who would discover and dredge them up to public view, if only to debase them. As Silius says of two of Sejanus's clients,

> There be two,
> Know more, then honest councells: whose close brests
> Were they ripp'd vp to light, it would be found
> A poore, and idle sinne, to which their trunkes
> Had not beene made fit organs. (I.23-7)

The secret, once mined, becomes a paltry thing, but the violence of such images suggests the passion for revelation that drives even the best men in this play. Discussing 'the heart of [Sejanus's] designes' (I.251) on the lives of the Germanican heirs, the ordinarily restrained Arruntius explodes in a frenzy of metaphoric anatomizing:

Tyrant and Text in *Sejanus*

> By the gods,
> If I could gesse he had but such a thought,
> My sword should cleaue him downe from head to heart,
> But I would finde it out: and with my hand
> I'ld hurle his panting braine about the ayre,
> In mites, as small as *atomi*, to'vndoe
> The knotted bed – (I.252-8)

Only slightly less gory than Arruntius's imagined brain-splattering assault on Sejanus is Drusus's threat to crucify his bloated body:

> I'le aduance a statue,
> O'your owne bulke; but 't shall be on the crosse:
> Where I will naile your pride, at breadth, and length,
> And cracke those sinnewes, which are yet but stretch'd
> With your swolne fortunes rage. (I.570-4)

There is nothing Christ-like or even vaguely heroic about this broken body. The only bodily 'sacrifice' that Sejanus ever makes for the Roman state takes the form of sodomy, not bravery. Silius may legitimately boast of a Coriolanus-like solitary charge into the enemy troops that left him with 'forward markes, wounds on [his] brest, and face' (III.263).[12] Sejanus, on the other hand, came off from his encounters with only the 'backward ensignes of a slaue' (III.262).

The brutally anatomized sexual, gustatory, excretory, and other functions of the human body render grotesque Sejanus's attempts at self-valorization through the construction of heroic statues to himself. These emblematized forms of Sejanus's body become a focus for political debate in the latter acts of the play, but even they are soon smashed to pieces, thereby presaging the hero's dismemberment. When Tiberius reports that one of the statues 'sends forth / A smoke, as from a fornace, black, and dreadfull,' Sejanus orders that 'the head be taken off,' but this symbolic beheading has already been accomplished, and when it was, 'there leap't out / A great, and monstrous serpent!' (V.29-37). Here, if ever, is a metaphorized human form ripe for interpretive construction. But the available readings are almost too easy, too commonplace, and Sejanus scorns the popular imagination that has superstitiously constructed his monstrosity and destruction. In a brilliant show of antique hybris he defies augury and propels his body rapidly forward to its ultimate textualization and disintegration. The state's inscription of his body will soon be complete.

Writing within a few years of the probable date of composition of *Sejanus*, Edward Forset set down the following prescription for proper statecraft: '*The vttermost extent of mans vnderstanding, can shape no better forme of ordering the affayres of a State, than by marking and matching of the workes of the finger of God, eyther in the larger volume of the vniuersall, or in the abridgement thereof, the body of man.*'[13] The form of the body politic, that is, should be based on a reading of divine creation, both macrocosm and microcosm. The authors of state policy, then, create a kind of mediating text between the vast volume of Nature and the abridged version, man's physical body. The dramatist who represents this process, I want to argue, performs an analogous function, creating texts that mediate between the larger volume of human history and immediate political situations. In *Sejanus*, Jonson's selection and redeployment of ancient history set up parallels with a body of political thought and action in his own time.

Assiduous paralleling has always been the stock-in-trade of political commentators. Great and greatly textualized historical figures from Coriolanus and Alcibiades to Elizabeth I ('I am Richard II. Know ye not that?') attest to this widely acknowledged truth. And the suspicion of politic paralleling falls even on those who are not trying to forge telling political links between the present and remote ages, people like William Hazlitt, who could not ply his trade of literary lecturer and excerpter without worrying that speeches he selected from *Sejanus* might 'look double to squint-eyed suspicion.'[14] The Earl of Northumberland's suspicions may also have been causing him to see double meanings in the play when he had Jonson summoned before the Privy Council in 1603. On the other hand, it may be that any play created from accounts of state secrets and the readily corruptible bodies of Roman princes necessarily would have been read by Jonson's interpretive community as a reflection of the deformities of his own time.[15]

Perhaps no single metaphor appears with such frequency in the political discourse of the period than that linking the state with the human body, sometimes strong and healthy, sometimes deformed. Machiavelli and Guiccardini, François Ier and Jean Bodin, Hooker and Hobbes all exploit this commonplace link between singular man and politic mankind under the aspect of 'natural' form. The particular, though by no means unique, spin that Jonson puts on the body-state metaphor in *Sejanus* is to represent both human and governmental forms as texts for interpretation and, eventually, for obliteration. Just as words can be violently torn out of context and misappropriated, so too can human beings subjected to unscrupulous authority be mutilated and dispensed with in Tiberian Rome. Could such violence against persons and texts have been countenanced in Jacobean England?

On at least one occasion when King James wrote about the metaphor of the body politic, his explication considered the possibility of its mutilation: 'And for the similitude of the head & the body, it may very wel fall out that the head will be forced to garre cut of [i.e. to cause to be cut off] some rotten member ... to keepe the rest of the body in integritie. But what state the body can be in, if the head, for any infirmity that can fall to it, be cut off, I leaue it to the readers judgement.'[16] Not surprisingly, James justifies political dismemberment only of the members. He assumes that no reader could imagine a decapitated state, though within half a century Englishmen would find themselves in one. Well before that bloody period, indeed just shortly after the ill-fated stage première of *Sejanus*, the Earl of Shrewsbury wrote to the Earl of Kent recommending a particularly Draconian way of dealing with the peasants during the Midlands Revolt of 1607: 'Neyther ... use any perswation at all till you have some 40 or 50 horss well apoynted, which will run over and cutt in peeces a thousand of suche naked roges.'[17] The Earl abstracts and objectifies the opposing social inferiors into an unthinkably large number of body parts. His letter highlights similarities between the threats of mutilation that were a feature of the rhetoric of Jacobean aristocratic retribution and the politicized violence of Senecan tragedy and such plays as *Sejanus*, which derives enormous power from a description of dismemberment.

Following book IV of Tacitus's *Annals*, from which Jonson derived most of the story of Sejanus, there occurs a hiatus in the text. The reversal of Sejanus's political fortunes and his violent death are missing from the manuscript sources. Jonson fills in the gap largely from Dio Cassius's *Roman History*, but for the climactic account of his hero's dismemberment, Jonson turns to an entirely different classical life, Claudian's of the tyrant Rufinus. In Claudian he found a detailed account of a Roman mob rending their former leader limb from limb: 'They stamp on that face of greed and while yet he lives pluck out his eyes; others seize and carry off his severed arms. One cuts off his foot, another wrenches a shoulder from the torn sinews; one lays bare the ribs of the cleft spine, another his liver, his heart, his still panting lungs. There is not space enough to satisfy their anger nor room to wreak their hate.'[18] Jonson kept Claudian's text completely intact, representing it not as dramatic action (the Renaissance stage would try the occasional head or hand or heart, but never a whole dismembered body) but as a narrative delivered by one Terentius. Terentius describes the mob, themselves apparently dismembered into 'A thousand heads, / A thousand hands, ten thousand tongues, and voyces' (V.811-12) all at their bloodthirsty work:

> These mounting at his head, these at his face,
> These digging out his eyes, those with his braine,
> Sprinkling themselues, their houses, and their friends;
> Others are met, haue rauish'd thence an arme,
> And deale small pieces of flesh for fauours;
> These with a thigh; this hath cut off his hands;
> And this his feet; these fingers, and these toes;
> That hath his liuer; he his heart: there wants
> Nothing but roome for wrath, and place for hatred! (V.818-26)

What strikes me most forcefully about these lines is not the 'savage coolness of an anatomist,' attributed by Gibbon to Claudian and thence by Herford and the Simpsons to Jonson,[19] but the total absence of the anatomist's systematic and orderly presentation of the human body and its parts. Rather, this human being is a jumble of eyes and toes and livers and odd bits presented as parodies of courtly 'fauours' by some grotesque antimasque's triumphant rout. The economy of the body politic that values heads above toes has been utterly demolished in a moment that Jonson has deliberately prepared his audience for through a pattern of iterative imagery of body parts.[20]

Sejanus and Tiberius have precipitated one of those moments in history when, in Yeats's words, the centre cannot hold. Indeed, there is no centre, no integrity in this political combination or conspiracy, because the body politic that they have constructed is a two-headed monster. The con-spiracy, the act of breathing together (that is, of whispering secrets), is impossible to sustain because the polysemous property of language permits competing versions of what is going on to leak out, no matter how close a watch the conspirators keep.

In her stimulating chapter on *Sejanus*, Gail Kern Paster points to an important connection between the body politic and the body sexual in the play, calling dismemberment 'Sejanus's consummate accomplishment as "noted pathick" [male prostitute] – a final act of submission to the state.'[21] Indeed, dismemberment had been a strategy for representing the eroticized female body in poetry since Petrarch's *Rime sparse*, as Nancy J. Vickers has argued.[22] By *dis*membering the beloved in order to *re*member her, Petrarch set the pattern for subsequent lyric poets' enumeration of idealized but often scattered female body parts – eyes, arms, hair, feet. According to Vickers, the technique of fragmenting the female Other through textualization is an attempt to counter a threat felt by men. It also serves as a response to political threats in *Sejanus*.

The body politic in *Sejanus* has not just been turned topsy-turvy or inside out. It has been chopped into messes, and there is no telling head from foot, inside from out. Sejanus, the man who would be king, has effectively been marginalized through a textual strategy that Jonson initiates early in the play and expands as he builds toward the play's climax. An example of what I have called textualization occurs in act IV when a senator of Sejanus's faction refers to 'Fresh leaues of titles' and 'large inscriptions' (IV.430), Tiberius's most recent addenda to the already lengthy text of his current court favourite's honours. This process of inscribing Sejanus reaches its point of crisis in Tiberius's 'huge, long, worded letter' to the senate in act V. There, Sejanus, who had for some time permitted himself to become the epistolary creation of the absent emperor, falls prey to Tiberius's intentional verbal ambiguity, a 'doubling line' (to borrow Lepidus's earlier phrase [IV.465]), praising him on one hand and damning him on the other in a pyrotechnic display of self-deconstructing prose.

In *Sejanus* the authorizing power is so inaccessible as to make it irresistible. There is no choice for Silius, Cordus, and Sejanus but to become footnotes in the great, self-authored life of Tiberius. On the matter of Tiberius's political stability, I differ considerably from those who believe that Tiberius is seriously threatened by Sejanus or any other political dissident.[23] His word alone is finally heard. Competing texts such as Cordus's annals, as we noted earlier, are suppressed, indeed, sought out and burned.

The political threat posed by texts and textualizing was a crucial question for Jonson in 1603, when *Sejanus* was first performed, and it claims a central place in the play, namely Cordus's lengthy trial in act III, which we examined earlier. Writers were forging and (selectively) revealing their political agendas by authorizing the texts they chose to cite, by the historical events they chose to represent, even by the literary styles they chose to adopt. Jonson, aspiring writer of panegyrics for the new monarch, was textualizing his political self in *Sejanus*, and he must have been aware of the risks he was running.[24] Anxiety that his plays would be misconstrued came from two opposite directions. If he feared that ordinary audiences would not be able to interpret his work,[25] he worried equally that state spies would. Like political prisoners, texts were racked until they revealed the plot (or character parallels or incitements) suspected by state-authorized interpreters. This was to have one's political self retextualized in the most dangerous way. The best defence against this political reinscription was, Jonson discovered, to craft his own texts with extreme caution, a form of self-censorship that went beyond tact. A recusant whose career had been dogged fiercely by government spies and who had spent much of his life as soldier and writer living on the margins of society, Jonson hit, for example, on the expedient of wrapping his Tacitean tragedy in a protective cloak of textual accuracy and antiquity. To this end, he published the quarto of *Sejanus* (1605) in a heavily marginated form that identified his sources so as 'to shew [his] integrity in the *Story*.'[26] The marginal annotations insulated him in a technical sense from charges of self-interest, but as author, Jonson was never simply a transparent glass allowing a clear view of a hermetically sealed political antiquity. As Annabel Patterson has pointed out, Jonson was not arguing in Cordus's courtroom defence for what Jonas Barish calls the 'disinterestedness of historical writing' but rather for monarchial toleration of a wide spectrum of historical biases.[27] Jonson, that is, felt the need to be no more 'objective' than his sources as he went about his task of redrafting ancient histories for the modern stage. For the humanist, the basic needs and values of people living in a civilized community do not change radically over twelve hundred years. Nor do the oppressive tactics of rulers and government censors. It was this latter perception that made Jonson very nervous indeed. His primary concern was not to detextualize history and the self but to control contextually the derivable meanings and applications of a variety of texts. This is an important function of his dedications, prefaces, inductions, epilogues, and marginalia. We will trace some of the reasons for his caution more fully in conjunction with *Volpone*, but for now we should keep in mind that, being in several key senses a more marginal writer than Shakespeare or even Middleton – religiously, aesthetically, financially – Jonson felt the greater pressure to control the published word.

The kind of anxiety at being relegated to the edges of court society and harassed by ecclesiastical authorities that has been extensively documented in the case of John Donne likewise coloured Jonson's life and work, particularly his representation of such political dissidents as Sejanus and Catiline.[28] In the case of the former he began with a figure of only marginal significance to the overall career of Tacitus's Tiberius, and at the dramatic climax of his play, he showed that figure being ruthlessly shoved to the edges of power through the agency of a letter.

Tiberius's letter, written from his place of lecherous retirement on the Isle of Capri, is a masterpiece of reinscribing his political lackeys with the complicity of his audience, the Roman senate. He begins by claiming as his own precisely the defence of liberty of the press enunciated by Cordus during what was basically a censorship trial. Cordus had argued that the virtuous ruler should permit and then ignore slanderous reports: 'obloquies / If they despised bee, they dye suppresst, / But, if with rage acknowledg'd, they are confest' (IV.439–41). Tiberius disarms potential accusations of intolerance in advance by announcing in his letter that he is busily ignoring criticism of his protracted absence from Rome: *'Neyther doe these common rumors of many, and infamous libels published against our retirement, at all afflict vs; being born more out of mens ignorance, then their malice: and will, neglected, finde their owne grave quickly; whereas too sensibly acknowledg'd, it would make their obloquie ours'* (V.556–61). Tiberius then raises point after point against his supposed favourite, Sejanus, culminating in a reference to that overreacher's ambition to become great Caesar's son-in-law. By turns the letter suggests that Tiberius is tempted to treat these crimes leniently, perhaps too leniently, and that the senate is free to take a harder line. In his *'long doubtfull letter'* ('The Argument,' line 36), Tiberius presents himself as a study in ambiguity. As Giovanni Manzini writes of Tiberius, 'One while he praised *Sejanus* in his letters, and yet sometime writing backe hee blamed him, magnified other of his favourites, and depressed others: To conclude, the whole Court depended on the uncertainty of his practises, which had nothing regall in them, but doublenesse.'[29] Tiberius is of at least two minds and, having pointed the way for Sejanus's punishment, allows the senate to act for him. In language derived from a letter quoted by Tacitus and Suetonius, Tiberius records his feigned, 'damned-if-I-know-what-to-do' sense of impotence: *'What wee should say, or rather what we should not say, Lords of the Senate, if this* [reported accusation against Sejanus] *bee true, our gods, and goddesses confound vs if we know!'* (V.604–6). But senators know what to do in a case like this. To the delight of Arruntius, allowed court fool and cynical presenter of the scene, they slip and slide and creep away from the infected Sejanus. Macro, Tiberius's new puppet, enters to continue the business of marginalizing Sejanus, a procedure that ends, as we have seen, with his literal dismemberment.

It will have become clear by this point that the making and marring of texts, bodies, and state power in *Sejanus* is in the hands of men only. Sometimes they band together in secret 'combinations,' drawing their strength from inside information and carefully excluding political adversaries, senators (even of their own faction), and women. The information is gathered from spies and informants, men whose motives are seldom made clear but who occasionally invoke loyalty to the state as their excuse for personal treachery. Knowledge gained by such secret means sends waves of anxiety through those excluded from public power and still greater waves of confidence through those, like Sejanus, who believe themselves firmly entrenched in the inner circle of decision-makers. These, at least, seem to be the consequences of an epistemology of male conspiracy run successfully from the top down.

But these particular combinations prove impossible to maintain. Shared confidences work against the still deeper epistemology of secrecy, and the conspiracies begin to break down. What had originally seemed a stable, efficient combination of political members – represented partly by the texts of certain Roman writers and partly by the physical body of Tiberius's political creature, Sejanus – is torn asunder in a violent explosion that affects Roman men and women alike. Jealousy and competition over the possession of women, physical prowess, and the accumulation of imperial favours destabilize the various state cabals from below, while the urge from above to deny information to others leads to the formation of fresh alliances and eventually to each man's withdrawing into the cocoon of his own private indulgences. The available options are to remain tight-lipped or, following Tiberius's model, to speak in puzzlingly non-directive directives. What looks, then, at first blush, like a generally progressivist critique of Tiberius's reign of terror finally permits the man with real power to perpetuate it with a highly effective combination of silence and indirection. Jonson's appeal for the historian's privilege (Cordus's and his own) rests firmly on a foundation of aristocratic, meritocratic, and patriarchal prerogative. His version of legitimate discourse acknowledges the power as well as the perniciousness of self-stabilizing rule.

The handful of female characters in *Sejanus* are incapable of either available strategy for self-maintenance, silence or indirection. The men in power either use these women and cast them aside or simply cast them aside without bothering to use them. Livia, wife of Drusus, Senior, falls into the first category, the used and discarded. In chapter 1 we observed her cosmetic concerns and her willingness to betray her husband's secrets to Sejanus. She is portrayed as being totally, vainly vulnerable to the blandishments of the rising young star in the government of Rome. And Sejanus loses no opportunity to point out that her own husband has, by comparison, completely lost his brilliance.

> Such a spirit as yours,
> Was not created for the idle second
> To a poore flash, as Drvsvs; but to shine
> Bright, as the Moone, among the lesser lights,
> And share the sou'raigntie of all the world.
> Then Livia triumphs in her proper spheare,
> When shee, and her Seianvs shall diuide
> The name of Caesar; and Avgvsta's starre
> Be dimm'd with glorie of a brighter beame:
> When Agrippina's fires are quite extinct,
> And the scarce-seene Tiberivs borrowes all
> His little light from vs, whose folded armes
> Shall make one perfect orbe. (II.33-45)

His fantasy of their perfect political and sexual 'orbe,' purged of all grosser elements (the flash-in-the-pan Drusus, the over-the-hill Augusta and Agrippina, the lesser satellite Tiberius), is the heterosexual counterpart of the male bonding that characterizes the play's other 'combinations.' But the flight of Sejanus's astronomical rhetoric is immediately interrupted by the knock on the door that is the final terror of all who live in a state driven by secrecy. 'Who's that? ... / Looke, 'tis not Drvsvs? Ladie, doe not feare,' says Sejanus, terrified, then scrambling to recover his manly control of the situation, of the woman. But Livia doesn't need his reassurances: 'Not I, my lord. My feare, and loue of him / Left me at once' (II.45-8). Even in the midst of an adulterous assignation, Livia is more open and straightforward than Sejanus. She knows where she stands and says so, while the fearful Sejanus, by contrast, hops to the summons of his emperor. While not a flattering representative of women, Jonson's Livia appears to know her own mind, and the treachery of her actions is partly drawn off onto her sycophantic physician, Eudemus. It is Eudemus who, having (s)lavishly praised her transfer of affections and loyalties from Drusus to Sejanus, concludes that her actions are so wise that she will be regarded as other than a woman:

> The ages that succeed, and stand far off
> To gaze at your high prudence, shall admire
> And reckon it an act, without your sexe:
> It hath that rare apparance. (II.91-4)

Despite Eudemus's feeble effort to upgrade (in his eyes) her sex to male, Livia remains firmly fixed in the audience's mind as the woman who gets a make-over on stage in act II and then is heard from no more.

More promising as a sincere and forceful opponent of the reign of secrecy is Sosia, wife to Silius. On his way to his death before the senate, Silius commends Sosia to the keeping of Agrippina, whom, he says, his wife admires faithfully. But Sosia is something of a loose cannon, pronouncing her Germanican allegiance without regard to the consequences for all concerned:

> shee is bold, and free of speech,
> Earnest to vtter what her zealous thought
> Trauailes withall, in honour of your house;
> Which act, as it is simply borne in her,
> Pertakes of loue, and honesty, but may,
> By th'ouer-often, and vnseason'd vse,
> Turne to your losse, and danger. (II.436-42)

In a highly gendered metaphor, Sosia's guileless thoughts 'trauaile' to give birth to weighty political matters. Her untutored tongue is free but also dangerous. In point of fact, however, Jonson gives Sosia only one half-line in the entire play, an approving finish to Nero's line about a suitable reception for Sejanus's informants:

> NER. 'Twere best rip forth their tongues, seare out their eies,
> When next they come. SOS. A fit reward for spies. (II.477-8)

The passion to mutilate the oppressors is, as we have seen, focused finally on the person of Sejanus. As for Sosia, she is heard of only once more, in a list of victims of Tiberius's and Sejanus's all-consuming lusts (IV.20). Like the other women in the play, she becomes mere text, a reported, absent presence, a bit of recent history.

The most important woman in the history of the period is Agrippina, widow of Germanicus, mother of the opposition to Sejanus, and a prominent figure in Jonson's play. She and her friends bear the brunt of the spying and the tireless construction of accusations used to enforce male power. Being a woman of wit as well as principle, she enjoys for a moment the possibility of baffling her accusers by actually doing some of the horrendous things she is said to be doing, but finally she acknowledges that she is an offence to the state simply by being. She begins her meditation by recommending that her particular 'combination' be dissolved as being impossible to maintain:

> Let vs fall apart:
> Not, in our ruines, sepulchre our friends.
> Or shall we doe some action, like offence,
> To mocke their studies, that would make vs faultie?
> And frustrate practice, by preuenting it?
> The danger's like: for, what they can contriue,
> They will make good. No innocence is safe,
> When power contests. Nor can they trespasse more,
> Whose only being was all crime, before. (IV.34–42)

The contestation of power to which she refers denies the difference between guilt and innocence. Indeed, in the wake of the slaughter of Sejanus, the multitude, having been loosed at Tiberius's implicit behest, turn their ferocity on Sejanus's children:

> A sonne, and daughter, to the dead Seianvs,
> (Of whom there is not now so much remayning
> As would giue fastning to the hang-mans hooke)
> Haue they drawne forth for farder sacrifice;
> Whose tendernesse of knowledge, vnripe yeares,
> And childish silly innocence was such,
> As scarse would lend them feeling of their danger:
> The girle so simple, as shee often askt,
> *Where they would lead her? for what cause they drag'd her?*
> Cry'd, *shee would doe no more. That shee could take*
> *Warning with beating.* (V.839–49)

The girl's offer to accept a beating and promise never to repeat the wickedness that in fact she had not committed figures not only the naïveté of children and the accepted violence against women, but the victimizing of all subjects outside the secret circle of male power. The nuntius continues his tale of the rape of innocence, laying a grotesque perversion of Roman statutes at the feet of the new tyrant, Macro.

> And because our lawes
> Admit no virgin immature to die,
> The wittily, and strangely-cruell Macro,
> Deliuer'd her to be deflowr'd, and spoil'd,
> By the rude lust of the licentious hang-man,
> Then, to be strangled with her harmlesse brother. (V.849-54)

Here is the antithesis of Foucault's spectacle of the scaffold: state authorized child-pornography in the form of 'snuff' theater that makes no attempt to legitimize power, only brutally to use it. The children's mother, Apicata, finds her children's bodies 'spred on the degrees' of the Gemonian Steps (V.860) and offers up a shattering lament which, in Jonson's play, far outstrips anything in his source:

> After a world of furie on her selfe,
> Tearing her haire, defacing of her face,
> Beating her brests, and wombe, kneeling amaz'd,
> Crying to heauen, then to them; at last,
> Her drowned voyce gate vp aboue her woes:
> And with such black, and bitter execrations,
> (As might affright the gods, and force the sunne
> Runne back-ward to the east, nay, make the old
> Deformed Chaos rise againe, t' ore-whelme
> Them, vs, and all the world) shee fills the aire;
> Vpbraids the heauens with their partiall doomes,
> Defies their tyrannous power, and demands,
> What shee, and those poore innocents haue transgress'd,
> That they must suffer such a share in vengeance. (V.861-74)

A terrible feature of this stunning lament is that Apicata has no voice in it. She has been textualized into third-person narration to be delivered by a nameless messenger in the grand manner of ancient tragedy. However pitiful the plight of women in *Sejanus*, it is a plight largely appropriated by male voices.[30]

The most prominent female figure in Jonson's dramatic climax is Dame Fortune,[31] and she too speaks through a male intermediary, the flamen or priest:

> *Great mother* Fortvne, *Queene of humane state,*
> *Rectresse of action, Arbitresse of fate,*

> *To whom all sway, all power, all empire bowes,*
> *Be present, and propitious to our vowes.* (V.178–81)

But the statue on the altar of the 'Queene of the humane state' turns away from the representatives of the Roman state, striking terror into the hearts of all except Sejanus, who sneeringly calls her a 'peeuish gigglot' or harlot (V.206). His mocking interpretation of the prodigy is that Dame Fortune turned away in shame before his own superior deity. Lepidus further debases and demystifies the goddess, attributing her power solely to men's folly. Asked who would trust in her, he replies,

> They, that would make
> Themselues her spoile: and foolishly forget,
> When shee doth flatter, that shee comes to prey.
> Fortune, thou hadst no deitie, if men
> Had wisedome: we haue placed thee so high,
> By fond beliefe in thy felicitie. (V.730–5)

The last vestige of female authority having been stripped away, the stage is set for the public rape and execution of Sejanus's daughter.

Jonson continued to exclude women from the effective power combinations in his next two plays, *Volpone* and *Epicoene*, the latter being an elaborate joke about the silent woman. Conspiracies continue to dominate the dynamics of these plays and to suggest, as they had in *Sejanus*, parallels with the tastes and values of Jacobean London. Particularly suggestive in this regard is the Sir Politique Wouldbee subplot in *Volpone*, an action that we will see raises complicated issues of state paranoia and counter-intelligence.

The element of suspicion that is endemic to conspiratorial actions in Jonson's Roman tragedy takes slightly different forms in the succeeding comedies, but it keeps pulling men out of the combinations that had both fostered secrecy and engendered the impulse to share secrets beyond the bounds of the conspiring group. This impulse is at the root of the distrust of language shared by Jonson's most brilliant manipulators of power. While Tiberius carries out his program of violating others' bodies by representing himself as remote from his ambiguous judgments and directives, Volpone represents himself to the world as deceased, and, unlike Tiberius, relinquishes power to his servant. The drive toward self-cancellation that Jonson represents in societies controlled by secrecy creates, in both plays, a sharp, though not an undermining, critique of aristocratic authority.

CHAPTER THREE

The Play of Conspiracies in *Volpone*

At the heart of the representation of self on the seventeenth-century English stage lies a secret, or rather, a series of secrets. We have seen that the self is conceived of in plays such as *Sejanus* and *The Changeling* as an area of knowledge to be carefully guarded and to be shared only at enormous risk. Secrecy is the last bastion of self-preservation for the imperial minion, Sejanus, plotting his coup against his mentor, just as it is for Beatrice-Joanna, moving through the deadly changes of her wedding dance. Images of self-realization, especially in tragedies of the period, feature isolation from, not integration with, the ambient culture. The outcasts of myth, fiction, and history who knew how to keep their own counsel figure prominently among the models of tragic self-definition whether for military deeds, like Coriolanus, or domestic ones, like the Duchess of Malfi. The much misunderstood, often dubious centre of their power is their integrity, the part of their existence that cannot be shared with mother or brother, spouse or lover. This is the secret of self-preservation.

But if it promises to preserve the inviolability of the self, secrecy also creates the occasions for self-publication, the sharing of powerful secrets. As the tension of silence and private conspiracy mounts, and intrigue overtakes the larger commonwealth, the individual proves incapable of containing him- or herself. The force behind the scenes – for example, Mosca behind Volpone's deceits in the play we turn to next – is impelled into the public arena by a powerful sense of self that requires, in theatrical terms, an audience.

Secrecy is central not only 'to the planning of every form of injury to human beings,' as Sissela Bok maintains, but also to the complementary, sometimes conflicting, desires for self-protection and self-publication and to the impulse to interpret texts and the authors imagined to lie behind them. Integral to such plays as *Sejanus*, *Volpone*, and *Catiline* is the rhythm of concealment and revelation that informs the production and reading of any written text. The theatre is, in one sense, an extension of the dramatist's text, its voicing and enactment. While English Renaissance plays were themselves texts, in the first instance, highly unstable scripts used in the playhouses, they also *contained* texts in the form of embedded letters, plays-within-plays, and what I have called 'textualized' characters. Behind the characters, written and animated, in Jonson's texts, are concealed private desires, aspirations often critical of the state and strongly reminiscent of the conflicts of individual and public polities that dot early seventeenth-century English history. The interplay of *Volpone* and the Gunpowder Plot is a revealing case in point.

In 1980 at the Oxford Playhouse, Nigel Levaillant played Volpone with his legs in that unnaturally turned-out position characteristic of tight-rope walkers, ballet dancers, and swordsmen. He tilted his head just so, as though posing for a vaguely inspirational portrait, and he caressed certain strategically placed words in Jonson's blank verse lines with richly operatic tones. I mean he *hammed* his way – stylishly, successfully – through the first three acts. And he took his cue for theatricality directly from Jonson's text:

> What should I doe
> But cocker vp my *genius* ...? (I.i.70-1)

> Now, my fain'd cough, my phthisick, and my gout,
> My apoplexie, palsie, and catarrhes,
> Helpe, with your forced functions, this my posture,
> Wherein, this three yeere, I haue milk'd their hopes. (I.ii.124-7)

> But, were they gull'd
> With a beliefe, that I was Scoto? MOS. Sir,
> Scoto himselfe could hardly haue distinguish'd! (II.iv.34-6)

> I am, now, as fresh,
> As hot, as high, and in as iouiall plight,
> As when (in that so celebrated *scene*,
> At recitation of our *comoedie*,

> For entertainement of the great Valoys)
> I acted yong Antinous; and attracted
> The eyes, and eares of all the ladies, present,
> T'admire each gracefull gesture, note, and footing. (III.vii.157-64)

If there was one thing that Volpone and Mr Levaillant enjoyed doing, it was performing. So exclusive was their absorption in acting that one felt right from the start that, while histrionics was the actor's bread and butter, it would be the Magnifico's undoing. Given enough time, Volpone would, and did, upstage himself.

But Volpone's theatrical genius has perhaps been overstated in the critical literature and in production. In fact, the character-actor analogy is somewhat inaccurate because the success of Volpone's performance depends on his *not* being recognized as a performer by the other characters. Furthermore, *all* the characters, not just Volpone, disguise their true desires and intentions in their attempts to control others. The real crux of the matter, then, is not so much Volpone's theatricality as the largely unquestioned assumption that men and women in the world of this play will pursue their own goals in secret. Secrecy is the societally condoned habit of mind that intensifies greed, lust, affectation, and mistrust. The dramatic mimesis of secrecy in *Volpone* is conspiracy, in which a small group schemes together secretly to deceive the rest of society. In each conspiracy Jonson uses techniques of the theater – disguise, plotting, and suspense – to comment satirically on those hidden forms of social intercourse invented and perpetuated by people for self-serving ends. In place of a shared community of interests, *Volpone* postulates a rivalry of conflicting ones, pursued through fraudulent shows of mutual concern. An interlocking set of conspiracies creates a distinctive pattern of personality and plot in *Volpone* that demonstrates the fragility of familial as well as patron-client bonds in a community devoid of mutual trust.

Volpone's deceptions are normative in the fictional world of Venice, a world that not only tolerates but richly rewards secrecy.[1] Mosca repeatedly acts in collusion with others, occasionally with three or four factions at once. The three *captatores* (legacy-hunters) feign devotion to their 'sick' potential benefactor, Volpone, and offer him restoratives prepared to kill him. We can never be quite sure who Volpone's three freaks are: they have no clear-cut identities apart from the roles they play in the embedded fable of metempsychosis. Even Bonario and Celia have their public faces of pristine innocence while offering, in one case to spy on his father, in the other to prevaricate in collaboration with Volpone. The four *avocatori* appear to be seeking justice even as they try to forge alliances with Mosca *sotto voce*. The entire collection of secondary characters constitutes a society that perverts privacy into secrecy, theatrical flair into cynical conspiracy. The aside, the secret strategy session, and the whispered suspicion of plots and counterplots set a tone of uneasiness, of dis-ease in the play.

I propose to consider in this chapter, first, the inclination toward secrecy in Jonson's London immediately preceding the first performance of Volpone; second, the specific theatrical strategies based on conspiracy that he built into the play; and, third, the two modes of discovering conspiracy – one false, one true – that he employed to end his comedy. Studying the ways that these conspiracies involve fictional characters and their audiences can help us to see how Jonson's art can co-opt, comically diminish, and hence discredit the bias toward secrecy in a culture being propelled by its collective anxiety, in particular by its xenophobic anti-Catholic hysteria.

Without relying too heavily on biographical information, which is at best incomplete, at worst a reflection of Jonson's conscious attempts to cut a controversial figure, I believe that we can see in *Volpone* something of Jonson's own frustrations in a world that conducts its business under a veil of secrecy. In the immediate wake of the Gunpowder Plot, when *Volpone* was being composed and played, the hunt for Jesuit sympathizers created particularly treacherous undercurrents in English society.

Jonson became connected with the investigation of the Plot two days after Guy Fawkes's arrest in awkward proximity to thirty-six barrels of powder in a cellar adjoining the Houses of Parliament, where King, Lords, and Commons were to gather the next day, on 5 November 1605. A particular Catholic priest was wanted for questioning in connection with what was immediately and widely known as a papist conspiracy, and Jonson, a known recusant, agreed to contact the priest on behalf of the Privy Council. On 8 November he wrote to the Earl of Salisbury that he was unable to communicate with the priest in question and expressed his outrage that anyone connected with his adopted religion could contemplate such a heinous attack on the established authority of England.[2] He seems to have taken this matter very seriously, but at the same time in *Volpone* he pokes fun at the bizarre, counter-conspiritorial mind-set that emerged in response to the Plot. This is especially evident in the subplot involving Sir Politique Would-bee, the English informant abroad, who is intrigued by, among other things, techniques for passing state secrets concealed in cabbages, musk-melons, and a hollow toothpick (II.i.67-80). Just as the gunpowder treason was widely advertised to have been foiled by divine revelations to King James, so too is Sir Politique prepared to believe that secrets have been recently revealed through such prodigious signs as a new star in the heavens, whelping lions, a whale, and porpoises far up the Thames (II.i.33-52). The upshot of this action is Peregrine's 'counter-plot' (IV.iii.24) against Sir Politique in which he tells the hapless knight that there is

>   a spie, set on you:
> And, he has made relation to the Senate,
> That you profest to him, to haue a plot
> To sell the state of *Venice*, to the *Turke*. (V.iv.35-8)

Sir Politique protests that he has no such international intrigues recorded among his papers, which are 'but notes, / Drawne out of play-bookes' (V.iv.41-2). And so the potentially earth-shaking Gunpowder Plot and its underground investigators are revealed in the mirror of the stage to feed off one another. The terror that forces Jonson's English knight to creep into his 'politique tortoyse' shell (V.iv.80), where he is soundly drubbed, is perhaps no more foolish than the creeping paranoia that still gripped London in March 1606, the most probable date for the first performance of *Volpone*.[3]

Like secrecy, state paranoia is an extraordinarily complex phenomenon. It differs in its operation from the individual mental derangement whose effects are largely unpredictable, uncontrollable, and disabling. What I am concerned with here, and what Jonson was concerned with in *Volpone*, is a set of socio-political responses triggered by threatening public events, responses that can be manipulated by original reports of the events and by their subsequent redaction, including various forms of licensed and unlicensed popular entertainment. As Lacey Baldwin Smith points out, paranoia in this sense in the Renaissance could at times be a 'healthy,' self-protective, systemic response to internal and external threat: 'paranoia was not of necessity the figment of a deranged and overactive imagination, nor was it solely the product of educational and ideological conditioning.'[4] It is the case that violently reactive investigative schemes fostered in Elizabeth's reign by men like Cecil undoubtedly served to protect the ideological ends of power and privilege which Jonson also served and from which he benefited through the middle portion of his writing career. In the case of the Privy Council's investigation of the Gunpowder Plot, Jonson personally responded with support and enthusiasm for the English cause. Still, he retained sufficient distance from this elaborate state apparatus to be critical of the hysterical response that its counter-measures fostered in the citizenry. While his correspondence with Privy Council distinguishes earnestly between acceptable and unacceptable behaviour for English Catholics, he found it desirable to employ his skills as a writer of comedy to defuse the indiscriminate anti-papism being driven by the engine of state paranoia.

Typical of the scare-literature being written in London at the time is William Leigh's *Great Britains great deliverance from ... popish powder*, entered in the Stationer's Register in January of 1606. With clear hindsight Leigh berates Englishmen for having ignored their sacred duty to remain vigilant in spying out papists.

> We should haue seene these miscreants, neuer sated with the bloud of the Saints, til they had changed our religion for superstition, our knowledge for ignorance, our preaching for massiing [sic]; our subjects for Rebels, our Councellors for conspirators, and so haue brought vpon vs, and ours: A most wofull Sabaoth, when both the lawes of God & man (which are the sinewes of a sanctified state) had beene dissolued, and silent. (sig. B2)

There is a hint of the satirist's reforming zeal in Leigh's catalogue of Roman ambitions, but more of the government official's readiness to find a foreign papist under every Protestant bed, as appears clearly in his subsequent appeal to English fears: 'Againe, take heed of them, for they are busie bodies, and walke inordinately amongst you: they are impatient of our profession, great peace, and much plentie' (sig. D4v).

We might add here that although busybodies of whatever persuasion were often targets of scorn in Jonson's comedies and epigrams, he would certainly not have subscribed to William Leigh's solution that 'I will fight against you with your owne weapons, and I wil weary you in your owne waies' (sig. C2v). Jonson's abhorrence of this kind of doing unto others, fighting secrecy with secrecy, goes some way toward explaining the pattern of personality and plotting in *Volpone*. Jonson had been personally harassed by government informers while in prison, and he was cited for recusancy before the Consistory Court of London on 10 January 1605/6.

> Presented, that they [Jonson and his wife] refuse not to Come to divyne servis but have absented them selves from the Co[mmun]ion beinge oftentymes admonished w[hi]ch hathe Continued as farr as we Can learne ever since the kinge Came in[;] he is a poett and is by fame a seducer of youthe to ye popishe Religion.[5]

Even under this rather commonplace kind of surveillance and interpretation of his private actions, Jonson developed a deep distrust of 'politique *Picklocke*[s] of the *Scene*' (*Bartholomew Fair*, Induction, line 138), men who would search his public utterances for subversive meanings.

Jonson's fellow poet, John Donne, likewise embraced Roman Catholicism and had, during the reign of the old Queen, fashioned the world of the frightened recusant into the stuff of satire.[6] The speaker of Donne's *Satyre IV*, pumped for his opinions by a chattering courtier of the Sir Pol species, had felt 'One of our Giant Statutes ope his jaw / To sucke me in' (lines 132–3), and in the closing lines of the poem admits that 'I shooke like a spyed Spie' (line 237), quite without reason. Several characters in *Volpone* eventually suffer the fate of the 'spyed Spie' when Volpone himself reveals their illegal, clandestine activities. This was a recognizable category of courtiers in Jonson's dramatic vocabulary.

Volpone marks the beginning of Jonson's penetrating analysis of the specific problems of his secrecy-ridden society on the comic stage. In this play, the conspiracies take the form of earnest financial fraud, medical quackery, courtroom perjury, and sexual assault, among others. While similar forms of violence and deceit occurred, for example, in Jonson's early plays based on Roman intrigue comedy, his understanding of the moral implications of conspiracy was different in his middle plays. He gives new meaning to 'intrigue' comedy. In the early play, *Every Man In His Humour* (1598), for instance, Musco, like the conventional much-abused slave of Roman comedy, bounces back irrepressibly with fresh schemes that the audience wishes to see succeed. As in the classical models, the servant in *Every Man In* usually works alone to achieve limited goals that help to foster a light-hearted complicity with the audience through his asides, soliloquies, and whatever winks, grins, and shrugs the actor can use to ingratiate himself with the audience.

In *Volpone*, by contrast, nearly everyone in the play has become his or her own Musco, and the trickster's alliance with the cause of young love has become at once vestigial and unsavoury. The audience can no longer relax into a winking conspiracy. In the tinny casuistry of Corvino's pandering, the smug chuckle of Mosca's encomium on parasites (III.i.1-33), and the cynical gloating of the inventory scene (V.iii), Jonson lets his audience hear the hollowness of laughter at human exploitation, however cleverly executed, and he shows us the moral maze of an easy complicity. Such pleasures of comedy, like laughter itself when divorced from judgment, are denied Jonson's audience. His comments on the subject of mindless laughter in *Discoveries*, as well as in the plays and prologues, are devastating: 'the moving of laughter ... is rather a fowling for the peoples delight, or their fooling. ... This is truly leaping from the Stage to the Tumbrell againe, reducing all witt to the originall Dungcart' (*Disc.*, lines 2629-31, 2675-7). This view of the abuses that stage comedy was prone to suggests why Jonson might have turned from the rather raucous humour of his comical satires *Cynthia's Revels* (1600) and *Poetaster* (1601) to the vicious ironies of *Sejanus* (1603), the first play in which he treated conspiracy as a tragic theme. Later, after treating the subject comically in *Volpone* (1606), *The Alchemist* (1610), and to a lesser extent in *Epicoene* (1609), he returned specifically to the fatal effects of conspiracy on the body politic in his tragedy, *Catiline His Conspiracy* (1611).

In order to trace the subtle play of conspiracy that I believe underlies the comic structure and social satire of *Volpone*, I will look closely at the dialogue in several brief episodes that shape audience expectations going into the play's climactic trial scenes. Each of these episodes incorporates not only the theatrical talents of the chief conspirators, Volpone and Mosca, but also definite hints of the debilitating effects of conspiracy on all the characters, especially on their family relationships. Each meeting between Volpone and one of the spying *captatores* in the first act is preceded by private conversations, first between Mosca and his master, then between Mosca and the gull. The presentation of bribes to Volpone and the furious negotiation for assurances of the inheritance are extensions of the terms and motives worked out in the preceding private conspiracies. In the play's second scene, for example, Mosca announces to Volpone that Signior Voltore is waiting outside to see him. Master and servant then mock the legacy-hunters for their animal rapaciousness, crude disguises, and gullibility.

> VOL. Now, now, my clients
> Beginne their visitation! vulture, kite,
> Rauen, and gor-crow, all my birds of prey,
> That thinke me turning carcasse, now they come:
> I am not for 'hem yet.
> ...
> MOS. Hood an asse, with reuerend purple,
> So you can hide his two ambitious eares,
> And, he shall passe for a cathedrall Doctor. (I.ii.87-113)

Mosca's caricature of Voltore as an ass disguised as a learned doctor of philosophy not only mocks the lawyer's ambition but also reveals that Mosca is aware of other 'fine delusiue sleights' (I.ii.95) abroad than the one he and Volpone are devising to cheat Voltore.[7] The hooded gull is himself a would-be conspirator. Acting on this awareness, Mosca pretends in the opening lines of the next scene to conspire with Voltore against Volpone and the rival *captatores*: 'Onely you / (Of all the rest) are he, commands his loue' (I.iii.1-2). Then, during the central section of the scene, Mosca plays confidant to Voltore and Volpone simultaneously:

> (MOS. You are his heire, sir.
> VOLT. Am I?) VOLP. I feele me going (vh, vh, vh, vh.)
> I am sayling to my port, (vh, vh, vh, vh?)
> And I am glad, I am so neere my hauen.
> MOS. Alas, kind gentleman, well, we must all goe – (I.iii.27-31)

While Mosca's asides to Voltore suggest conspiracy between them, his faithful echoing of Volpone's platitudes on the inevitability of death signals to the audience his deeper conspiracy with his master. The effect of these multilayered conspiracies on the projected and perceived personalities is purely constrictive. The expansiveness we ordinarily associate with game- and role-playing is smothered in secrecy. Volpone and Mosca discuss greed and imminent death with mindless banality; Voltore pretends to be taken in by their cant, while at a deeper level he is *actually* being duped. The atmosphere of conspiracy permits people to show only one side of their personalities. Potentially multifaceted personalities become diminished when secrecy is the norm at all levels of social intercourse.

The same pattern of entwined conspiracies is repeated in the interviews with Corbaccio and Corvino with even more chilling effect than the constriction of personality we have just seen: first, Mosca schemes genuinely with Volpone (though always keeping his options open), then falsely with the visitor, and finally with both together. The effect is to place Mosca in the pivotal position of all character relationships, even while Volpone holds centre stage in a series of plays within the play. Mosca even succeeds in inducing Bonario to eavesdrop on his father, much as Iago conspires with Othello against Cassio and Desdemona, though Mosca daren't promise ocular proof:

> if you
> Shall be but pleas'd to goe with me, I'le bring you,
> (I dare not say where you shall see, but) where
> Your eare shall be a witnesse of the deed;
> Heare your selfe written bastard: and profest
> The common issue of the earth. (III.ii.60–5)

Exactly why Mosca shares this confidence with Bonario is not immediately clear. Bonario has begun the scene accusing Mosca of baseness, but Mosca easily turns the charge aside. He may perceive some financial gain as well as sheer mischievous pleasure to be got from turning son against father.[8] While Mosca is out of Volpone's house conspiring with Bonario, Lady Politique Would-bee visits and easily dominates the unsupported Volpone. Only the servant's timely return keeps this significant variation of the pattern of Volpone-Mosca pre-conspiracies from being a disaster. Mosca's solution to the problem is to send Lady Would-bee chasing off in search of yet another conspiracy, the alleged assignation between her husband and a Venetian courtesan. What she stumbles into on the Rialto is not the conspiracy she expected, but another one: her husband keeping close counsel with a counterfeit English spy, Peregrine, whom she mistakes for 'A female deuill, in a male out-side' (IV.ii.56).[9] Even this apparently inconsequential and totally misconstrued conspiracy will subsequently be turned to Volpone's purposes in the first trial scene. Like the fanatical anti-papist William Leigh, Lady Would-bee imagines conspiracy to be lurking everywhere and is all too eager to testify against those she suspects. Her zeal to uncover intrigues and to share in Volpone's 'possessions ... and much plentie' only prevents her from seeing who the real conspirators are, however.

The basic purpose of conspiracy that emerges from the episodes I have reviewed so far is to outwit one's rivals by obscuring one's real motives. The basic absurdity that renders these actions comic is that the instigator of conspiracy must employ the aid of another, or others, for two reasons: to gain credibility by generating an apparent consensus (that is, the conspirator's tales assume the ring of truth by being repeated by his cohort), and to provide him an appreciative audience in an action that would otherwise lose the thrill of performance. The fundamental contradiction between reliance on a fellow conspirator and clandestine pursuit of a selfish prize becomes the central element of closure in Jonson's comedy, as we shall see. In the short run, however, conspiracy provides gratification and applause as well as release for the conspirators' hostility toward the rest of humanity.

Patterns of performance and conspiracy deepen and darken into the arrangements for a gruesome travesty of offering the gift of heavenly love (the merchant's wife is named Celia, the heavenly one) to the supposedly dying old lecher, Volpone. The sequence begins as a conspiracy between Mosca and the merchant, Corvino. Mosca reports that his master has been temporarily revived by a dose of Scoto's magic remedy and that the 'colledge of physicians' (II.vi.27) has now supposedly prescribed a young woman, 'Lustie, and full of iuice' (line 35), to restore Volpone's vitality. Corvino is particularly distressed to learn that a rival *captatore*, one Dr Lupus, has already offered his daughter for the purpose. Mosca patiently nurtures the seed of an idea in his gull's mind: Corvino's wife will meet the requirements admirably, and the reluctant husband can rationalize away his moral scruples (actually his jealousy) if only he can convince himself that he will win the prize of Volpone's inheritance by pandering for his own wife. Playing the appreciative audience, a role he is much practised in, Mosca waits for Corvino to unfold the plot, as if it were his 'owne free motion' (line 95), and applauds him enthusiastically for thinking of the very thing that Mosca himself would have suggested were he not reluctant to 'seeme to counsell' Corvino (line 82). Mosca has so artfully arranged the conspiracy to get Celia for his master that Corvino is satisfied that he himself is the source of a powerful idea, the distributor of benefits, and the certain winner of a still grander prize, yet to be awarded.

When Corvino all but shoves his wife into Volpone's bed chamber and then withdraws with Mosca in III.vii, Volpone is abandoned, for the second time in the play, to his own devices, and things go just as badly as they had in the interview with Lady Would-bee. Having lost his chief conspirator, Mosca, he tries to cast Celia in that role, with disastrous results. He confides that it was he, Volpone, who appeared that very morning at her window in the shape of a mountebank. That masquerade having worked so successfully, he proposes that, together, they continue to baffle the jealous husband. He boasts that

> before
> I would haue left my practice, for thy loue,
> In varying figures, I would haue contended
> With the blue Protevs, or the horned *Floud*. (III.vii.150-3)

Certainly Volpone's claims are a fitting extension of his past Protean performances, but this time he has conspired with someone who does not share his hostile delight in deception. His analogies between himself and Proteus and the river-god Achelous, who fought in many shapes to win Dianeira, are utterly presumptuous, pride being not so much an isolated flaw as a basic axiom of Volpone's character. His attempt to replay the lusty young hero of an Ovidian entertainment, as in William Gager's university play, *Ulysses Redux* (1592), simply makes Volpone look awkward and foolish.[10]

> I am, now, as fresh,
> As hot, as high, and in as iouiall plight,
> As when (in that so celebrated *scene*,
> At recitation of our *comoedie*,
> For entertainement of the great Valoys)
> I acted yong Antinovs; and attracted
> The eyes, and eares of all the ladies, present,
> T'admire each gracefull gesture, note, and footing. (III.vii.157-64)

Celia retreats before his torrent of words and his fancy footwork; for Jonson's purposes she need do nothing more to encourage Volpone's tirade to solidify the audience's impression of his folly.

Volpone continues his virtuoso performance with the famous *carpe diem* lyric adapted from Catullus ('*Come, my* Celia, *let vs proue*'), charming in itself but devastating to his cause in this context. The middle section of the song, often ignored by interpreters of the play, extends Jonson's exploration of deceit, spying, and conspiracy into the arena of supposed lovers' 'wile[s].'

> *Cannot we delude the eyes*
> *Of a few poore houshold-spies?*
> *Or his easier eares beguile,*
> *Thus remooued, by our wile?* (III.vii.176-9)

The theme of the entire song is not love but the urge to 'delude': first Time, the destroyer, then the jealous husband, and finally an entire society's system for spying out 'crimes' (line 183). The social divisiveness that Volpone advocates in the song compounds itself ironically when the effect of the song is further to alienate the 'beloved.'

The more Celia 'droopes' and prays for some calamity to end the assault, the more Volpone persists in building his vaguely nauseating word-worlds of inedible private banquets, finally setting the whole thing 'whirl[ing] round / With the *vertigo*' (lines 218-19). He imagines that while his dwarf, eunuch, and fool perform a dizzying dance,

> we, in changed shapes, [shall] act Ovids tales,
> Thou, like Evropa now, and I like Ioue,
> Then I like Mars, and thou like Erycine,
> So, of the rest, till we haue quite run through
> And weary'd all the fables of the gods. (III.vii.221-5)

Volpone's choice of mythological rapes as examples of romantic apotheosis reminds the audience of a sordid reality that Volpone seems totally to have forgotten. Try as she may, Celia can produce no arguments to deter Volpone from his high-flown imaginings. He sees her only as his partner in fable and conspiracy, and her demurs have no place in that script.[11] Only inadvertently does she bring Volpone down with a jolt when she offers to report him virtuous, thereby actually offering to enter, on her own terms, his conspiracy to deceive the world. Volpone is flabbergasted: 'Thinke me cold, / Frosen, and impotent, and so report me?' (lines 260-1). Having thrown aside his mask of diseased incapacity at the beginning of the scene, the self-styled virtuoso in sexuality feels he must now at all costs establish his credentials as a lusty scoundrel. In a marvellously comic show of misplaced loyalty, he refuses to disgrace the reputation of all Italian lechers. Later he is to sweat profusely as he sits helplessly by in his invalid's chair at the *scrutineo* while his lawyer scorns the very notion of his sexual prowess. Are these palsied hands 'fit to stroake a ladies brests?' demands the advocate; and when the trial is over, Volpone needs strong wine to steady those shaking hands and to dispel the heart-sick humour that he is indeed past his prime (IV.vi.27-8; V.i.11-12). Confronted with Celia, he had to prove himself a virile villain, but his supposed erotic poetry ironically vitiated that intention. He emerges from the seduction scene as one who lacks not only good sense but also real passion.

The blighting of sexuality and the comic deflation of the main character are, then, two direct consequences of the conspiring habit of mind in *Volpone*. We have also seen the disturbing effects of conspiracy on the bonds between father and son (Bonario and Corbaccio) as well as husband and wife (Corvino and Celia). To this list we can add Lady Would-bee's unconscious travesty of humanist learning as she uses books and ideas as tokens to gain entrance into what she imagines to be the closed circle of the Venetian intelligentsia. Similarly Sir Politique's fascination with the latest gossip about London's secret agents leads him to view life as an extended game of clever mechanical devices.[12] While the discovery and mocking of Sir Politique's 'secrets' can be achieved by a simple, farcical unmasking action in the subplot, unravelling the more serious consequences of conspiracy in the main plot involves Jonson and his audience in more elaborate indirections.

Bonario's intervention during the seduction scene proves to be one step, but a false one, in the process of discovery. He foils Volpone's seduction attempt at the last minute, commanding him, 'Forbeare, foule rauisher, libidinous swine, / Free the forc'd lady' (III.vii.267-8). The diction and cadence of his speeches, borrowed from heroic romance, provide one final humorous touch in the scene.[13] Like the lyricism of Catullus and the eroticism of Ovid, the heroism of Spenser's Red-Crosse Knight is ridiculously out of place in Volpone's bedroom. The dashing lone hero has no serious answers for this society where everyone lurks in dark corners and no one much regards the law. Even the denouncer of foul ravishers has turned spy in a way that breaches the 'bond ... 'twixt son and father' as surely as does the more famous action of the contemporary play, *King Lear*. The collapse of social bonds and contracts under the pressure of conspiracy is given special ironic force in *Volpone* as well as *King Lear* by the inclusion of formal trial scenes.

Volpone and his allies are brought to trial twice in the course of the action, the first time immediately following the abortive seduction scene. Jonson had used trial scenes in his comical satires as a way to present in orderly fashion key issues such as courtly pretension (*Cynthia's Revels*) and false art (*Poetaster*). In these plays spokesmen for justice passed judgment and assigned punishments. The courtroom scenes in *Volpone* serve a different purpose, however. In these scenes the central issue of conspiracy is dramatized, not merely commented on. The courts and pseudo-courts of Jonson's middle comedies are hardly models of the orderly dispensation of justice. What strikes the *avocatori* in *Volpone* as a temporary procedural problem – lack of order in the courtroom and of clarity in the proceedings – in fact mirrors and even ratifies the violation of familial, sexual, and financial bonds in the first three acts. In the course of the second trial one perplexed judge exclaims, 'This same's a labyrinth!' and another echoes the sentiment, saying, 'This is confusion' (V.x.42, 47). The point of this consternation is not simply the judges' obtuseness but the ease with which a community given to secrecy can be divided against itself. The well-spring of the confusion is, as always in Jonson, the human tongue divorced from truth. To be persuasive in a world such as Volpone's Venice, the fast-talker need only slightly skew one basic premise of rhetoric – that speech should be adjusted to suit the particular audience – by spinning out a different tale for each faction of hearers. The inventive deceits of such speakers will not be confined by the bond of any oath administered in the courts.

The professional tongue-wagger in the courtroom is Voltore, Volpone's lawyer and aspirant to his inheritance. Early in act I Mosca marvels that Voltore is a man 'of so perplex'd a tongue, / And loud withall, that would not wag, nor scarce / Lie still, without a fee' (I.iii.63–5), and after the first trial he enthusiastically tells Voltore that his 'tongue [should be] tipt with gold' (IV.vi.64). Though Mosca's remarks are pure flattery, he also believes that under the circumstances words are golden; that is, without Voltore to orchestrate the conspirators, the fortune might have been lost. Yet Mosca also knows that the words of the golden-tongued lawyer are nothing but useful noise, a kind of verbal chaos that obscures for the moment the knavery of Volpone. 'We will but vse his tongue, his noise,' Mosca tells Corvino (IV.iv.11). As with Volpone's masterful obfuscation in the mountebank scene, Voltore's speeches in the present instance flow into the realm of insubstantial jargon. He asserts, with Corvino's nodded consent, that the wronged husband knew of a sexual liaison between Celia and Bonario; he then goes on to berate the young couple for presuming further on the willing cuckold's mercy.

> For these, not knowing how to owe a gift
> Of that deare grace, but with their shame; being plac'd
> So'aboue all powers of their gratitude,
> Began to hate the benefit: and, in place
> Of thankes, deuise t'extirpe the memorie

> Of such an act. Wherein, I pray your father-hoods,
> To obserue the malice, yea, the rage of creatures
> Discouer'd in their euils; and what heart
> Such take, euen, from their crimes. (IV.v.44–52)

The functional words in the speech are a series of nouns – 'shame,' 'malice,' 'rage,' 'euils,' 'crimes.' The only 'crime' named in the speech, however, is ingratitude for the rather dubious favour that has become in Voltore's account no less than a gift of grace. The richly emotive language of prosecution obscures what is really going on just as surely as Volpone's early promises of profit and declaration of love had done.

However prominent and pyrotechnical the advocate's art of obfuscation may be, the chilling fact remains that little ingenuity is required beyond a conspiracy of witnesses to make a mockery of innocence and judicial proceedings. Bonario and Celia place their entire trust in God and the law. Of course, they appear foolish to do so in the present circumstance, for it is the nature of the Fox and his cohorts to turn witty imposture against established communal authority. False testimonies from Celia's husband and Lady Would-bee, and Volpone's masquerade in the invalid's chair, plausibly make the accusing parties appear to the court as the accused, indeed the guilty parties. The legal monster of Donne's *Satyre IV*, who thrives only through the bad offices of spies and informers, is prepared to 'ope his jaw / To sucke. . . in' the play's young innocents. Bonario and Celia revert to ridiculously hollow special pleadings that the *avocatori* consider 'no testimonies' at all (IV.vi.18). These judges may have already revealed their dullness and will subsequently show their venality, but what member of Jonson's audience could have arrived at a different verdict after hearing only the evidence presented in the first trial? The plot seems to have come to a cynical and wholly repugnant conclusion, leaving Volpone to savour his successful up-ending of justice. Apparently Jonson has thrown Bonario's and Celia's 'unworldliness into the arena: hers to be mauled by the wolves, his to be applauded by the asses,' as one critic says, thus extending the beast-fable to include the audience's inhuman reactions.[14] But has Jonson discarded his foolish innocents cynically, or has he rather used them to demonstrate how easily justice may be subverted by craft and to force his audience to reject this inadequate ending to his comedy? If so, in rejecting the morally down-beat ending, we presumably reject all that it implies about the glamour of the trickster's life and the advantages of secrecy. Giving the audience what it may have thought it wanted in the triumph of villainy, Jonson in fact causes us to reject a cheap, conspiratorial victory in favour of another ending yet to come.[15]

To argue that Jonson establishes moral priorities by indulging the audience's secret desire for the Fox to escape punishment at the end of act IV is not to say that we must expect from his comedy only light-hearted forms of closure, what Jonson elsewhere called *'the Concupiscence of Daunces, and Antickes.'*[16] Instead, Jonson has used the double ending of his comedy to probe the most distasteful sorts of human commerce, to put the snaffle in the mouths of puritan theatre critics with a vengeance, and to make his viewers see more clearly the real values of communal living, including social hierarchy. To do this requires a further twist in the plot, the comic inversion of the master-servant relationship and a stunning moment of revelation.

Jonson revives his plot at the beginning of act V and prepares for a totally different ending to its comic deceptions than anything yet seen on the English stage. We glimpse for a moment the chink in Volpone's armour: the trickster's abiding fear that the infinite variety of identities he has found in his personal Pandora's box might vanish and the reality of a 'dead palsey' put an end to life's masquerade.

> A many of these feares
> Would put me into some villanous disease,
> Should they come thick vpon me: I'le preuent 'hem.
> Giue me a boule of lustie wine, to fright
> This humor from my heart. (V.i.8-12)

Earlier, Volpone had floated above life on an insulating layer of disguise and material objects – much gold, some furs, 'lustie wine,' Turkish carpets, down beds – that were continually being catalogued, as much to establish their volume as their value. There in the public courtroom in act IV, the insulation grew too thin for comfort, and the chill of fear replaced the heat of elation. Mosca, seeing his chance, cleverly mocks and feeds the fear ('But confesse, sir, / Were you not daunted?' [V.ii.38-9]) until Volpone feels himself constrained to overreach his past deceptions as a way of reasserting his faith in scheming. He volunteers to don the ultimate and ultimately terrifying disguise of death.[17]

> Go,
> Streight, giue out, about the streetes, you two,
> That I am dead; doe it with constancy,
> Sadly, doe you heare? impute it to the griefe
> Of this late slander. ...
> I shall haue, instantly, my vulture, crow,
> Rauen, come flying hither (on the newes)
> To peck for carrion, my shee-wolfe, and all,
> Greedy, and full of expectation – (V.ii.59-67)

The injunction to 'doe it with constancy' (i.e. to act consistently in character) reverberates ironically in context, since by making the servant his master, Volpone effectively destroys the shifting ground of his multiple conspiracies. He must remain permanently 'dead.' After all, while a dead man requires an executor of his will, the living no longer need the dead for economic benefit. Volpone has written himself out of the script, or rather, he may now speak *only* in asides or as another person – the ultimate trap of secrecy. The Fox will slip this trap, but only to be fixed with a final, until-death identity as a prisoner in chains.[18]

The uncasing action of act V repeats many of the events of the earlier acts but with a significant variation: elaborate theatrical pretences are renewed, but this time Volpone and Mosca abandon their practice of flattering and cajoling their dupes in favour of the more offensive tactic of gloating over the fools' disappointments. Like Peregrine stripping Sir Politique of his tortoise shell and then mocking his vulnerability in the subplot (V.ii), first Mosca, enthusiastically assuming the role of Volpone's heir in the inventory scene (V.iii), and then Volpone himself, disguised as an officer of the law (V.vi-ix), mock the foiled *captatores*. In the final trial scene Mosca holds his master's keys and title, indeed his very identity, publicly refusing to acknowledge his existence or to share the spoils of their confederacy. To the surprise of everyone on stage and in the audience, Volpone drops his disguise and calls down the law on the head of his upstart servant. This, Volpone's most desperate use of the Venetian legal system for his own purposes, is also his last, since it entails revealing the truth about his own deceptions as well.[19] With the possibilities of further conspiracy exhausted, the play comes to an end. The former conspirators are all stripped of their valuables and committed to various forms of incarceration and humiliation. The paranoid state certainly cannot claim responsibility for spying out fraud in this play. Rather, we see an instance, unsurpassed in the Jonson corpus, of what I earlier called the intersection of purposeful suppression with accidental discovery.

It has become fashionable, in the wake of Stanley Fish's affective reading of seventeenth-century texts, to argue that Jonson draws even his audience into a kind of conspiracy with his characters, only to surprise them with the sudden revelation that they too have sinned.[20] Though it is certainly true that Jonson was willing to surprise his audience on occasion (viz. the ending of *Epicoene*) and to insult their critical intelligence (as in the Induction to *Bartholomew Fair*), I am not convinced that the audience of *Volpone* is treated like this. The on-stage audience – those applauding conspirators – *are* stung in precisely this way, but almost anyone watching Jonson's play unfold can reasonably be expected to remain at arm's length from the theatrical spectacle that so enraptures and then disillusions Jonson's characters. We have already seen this kind of distance forced on the audience by the outcome of the first trial scene. Having been allowed backstage, so to speak, during the scenes of conspiracy to watch the preparation of scripts, costumes, and even makeup, we have been encouraged from the start to judge the actor's art with a critical eye. Far from glamourizing what Pico called 'our chameleon,' Jonson makes self-transforming conspiracy the chief butt of his satire.[21]

In *Volpone* Jonson has made a comic form, based on the conspicuous contrivance of intrigue comedy, where schemes self-destruct when their designers try to play life as a conspiratorial game devoid of serious consequences. The game is highly amusing to watch unfold, deeply satisfying to see concluded. It is concluded by an inadvertent shift to revelation in a society compartmentalized by secrecy. The shift is caused not by the intervention of an influential, easygoing, wittily outspoken advocate of civic harmony such as Justice Clement but rather by internal pressures in the society that force characters and plots to exhaust the resources of secrecy. The play makes no attempt to represent a just or humane society, and such a society can at best be imagined as the antithesis to Volpone's Venice. The techniques of theatrical discovery, including the act of unmasking and the virtual detheatricalizing of life as the play moves toward a conclusion in Volpone's epilogue, doubtless had, as they still have, a stinging relevance for an audience familiar with the antics of spies and informers. Both as Catholic recusant and as satirist, Jonson courageously disdained the cautious advice of timid men like his would-be intriguer, Sir Politique:

> not [to] tell a secret,
> On any termes, not to your father; scarse
> A fable, but with caution; make sure choise
> Both of your company, and discourse; beware,
> You neuer speake a truth – (IV.i.13–17)

The outcome of such secrecy, as we can see in *Volpone*, is the suppression of truth in matters of money, marriage, statecraft, and religion. Writing at a moment of acute political crisis in Jacobean England, immediately following the discovery of the Gunpowder Plot, Jonson implicitly attacked the conspiratorial excesses of both the counter-revolutionary Roman Catholic forces and the Protestant establishment. In so doing, he simultaneously managed to ridicule the false forms of theatricality that to his mind had infected the English stage and to create a comic form that remains 'neere, and familiarly allied to the time' (*Every Man Out of His Humour*, Grex, III.vi.200–1). Because the new form captured men in their most awkward public poses and their most conspiratorial whisperings, Volpone swings madly between being a shrivelled windbag and being a sinister threat to the integrity of anyone attracted to him. The temporary collapse of the clandestine community that had formed with Volpone as its 'centre attractive' afforded Jonson the chance to address, in their own terms, those critics who claimed that *'we neuer punish vice in our* enterludes' (Epistle to *Volpone*, line 116). Not that any true enemy of the stage would have been silenced by such a comic catastrophe, but it testifies to Jonson's passionate, even foolhardy, commitment to speaking out against those powerful conspiracies that undercut social trust.

Over against *Volpone*'s vision of a society shut up against itself we may place those open and 'liberall' societies that Jonson idealizes in the epideictic strains of his poems and masques. Jonson insists on protecting the principle of open expression in his own house when, upon 'Inviting a Friend to Supper,' he offers assurances that there will be 'no *Pooly*', or *Parrot*' there to spy or inform on his guests.[22] The same kind of liberality characterizes the hospitality afforded by the Sidneys at Penshurst.[23] In a more broadly symbolic form, the public rituals celebrated in Jonson's masques repeatedly enact the driving out of cloaked disrupters by the light of true nobility. In *Hymenaei*, performed the same year as *Volpone*, the gaudily over-dressed Humours and Affections are driven forth by the light of Reason, and at Truth's ultimate exposure of Opinion '*a striking light seem'd to fill all the hall*' (lines 876–7).[24] The masque's closing line records that 'Trvth in him [King James] make[s] *treason* euer rue' (line 944). Those treasons and their brutal suppression were Jonson's concern in *Sejanus* and the stuff of broad humour in the subplot of *Volpone*. In his next play, *Epicoene*, he was to figure secrecy in social and economic terms rather than expressly political ones. The highly theatrical gestures of fashionable London society threaten the values of restraint as well as openness in this farcical and deeply misogynistic comedy.

CHAPTER FOUR

Private Lies, Public Notice: *Epicoene* and Theatrical Deception

Most modern commentators find *Epicoene* a slighter and less engaging play than *Volpone*. Readers find its issues trivial, its characters unattractive, and its social attitudes offensive. It is seldom performed.[1] It almost seems as though Jonson took the marginal, topical, frequently cut subplot of Peregrine swooping down on the tortoise from *Volpone* and made it into the main action of his next play. The resulting *'comoedy* of affliction' (*Epicoene*, II.vi.37), a sometimes painful exercise in tormenting dim or anti-social characters, has found few champions. Dryden admired the play for its carefully crafted plot; Ray Heffner found richness in its central 'unifying symbol,' noise; Jonas Barish revelled in its rhetoric of antithesis; and I argued many years ago that the play significantly reshapes the traditions of the prose paradox.[2] In recent years the play has begun to find favour not so much as drama but as a demonstration piece for feminist and cultural materialist critics.[3] While there can be no question that women are a prime economic commodity in the London of *Epicoene*, as medium of exchange they are just part of a larger commerce between private intimacy and public appearances that Jonson places at the centre of the theatrical experience. In order to assign this curious play its full value, we need to understand not only the embracing social and economic forces at work in it but also the highly exclusionary dynamic of Jonson's play-text and its performance. In this play, unlike *Volpone*, the audience itself is excluded from the central secret of the plot, excluded by a trickster and a playwright who both play their cards very close to the chest. Understanding Jonson's decision to keep the mechanism of the comic catastrophe as a secret from his audience can explain some things about the cool reception it has received in the theater and the interest it has begun to generate among sociologically minded critics.

Midway through act I of *Epicoene*, Dauphine, who is about to be disinherited by his wealthy uncle Morose, explains to his cohort, Clerimont, why the matter of his inheritance should not have been shared with a third friend, Truewit: 'with the fewer a businesse is carried,' he explains, 'it is euer the safer' (I.iii.9–10). Truewit's 'franke [read: outspoken, unreliable] nature ... is not for secrets' (I.iii.4–5). So the intrigue starts from the general principle of exclusion for safety's sake. In the exchange that Dauphine calls 'businesse,' suppressed information is reputed to afford the best protection. And to an extent Dauphine is right. As soon as the free-swinging Truewit takes charge of arranging the traffic of the stage, everyone gets into everyone else's way and no one is safe. He turns the other characters against one another by imputing some threat to one faction or the other, only to denounce those made-up 'secrets' subsequently in public as a means of enhancing his own reputation for cleverness and control. But he himself gets stung in the closing moments of the play when Dauphine reveals what even the audience has not been told – that Epicoene, the wife he has supplied for his uncle, is a cross-dressed boy.

This fifth-act *coup de théâtre* raises some disquieting retrospective questions about the play, particularly about who knows what and when he or she knows it. In *Epicoene* such questions are made to appear more pressing than the usual nagging uncertainties attendant upon intrigue comedy – questions about what is happening or has happened off stage, why certain coincidences prevent crucial meetings from taking place, and why certain tricks fail while others succeed. In this case, the uncertainties about discrepant levels of knowledge and awareness extend beyond the characters to involve the auditors and the author as well.

If we consider first only what the speakers in the play themselves know, we can conclude that identities, like bits of information, are made up as the immediate situation requires. With the exception of the Dauphine-Epicoene ruse, there are no hidden identities and no genuine or effective secrets. Though the *dramatis personae* comprise an intensely self-regarding group of over-dressed and over-confident socialites, individual characters never reflect upon who they are. Oddly, in a play so concerned with the threat of intimate, private actions to subvert public identities and responsibilities, there is simply no mechanism for generating the illusion of a private self.

Characters never speak in soliloquy, though figures like Morose, Mrs Otter, and Truewit are inveterate monologists. However much the characters are represented as objects, often mechanical objects, they never objectify themselves through the dialogue of self and self in the way that Richard II or Hamlet does. Nor is this absence necessary to comedy. Shakespeare's Viola and Parolles, as well as Jonson's own Mosca ('I feare, I shall begin to grow in loue / With my deare selfe,' *Volpone*, III.i.1ff.), engage in significant moments of self-reflexivity. The closest anyone comes to self-revelation in *Epicoene* is when the curmudgeonly Morose reflects on his upbringing, and no one on stage appears to pay the slightest attention to this serious account of his personal history, which he presents as the history of his personality:

> My father, in my education, was wont to aduise mee, that I should alwayes collect, and contayne my mind, not suffring it to flow loosely; that I should looke to what things were necessary to the carriage of my life, and what not: embracing the one, and eschewing the other. In short, that I should endeare my selfe to rest, and auoid turmoile: which now is growne to be another nature to me. (V.iii.48–54)

Truewit responds by calling for the tumultuous, tormenting annulment proceedings to begin. Fashionable London seems to be no place for sensitive, secret selves. Self-awareness remains at the level of face creams and perukes.

The level of frustration and aggression, sexual and otherwise, is extraordinarily high in *Epicoene*. At the root of the theatrical representation of frustration is the discontent that Jonson's self-regarding dramatic speakers (and perhaps, too, the audience, as we will see shortly) experience when confronted with the public under-representation or downright misrepresentation of themselves, especially through purported secrets bandied about in public places. Without engaging in the doubtful critical activity of trying to locate and penetrate the psyches of Jonson's characters, we can say that this particular group exhibits something like the narcissist's desire to be beautifully and fully mirrored by the outside world and his annoyance when, invariably, this fails to happen to his satisfaction.[4] Eavesdropping on the boastful antics of Daw and La Foole, Madam Haughty fulminates with her friend Centaure about 'how our iudgements were impos'd on by these adulterate knights!' (IV.vi.1–2). The Collegiate Ladies feel called upon repeatedly to represent themselves and their reputations in a more favourable light than anyone else does. Likewise, Truewit feels compelled, in the face of all good sense, to reject Dauphine's characterization of his interfering attempt to dissuade Morose from marrying as an 'ignorantly officious' acting out of an 'absurd, weake part' (II.iv.70-1), claiming after the fact that he knew all along that his arguments would have the opposite effect and strengthen Morose's resolve to marry.[5] Both the fools and the tricksters who set them up have a ridiculously inflated sense of their own powers of perception and self-representation.

While characters' discrepant levels of awareness about what is going on offer grounds for the audience to distinguish tricksters from victims of deception, the ground of this distinction proves highly unstable. Plots initiated at cross-purposes by the three gallants demonstrate that they possess little more insider's knowledge than the boastful thirty-pound knights (Sir Jack Daw and Sir Amorous La Foole) and unruly women (Mrs Otter and the Collegiate Ladies) whom they imagine themselves controlling. Nor is the audience in a much more secure position than the gallants, for though they may know the very London streets and locations being staged and understand that the three gallants are serving as the in-play agents of the author-as-plotter, they also eventually learn that they have been taken in and mocked by the boy-in-disguise trick.

The question is bound to occur: Does the author as chief architect of the theatrical experience know what he has done to the audience-stage dynamic with this final act of deception and revelation? While most Renaissance playwrights appear to operate on the assumption that they haven't got the full effect from a theatrical disguise unless they have let the audience catch glimpses of the 'person' behind the mask some three or four times and have tantalized everyone with inopportune near-penetrations of the disguise (as in the case of Shakespeare's Rosalind/Ganymede, Marston's Altofronto/Malvole, and Middleton's Prince/Phoenix), in *Epicoene* we find an author who foregoes dramatic irony for what might be called theatrical irony. The audience does not share a superior position with the author but is instead duped by the same trick that undoes Morose. Who does this author think he is, anyway, or who do we think he is?

I have identified the author of the texts under study from my title onward, giving him a local London habitation and a name. The lyric poet who published under this name endowed himself with a 'mountaine belly and [a] rockie face,' while William Drummond of Hawthornden gave him an enormous superiority complex, supernatural prescience in the death of his son, and a big toe capable of serving as a late-night battleground for a small army.[6] It should be clear by now that we have been in the realm of fantastic authorial (self-)construction almost from the start. Jonson the brick-layer's son, Jonson the classicist, Jonson the anal retentive, Jonson the recusant, Jonson the exposer of secrets – all these authorial personae have served the purpose of permitting subsequent readers to assign a corpus of texts to a single responsible agent and to facilitate a hermeneutic of interpersonal communication, however misleading, from 'author' to 'reader-auditor.'[7] At our own risk we can infer the author's existence and personality from the play-texts published under his name, and we can imagine that we hear one or other of his voices speaking through the prologues printed with the plays, including the two that accompany *Epicoene*. The speaker of the second of these assures us that 'he knowes, *Poet* neuer credit gain'd / By writing truths, but things (like truths) well fain'd.' Now you see him in truth; now you don't. In the same prologue he also issues the following warning: 'On forfeit of your selues, thinke nothing true: / Lest so you make the maker to iudge you' (*Another* [Prologue], 9–10, 7–8). Now you see *yourself*; now you don't. These sentiments, '*Occasion'd*,' as the marginal note tells us, '*by some persons impertinent exception*,' turns the author-maker into the judge of his critics.[8] His best defence is, as usual, highly offensive. While protecting his play from critical scrutiny (which he calls 'wresting' or interpretive wrenching out of shape), he hints that his critics have a deep-seated urge to represent themselves on stage, indeed to imitate his characters and to share their humiliation. Though in this account of the theatrical event Jonson is both maker and judge, he is hardly God-like in his creation or his judgment. Nor is he what Stanley Fish defines as the author-as-good-physician.[9] He neither rules nor cures the London fools and fops to whom he gives language. Rather, he remains in the shadows, a frustrated and grumbly fellow Londoner. One might imagine him in an Alfred Hitchcock cameo, arriving on stage as a mute but restive servant in the background of the pseudo-legal wrangling at the end of *Epicoene* or as one of the respectable folks from down the road who at the end of *The Alchemist* gather in front of Lovewit's house to exclaim incoherently about the carryings-on during the master's absence. In *Epicoene* he builds in numerous complaints about his neighbours, but he pretty much lets them sort out their own fictional business by themselves, either alone or in small conspiratorial groups and without the aid of the figures of judgment in earlier plays like *Every Man In His Humour* and *Cynthia's Revels*.

All this has tended to leave audiences and critics of *Epicoene* with a somewhat bitter taste in their mouths, perhaps feeling ill represented and often saying that the play trivializes and commodifies everything it touches and kills comedy with gratuitous torments. As recent feminist critics have argued, the most frequent objects of trivialization and commodification in the play are Jonson's female characters. For example, Morose treats his bride-to-be as a statue in act II, scene v, slowly circling Epicoene and appraising her value in an extended monologue that is validated by Mute's bows and Epicoene's curtsies. Then, upon hearing Epicoene speak her mind in act III, scene iv, Morose declares her 'a manifest woman' (42), reconstructing his own earlier action as though it were Epicoene's act of self-concealment and her subsequent speech as the true manifestation of her as a woman. As in Browning's 'My Last Duchess,' a too-confident male speaker feels that he alone can put aside the curtain to reveal the imputed secrets of a woman's heart or tongue, and as in Browning's poem, Jonson's readers have good reason to be suspicious of this deeply gendered revisionist history.

A simpler case for understanding the place of secrecy in the commerce of sex and sexual identity in *Epicoene* is the mutual humiliation of Mrs Otter and her husband in act IV, scene ii. Clerimont sees to it that Tom Otter gets drunk with his companions Daw and La Foole and his three absurd beer mugs – his bull, bear, and horse. In his jovial mood, egged on to talk about his wife, he is prepared to reject the concept of wife altogether, claiming only to 'haue a cook, a laundresse, a house-drudge, that serues my necessary turnes, and goes vnder that title.' He goes on to say that 'Wiues are nasty sluttish *animalls*' (IV.ii.51-6). At this point Truewit brings on Mrs Otter to eavesdrop on her husband in his expansively misogynist mode. He boasts that he married not a woman but her £6,000 and that he has not kissed her 'these fortie weekes' (IV.ii.78-80). But it is not until he begins to betray the secrets of her toilet that Mrs Otter steps out and hits him, calling him Judas for offering to betray her confidence (IV.ii.118). Otter has used the secrets of his wife's inner sanctum to gain credit with his male friends, describing her pots of face creams and her Blackfriars' false teeth, Strand eyebrows, and Silver Street hair and concluding that 'Euery part o' the towne ownes a peece of her' (IV.ii.91-5).[10] The privacy of the boudoir has been exploded into the publicity of the whole town, thus realizing a private anxiety that, as we shall see, has haunted Mrs Otter's dreams. Her secrets, however much exaggerated or made up, are demystified and debunked among Tom's drunken fraternity, but they are also robbed of some of their force as satiric revelation when Otter tries to unsay everything he has just said while being thrashed about the ears by this 'Mrs. Mary Ambree' (IV.ii.123), this ballad-heroine soldier-in-disguise. Power is not, then, permitted to be a private matter of what goes on behind closed doors but is transformed into the public occasion of revelation and humiliation. As David Underdown has shown, such public acts of humiliation were powerful forms of social control for both scolding wives and henpecked husbands in early modern England.[11]

The other clear instance of men mystifying women and subsequently exposing and mocking in order to enhance their own standing in the community is the treatment of the Collegiate Ladies by the trio of gallants. This group of women is the source of tremendous worry and tireless secret-making among the young men. The 'colledge,' as Truewit defines it, is

> an order betweene courtiers, and country-madames, that liue from their husbands; and giue entertainment to all the *Wits*, and *Braueries* o' the time, as they call 'hem: crie downe, or vp, what they like, or dislike in a braine, or a fashion, with most masculine, or rather *hermaphroditicall* authoritie: and, euery day, gaine to their colledge some new probationer. (I.i.75–81)

Truewit imputes all manner of transgression to these women, from his initial characterization of the group as a kind of secret Catholic lay 'order' to his allusion to the mysteries of the hermaphrodite. They are said to inhabit a geographical and social space somewhere between 'courtiers' and 'country-madames,' an ambiguous terrain that raises suspicions in Truewit, the would-be enforcer of society's heterosexual, patriarchal standards for gender-role behaviour. What these women actually do, according to Truewit's account, is live apart from their husbands, consort with fashionable young men (like himself), express their opinions publicly ('crie down, or vp'), and permit other women to join them.[12] One 'new probationer' will be Mistress Morose, who Truewit subsequently reports is being instructed in 'the colledge-Grammar' (presumably a code for female speaking) and who will know 'all their secrets instantly' if she passes an initiation ritual (IV.i.29–31). The play ends with Truewit's threat that if the ladies 'haue discouer'd any mysteries to this yong gentlemen [Epicoene],' these shared secrets will soon come home to roost when the boy comes of age and becomes a 'visitant' to their salons (V.iv.247-51). Truewit wants to insist to the very end that gender-encoded, gender-destabilizing secrets have been leaked into the public domain. His repeated attempts to cry down assertive women and to pry into their imagined secrets may well reflect male uneasiness resulting from the increased value placed on private space and private experience, including marital intimacy, in early seventeenth-century England.[13]

The invasion of private space is both fantasized and enacted by Truewit in his scene-long anti-marriage tirade, recited to dissuade Morose from marrying and begetting an heir as a means of disinheriting his nephew, Dauphine. Truewit explodes into Morose's muffled inner sanctum, propelled in his speech by the full force of centuries of misogynist rhetoric, which he updates to 1609 London. His vehemently expressed antipathy to marriage is, one feels, more than a ruse to protect his friend's patrimony. He appears to be acting out a private dread of that strangely attractive, socially necessary hobgoblin called Marriage with which he tries to scare Morose. Why, he demands, should Morose 'follow this goblin *matrimony*'? (II.ii.32). Where would he expect 'to find a chaste wife, in these times? now? when there are so many masques, plaies, puritane preachings, mad-folkes, and other strange sights to be seene daily, priuate and publique?' (II.ii.33-6). Truewit hits his rhetorical stride with a series of conditional clauses followed by predictions of dire consequences: if Morose's wife 'be faire, yong, and vegetous, no sweet meats euer drew more flies. ... If foule, and crooked, she'll ... buy those doublets and roses, sir. If rich, ... shee'll raigne in your house. ... If noble ... If fruitfull ... If learned ... If precise ...' (II.ii.66-80). The litany is to be found, among other places, in catalogues of paradoxical encomiums demonstrating that the fair, rich, noble, or fertile woman makes the worst wife.[14] Truewit also raids Juvenal's sixth satire for his anti-woman material, always stressing the consumerist values of contemporary London society. Morose, he claims, will have to pay for sex by the half-hour with his wife: 'you shall lye with her but when she lists; she will not hurt her beauty, her complexion; or it must be for that iewell, or that pearle, when she do's; euery halfe houres pleasure must be bought anew' (II.ii.93-6). And then there is the bogey man of a wife's secret, other life: she will 'goe liue with her she-friend, or cosen at the colledge, that can instruct her in all the mysteries, of writing letters, corrupting seruants, taming spies' and she will go 'in disguise to that coniurer, and this cunning woman' (II.ii.102–4, 125–6). The attempted demonization of women through the spectre of unnatural female alliances fails of its immediate purpose, however, and Truewit is left to scramble to re-establish his credibility with his friends.

The process of mystifying and demonizing the female Other includes an elaborate justification of violence against women in the courtship battle. Truewit explains to his friends that 'A man should not doubt to ouer-come any woman. Thinke he can vanquish 'hem, and he shall: for though they denie, their desire is to be tempted. ... Though they striue, they would bee ouer-come' (IV.i.72–83). When Clerimont objects that 'a man must beware of force,' Truewit answers, 'It is to them an acceptable violence, and has oft-times the place of the greatest courtesie' (IV.i.84–6). Truewit's version of the no-means-yes response constructs all women as what Macbeth calls 'imperfect speakers' (*Macbeth*, I.iii.70), his phrase for the witches who tantalizingly reveal partial truths about his future with paradoxical speaking. Truewit's violence may be slightly more 'acceptable' to modern audiences than Macbeth's because it is not life-threatening, but, like Macbeth's manipulations of and by gender, Truewit's speech reveals more about him than about the women onto whom he projects his fantasy of desire. As happens repeatedly in *Epicoene*, the discourse of having secrets generates its Other, the discourse of revealing others' secrets.

It would appear that David Miller's idea of a secret self immune from the otherwise ubiquitous forces of cultural construction, which we considered at the end of chapter 1, is unavailable in the face of a secret-making, secret-revealing strategy such as Truewit's. '*Art's hid causes*' (I.i.95), those mysteries that heighten and enhance human experience, are reduced to superficial cosmetics in this play, and the characters are able to make only a few ineffectual private preparations before confronting public humiliation. In particular, women exist either as secret self-painters, striving to make themselves into a male ideal of beauty (Mrs Otter) or as slaves to their secret sexual desires (the Collegiate Ladies).[15] But it would be a mistake to view this play as a sustained male assault on female integrity. The real contest is not the traditional battle of the sexes but rather rivalries for the affections of men. The real bonding is what Eve Kosofsky Sedgwick calls homosocial, and the most elaborately engineered plots are man to man.[16] Women may be convenient markers to define failures of the manly public self and threats to that image from the secret Other, but the real commerce of the play is strictly male.

The play's main action is the sustained attack of Dauphine and his two friends on his wealthy, reclusive uncle. The secondary action that shadows this one and adds a few crucial decibels to the assault on Morose's ears is the concocted rivalry between Sir John Daw and Sir Amorous La Foole. Both are private plots with anticipated public consequences, and both use women incidentally to sort out issues of reputation and inherited wealth in a man's world. Behind the appearance of heterosexual engagement there always resides the more or less open secret of homosocial desire, and along with that is more than a hint of homoerotic activity and fantasy. According to Truewit, Clerimont has 'his mistris abroad,' for public consumption, and 'his engle at home,' for private pleasure (I.i.24-5).[17] As we will see when we consider the larger social consequences of the heavily gendered actions of *Epicoene*, perhaps the most prominent institution in Jonson's society for transferring the secrets of homoerotic pleasure from the private realm to the public was the theatre. Ovid, Sr, in *Poetaster* is morally outraged at the thought that his son will join 'the common players' as a 'stager,' to become 'an enghle for players' (*Poetaster*, I.ii.11-16). In *Epicoene*, Clerimont's 'Boy' describes himself dressed player-like in a gown and wig, tossed into bed and kissed by the Collegiates, much to the annoyance of his jealous master (I.i.13-18). By the end of the play, the various actions intersect when Daw and La Foole are chastised for publishing their sexual conquest of Epicoene, whose wig and gown have just been removed to reveal a boy on the cusp of manhood. Here and elsewhere in the play, sexuality is presented under the aspect of excess, which is as much verbal as physical and which the three gallants both participate in and labour to expose in others.[18] The fact that they play fast and loose with the socially mandated secrecy surrounding sexual indeterminacy may account for some of the aggressive undervaluing of *Epicoene* by its critics.

The play's most vocal commentator on the spectacle of strained sexual identification and noisy chatter is Truewit, a devotee of the discourse of indifference. As Jonas Barish puts it, 'Truewit stalks folly purely for the pleasure of the chase, staking nothing but his wit.'[19] He presents himself as the antithesis of Morose's impassioned single-mindedness. Like so many other bipolarities in the play, this one tends to collapse under the pressure of theatrical revelations that work counter to announced self-images, but it is a convenient place to begin analysing the two sequences of exposure and torment engineered by Truewit: the Daw vs La Foole non-encounter in act IV, scene v, and the invasion of the unwanted wedding party that takes up much of act III. I will argue that in these scenes the London gallants, ostensibly under the direction of Truewit, misappropriate the functions of guardians of the public good and the methods of rural shaming rituals in ways that contribute to the very urban excesses that Jonson ordinarily strives to contain. By relying on repeated acts of theatrical concealment, Jonson's play participates in the privatization and destabilization of publicly observable standards of 'manly' behaviour.

It is important to notice that what I have called Truewit's discourse of indifference arises not from lethargy but from a strong impulse to bedevil a wide range of social and linguistic distinctions. While he argues passionately for doing 'nothing: or that, which when 'tis done, is as idle' (I.i.33-4), he points out with equal fervor that such realities as the plague and capital punishment can cause one 'to thinke, and value euery article o' [his] time, esteeme it at the true rate, and giue all for't' (I.i.29-31). His frequent recourse to paradoxical speaking is one aspect of his indifferent commitment to both sides of every issue. His even-handed (mis)treatment of Daw and La Foole is another aspect of this, as he serves as mediator between the two, trafficking in massive, 'unmanly' male egos.

The immediate motivation behind the torment of Daw and La Foole in act IV is revenge for their publicly denigrating Dauphine, who threatens, 'I'll beate 'hem. I'll binde 'hem both to grand Madames bed-posts, and haue 'hem bayted with monkeyes' (IV.v.14-16). In fact, Truewit has already devised the baiting and announces to Dauphine and Clerimont in characteristically theatrical terms:

> here will I act such a *tragi-comoedy* betweene the *Guelphes*, and the *Ghibellines*, Daw and La-Foole – which of 'hem comes out first, will I seize on: (you two shall be the *chorus* behind the arras, and whip out betweene the *acts*, and speake.) If I doe not make 'hem keepe the peace, for this remnant of the day, if not of the yeere, I haue faild once – (IV.v.30-6)

He deposits Daw in one small, dark room of Morose's house and La Foole in another, convincing each that the other is out to murder or at least to maim him. Standing outside first one door and then the other, he pretends to be attempting to restrain the fury of the supposed attacker while the two men yield up their swords and cower terrified in their respective 'studie[s]' (IV.v.82).

The scene is reminiscent of two such practical jokes in *Twelfth Night*, the enforced duel between reluctant rivals Sir Andrew Aguecheek and Cesario/Viola (*Twelfth Night*, III.iv.218-311) and the torment of Malvolio (IV.ii). The earlier of the Shakespeare scenes is generally much admired for the witty improvisations of its perpetrators, Fabian and Sir Toby, and the frantic improvisations of the unwilling and unskilled duellists. Viola's attempts to maintain a mannish bearing while dodging a fight strike audiences as charming, and the interruption of the duel by the valiant (if confused) Antonio preserves her secret and deflects the potential violence of the scene into another situation already fraught with dangers. While the issue of gender role reversal is also prominent in the *Epicoene* sequences, the second Shakespeare scene involving deceit and humiliation, the imprisonment of Malvolio, is closer to the Daw/La Foole-baiting in its mechanisms and its tone.

Jonson's scene of tormenting hapless pretenders to social status and erudition ('What's sixe kicks to a man, that reads Seneca?' asks Truewit [IV.v.293-4]) retains all the nastiness of the Malvolio-baiting and little of the charm of the Andrew-Cesario duel. Still, it has a good deal to say about how secret information becomes a dangerously two-edged instrument of ridicule in Jonson's plays. Truewit begins his *'tragi-comoedy'* by telling Daw that his life has been threatened by La Foole and by offering to conceal him until the threat can be neutralized. Daw entreats Truewit to be his 'mediator' with La Foole (IV.v.80, 121). Truewit in turn 'vnder-takes' (320) for La Foole, and a silly form of shuttle diplomacy unfolds, with intermediate stops to share the most recent conciliatory offer with Dauphine and Clerimont. Truewit, whose indifference obliterates all differences, bargains nonchalantly with the fools' proffered body parts.

> TRV. Well, I'll trie if he will be appeas'd with a leg or an arme, if not, you must die once.
> DAW. I would be loth to loose my right arme, for writing *madrigalls*.
> TRV. Why, if he will be satisfied with a thumb, or a little finger, all's one to me. You must thinke, I'll doe my best. (IV.v.122-8)

Once Daw has been shut away again, Truewit reports the offer of a 'left wing' to Dauphine, who immediately recommends taking it and is reprimanded, 'How! Maime a man for euer, for a iest? what a conscience hast thou?' to which Dauphine responds, 'as good maime his body as his reputation' (133-9). This kind of ghoulish jesting among the lads continues through the scene: 'Your upper lip, and sixe o' your fore-teeth' negotiated down to 'your two butter-teeth,' five kicks demanded and six offered, innumerable nose-tweaks received. The victims are enjoined to silence while the kicking and tweaking is going on ('No speaking one to another' [296]), and Dauphine is substituted for the supposed punisher each time. La Foole agrees to be blindfolded and tweaked 'in priuate' (323) so that he can subsequently disclaim any knowledge of the abuse should Daw decide to boast publicly of executing the humiliation (331-4). According to La Foole's solipsistic notion of secrecy, he can never be forced to confess to others what he hasn't seen with his own eyes. This epistemology of suppression replaces knowing with not-knowing as the goal of social relations. La Foole's isolation in the midst of frantic attempts to be heard in high society is figured in his temporary imprisonment in Morose's house and Truewit's efforts to force him into silence 'for this remnant of the day, if not of the yeere' (IV.v.35-6).

The public spectacle of humiliation, the tragicomedy mounted by Truewit for the entertainment of the Collegiate Ladies with the express purpose of silencing the chattering Daw and La Foole, amounts to a communally imposed form of censorship. While any sympathy for the victims would be impossible to justify on the basis of the play-text, Jonson must have been aware that his self-appointed custodian of public standards of taste, Truewit, runs the risk of himself appearing the fool for tormenting these dolts without ever sharing with them the reason that the community of wits sees fit to mock them. So far as Daw and La Foole are aware, they receive their beatings not because of their ignorant boasting but because they have inadvertently offended each other over the matter of party invitations. Truewit's travesty of a communally sanctioned process of mediation, conciliation, and punishment raises some troubling questions. For example, should the author of a theatrical jest conceal his object so thoroughly from his comic butts and his audience? Is a dramaturgical art that itself turns on secrecy a suitable instrument for exposing the mystifications that are so boggling English society in its newly generated enthusiasm for private selves, personal relations, and private spaces? The question of the satirist's responsibility engages Jonson more directly in this play than in any of the other middle comedies.

During all the physical and psychological goading of Daw and La Foole 'in priuate' and all the naming of parts (arms, legs, lips, teeth, noses), there is no mention of the private parts. But these are the ones most at risk in the 'ritualistic castrations' of Daw and La Foole in this scene and also of Morose in the post-wedding fiasco.[20] The public torment of Morose on the day of his highly secretive wedding amounts to a public gelding and raises some of the same questions about the social responsibilities of the dramatist as the Daw and La Foole sequences.

Some years ago Ian Donaldson made a major contribution to the critical literature on *Epicoene* in his book, *The World Upside-Down*, when he called attention to its many festive elements.[21] He pointed out that when Truewit summons everyone in Morose's neighbourhood to the matrimonial feast, he is reproducing the social ritual called 'charivari.' Donaldson also drew parallels between wedding festivities in the play and the marriage masques that Jonson was writing for performance at court at about the same time. The two types of ritual festivities, one rural and the other courtly, are very different, and Jonson is more concerned in *Epicoene* with the former than the latter.

The festivity called 'charivari' brought communal opprobrium, along with the riotous clamour of 'rough music,' to the doorstep of people thought to be violating acceptable standards of behaviour, particularly in the area of sexual and marital decorum.[22] Randall Cotgrave's *Dictionarie* (1611) defines 'charivari' as 'A publicke defamation, or traducing of; a foule noise made, a black Santus rung, to the Shame, and disgrace of another; hence, an infamous (or infaming) ballade sung, by an armed troupe, under the window of an old dotard married, the day before, to a young wanton, in mockery of them both.'[23] One effect of this activity was to place more or less private forms of behaviour on public show by having other members of the community act out absurd parodies of the individual or couple deemed to be behaving improperly. A second or third marriage, as well as one between an old man and a young woman, was a likely target for this particular communal shaming ritual. Similar rituals called 'skimmingtons' publicly ridiculed marriages in which a wife scolded her husband or was unfaithful to him. These impromptu displays of community disapproval usually involved such theatrical elements as mime, transvestite disguise, and rowdy interchanges between performers and spectators. Such occasions for enforcing community standards by publishing and punishing 'deviant' behaviour provided licence for drunken and disorderly conduct on the part of those imposing the sanction. The rituals were usually enacted by the young men of the village, whose aim was surely as much to mock the serious responsibilities of marriage and to enjoy the party atmosphere as to police the social standards of sexual propriety, gender differentiation, and social responsibility.[24]

We encounter a great many elements of rural shaming ritual in *Epicoene*. In an effort to turn folly against folly, obnoxious clamour against unnatural silence, festive rout against social isolation, Truewit designs a wedding party not to celebrate but to terminate a marriage that violates his sense of patriarchal decorum. He refuses to tolerate an old man marrying a young woman for the sole purpose of siring a child to inherit what Truewit believes rightfully belongs to his friend Dauphine. The direct approach – scaring off Morose by warning him about the tribulations of marriage – having failed, Truewit turns to rowdy celebrations following the wedding to drive home his 'left-handed cries' (III.v.20) against marrying. Rather than permit the newly-weds to creep off to enjoy the 'delights ... and silence of the night,' he insists that Morose partake of 'other open pleasures, and jollities of feast, of musique, of reuells, of discourse' (III.v.48–51), knowing full well that these are precisely the activities that will make Morose regret ever having taken a bride. When *'Musique of all sorts'* (SD III.vii.3) arrives and *'The Drum and Trumpets sound'* (SD III.vii.46), the allusion to the 'rough music' involved in country rituals of public humiliation is unmistakable.

The festive protest amounts to a concerted assault on a wealthy city tyrant who would enclose within the preserve of his sound-proofed house a fortune and a nuclear family. Such grasping behaviour may be seen as analogous to that practised by wealthy landowners in English pastoral communities, behaviour that led to planned, disorderly acts of resistance – at first, perhaps, 'festive' demonstrations, later bloody riots – against land enclosure. The more or less organized, often drunken and angry demonstrations of the underclasses against economic exploitation from above, the kind of revolt that had been recently erupting in the English countryside and would continue to do so for the next three decades, had provided a strong subtext for Shakespeare's *Coriolanus* the year before *Epicoene* reached the London stage.[25] The loud, jokey, holiday-like confrontations between the plebeians and the embittered, inflexible, tyrannical hero of Shakespeare's Roman tragedy are oddly similar to the raucous torment of Morose in Jonson's London comedy. Like Coriolanus, Morose has a momentary glimpse of self-awareness ('I forgot my selfe' [III.v.108]) in the midst of a furious outburst of cursing against the barber who broadcast his secret wedding plans. He feels overwhelmed by the insistent demands of his social inferiors, and, like Coriolanus, he lacks the imaginative flexibility to survive the social earthquake and tidal wave that are crashing around him. Confronted in his own house with the babbling Daw, Haughty, Centaure, Mavis, and Trusty, he wails, 'O, the sea breakes in vpon me! another floud! an inundation! I shall be orewhelm'd with noise. It beates already at my shores. I feele an earthquake in my selfe, for't' (III.vi.2–5). Like a commander who has lost control of his troops, Morose finds himself routed, after the midpoint of the play, first by the tongue-lashing of his supposedly silent new wife, next by the hilarious banqueters and musicians, and finally by a brace of lawyers who noisily debate the fine points of his marital humiliation before a gallery of spectators. Thus ever (one is tempted to conclude) are tyrants discomfited on the Renaissance stage, from Richard III to Leontes and from Tamburlaine to Sir Giles Overreach.

A complicating factor in most theatrical celebrations of the overthrow of tyranny by the indomitable spirit of the masses is that those masses are themselves often constituted of petty tyrants who in turn are driven by a variety of less-than-admirable motives. *Epicoene* can hardly be represented as the festive triumph of a happy, integrated community over a misanthropic outsider precisely because Jonson takes us behind the scenes of the wrangling plots and counter-plots to reveal that they are all initiated out of a desire by the various social splinter groups to achieve their own self-promoting ends. Consider, for example, the action of the charivari. No one in attendance, of course, has come to *celebrate* the marriage of the old skinflint to the silent young woman. Truewit, exhibiting the improviser's dubious gift for slipping easily into others' shoes, has made the characters believe that by joining the party at Morose's house they will be effectively snubbing someone who has insulted them. The great communal 'celebration' of Morose's marriage is, in fact, based on the premise of social exclusion and is punitive, not celebratory. The result of bringing together La Foole's 'quarter-feast,' the ever-squawking Daw, all the Collegiate Ladies, and the three gallants, along with a cacophony of musicians, at Morose's house is to create perhaps the loudest non-battle scene in English drama. As we have seen, like traditional country charivaris, the sequence transforms the supposedly long-awaited private moment of marital intimacy into humiliating public spectacle. Writing about charivari, Michael Bristol concludes, 'The counter-festive vocabulary of charivari provides the community with a system of critical resources through which marriage as a social arrangement and as a private form of sexuality may be either negated or reaffirmed.'[26] In this case marriage is negated, since what is publicized are the social and sexual inadequacies of the groom, who finally flees, 'shame-fac'd' (III.vii.26-7), to the rafters at the top of his house and later willingly proclaims his own impotence in order to nullify his marriage and to silence the clamour (IV.i.20-6). The charivari has all the elements that, according to Mikhail Bakhtin, characterize the subversively festive moment, including the unruly rumblings in the lower gut of the body politic. According to Truewit, 'The spitting, the coughing, the laughter, the neesing, the farting, dauncing, noise of the musique, and [Epicoene's] masculine, and lowd commanding, and vrging the whole family, makes [Morose] thinke he has married a *furie*' (IV.i.8-11). The overall effect in *Epicoene* is not social cohesion but rather clamorous fragmentation caused by the exclusive habit of conspiracy. There are disorderly forces at work here that simply defy containment.

The difficult interpretive problem in all this, then, is not identifying the homologous actions that link the world of Jonson's play to early modern social customs but rather determining what kinds of social work are performed by the importation of custom into this particular play.[27] It might be argued that Truewit produces a parodic version of a Jacobean court wedding masque and thereby claims for himself something like the monarch's power to banish disorder and to enforce his own ideal standards for the hymeneal moment. Opposed to this interpretation is the view that Truewit is enforcing conformity from below by inciting a rag-tag army of citizens to reject the puritanical tyranny of Morose. In either view the hierarchic arrangements on which familial and economic patriarchy relied would be re-established. The problem with both interpretations is that the three young gallants are engaged in a project that is eventually shown to be self-censoring, self-serving, and socially disintegrative. These young men do not assert control by invoking a respected form of authority from above; nor do they gain popular assent in the pursuit of socially harmonizing values demanded by a restless underclass. Instead, they humiliate and exploit *everyone*, including each other, because each one wants to emerge as the city's chief wit. Their efforts lack both the economic assuredness of courtly entertainment and the joyous country qualities of the skimmington or the charivari. Their secrecy is the revealing token of their uneasiness and their lack of moral authority. While achieving their immediate end of extorting Dauphine's inheritance from Morose, they fail to create a successful form of urban cultural corrective from the models provided by court and country. What they create instead is a deeply resonant set of anxieties about the possibility of any kind of privately felt, publicly endorsed sexual identity. The secret that Jonson explodes with the transvestite bombshell at the end of *Epicoene* leaves the social order of comedy something of a wreck.

There seems to be no place in this world of noise-making conspiracies for the private self to find a quiet retreat. Even when Dauphine dismisses a silenced Morose at the end of the play to 'be as priuate as you will, sir' (V.iv.215), there is the suggestion that the only fine and private place is, in fact, the grave, and that the next celebration for Morose will be his funeral. Jonson seems to take a fierce delight in invading every private space in London and loosing every silenced tongue to give the city, along with Morose, just what it deserves. In this play, with one notable exception (the author's own well-kept dramaturgical secret, about which I will say more shortly), Jonson strips the secret man of his illusion that he can be, as David Miller puts it, 'inaccessible to the culture that would otherwise entirely determine him.'[28] The inaudible, invisible self, free from cultural construction, is not to be found in *Epicoene*, even though the potential power of silence is the play's dominant image.[29]

Jonson's running title for the play, we should recall, is *The Silent Woman*. The open secret behind the phrase is the contrary 'truth' of paradox, the stereotyped notion that there can be no such creature as a silent woman. Women are assumed to be 'naturally' talkative. The misogynist satiric tradition out of which Juvenal and, following him, Jonson wrote disallows womanliness and silence in the same person, even though Renaissance handbooks regularly enjoined the ideal wife to strive for this goal that had been so carefully placed beyond her reach.[30] For women, silence is a cruel hoax, since the only truly silent woman, like the proverbial only good Indian in Hollywood westerns, is a dead one. Whether it be the ravished Lavinia with her tongue cut out, writing the names of her assailants in the dust with a stick guided by her mouth and her handless stumps, or the soft-voiced but plain-speaking Cordelia, the foreordained and ultimately silencing outcome is death. Even the silent woman depicted on English pub signs with her severed head tucked jauntily underneath her arm cannot but be dead. The silence of Epicoene is just a momentary trick of the plot, twice repudiated by subsequent developments, once when 'she' speaks out volubly at the charivari and again when the wig is removed to reveal her as a boy. During her quiet period, Morose construes her silence as consent, which we suspect to be just a preparation for some sort of plotted resistance to his tyrannical authority, the calm before the storm. But the plot and the resistance go deeper. They use the theatre to challenge the unspoken assumptions on which gender distinction, and especially male privilege, have stood for ages.

I have been concerned throughout this study with the paradoxical and highly theatrical activity of secret speaking, an activity carried playfully to the limits of intelligibility in *Epicoene* by the notion of silent speaking. The pregnant silence, as dramatists from Shakespeare to Pinter have amply demonstrated, may carry the seed of a great many unspoken truths, of both the assenting and dissenting varieties. Indeed, there is a venerable tradition – philosophical, rhetorical, and iconographic – of silent eloquence.[31] In this tradition, hidden persuasion and the power of secret wisdom were iconographically expressed by the gesture of silence, the index finger pressed to the lips. The silenced mouth both contains and expresses volumes of *arcana* to the Renaissance viewer. For instance, in a theological dialogue by Afinati D'Acuto entitled *Il muto chè parla*, translated by A.M. (probably Anthony Munday) in 1605 as *The Dumbe Divine Speaker*, the debate over the relative merits of speech and silence is resolved in favour of silently reading the Scriptures and speaking only to utter holy mysteries. As Jonson was well aware, the divine paradox of dumb speaking had immediate political reverberations for an English audience in 1609. When Cutbeard proposes to fetch a silent minister to marry Morose, Truewit mischievously suggests that he 'get one o' the silenc'd ministers' since 'a zealous brother would torment him purely' (II.vi.15–18). The reference is to puritan-inclining clergymen forced to leave the Church after 1604 for refusing to subscribe to the Thirty-Nine Articles and the King's supremacy. In Truewit's construction, these were preachers who could *really* preach your ear off. The most strictly silenced become the most voluble, while Morose's dumbshow wedding becomes the prelude to a flood of words. Whereas in *The Tempest* Prospero's speechless spirits are reported by Alonso to convey an 'excellent dumb discourse' through their eloquent gestures (III.iii.39), in Jonson's play every silent gesture is overwhelmed by the inanities of idle speech.[32]

Jonson pursues his demystifying parody of the commercial and prophetic language of the local *arcana Dei* by having his chief silence-seeker, Morose, babble wildly of impoverished knights like his nephew, lost in London's by-ways:

> No kinsman, I will now make you bring mee the tenth lords, and the sixteenth ladies letter, kinsman; and it shall doe you no good kinsman. Your knighthood it selfe shall come on it's knees, and it shall be reiected; it shall bee sued for it's fees to execution, and not bee redeem'd. ... It shall be the tenth name in the bond, to take vp the commoditie of pipkins, and stone jugs; and the part thereof shall not furnish it knighthood forth, for the attempting of a bakers widdow, a browne bakers widdow. (II.v.103–22)

Morose himself has taken on the voice of the newly enlarged 'silenc'd minister,' preaching economic damnation against his nephew. He adds the portentousness of the preacher's prophecy ('it selfe shall come on it's knees, and it shall be reiected') to the intimidating phraseology of business contracts ('the tenth lords, and the sixteenth ladies letter'; 'the tenth name in the bond'; 'the part thereof'). The superposition of puritan pulpit oratory on very petty bourgeois economics debunks both Christian and capitalist ideologies. The mysteries of both are rendered tawdry and improbable in Morose's ramblings.

Jonson reserves the mysteries of silence solely for his own playtext, which he dubs a *'dumbe peece'* in his dedicatory letter to Sir Francis Stuart, thereby wittily foregrounding the strong silence of its printed, as opposed to its less authorially controlled acted form. The privileged communication of a text to a literate aristocrat affords Jonson a greater chance to impart his private meanings and to have them properly understood than a performance could, even a private playhouse performance. In his prefatory conceit, the silence of reading protects him from being *'indanger'd by an vn-certaine accusation'* ('To the Truly Noble, by all titles, Sir Francis Stuart,' lines 15–16) such as the one levelled at him following a performance of *Epicoene* at Whitefriars and referred to in the margin of the second preface. For the moment, at least, he is content to pass over the contradiction that, through the technology of publication, his work is being released into the hands of any Jack Daw or city wife who can read and fancies him/herself a literary critic. He knows well enough that, as Truewit says, fashionable London ladies will 'censure *poets*, and authors, and stiles, and compare 'hem, Daniel with Spenser, Ionson with the tother youth' (II.ii.116–18). Finally, having released even his self-image into a nest of jabbering women and jackdaws, Jonson is left with just one last trick of his secret art tucked up his sleeve, that is, the real identity of his title character.

If it is impossible for Jonson's characters to preserve inviolate any silent, secret, inner space, it is equally impossible for them to locate any space in public London that is safe from noisy invasions. No matter what desperate measures Morose undertakes to turn his London townhouse into a private, silent sanctuary – negotiating 'treaties with the Fish-wiues, and Orenge-women' to stay away (I.i.150), running a sword through a passing fencer's drum (I.i.178), and requiring his servant to wait on him in 'tennis-court socks' (I.i.188)[33] – he finds noise secretly smuggled into his little world. That invading noise, moreover, is definitely gendered: the voices are those of the pair of effeminate knights, the Collegiate Ladies, Mrs Otter, and the suddenly garrulous 'silent woman' of the title. Jonson's idea of hell would seem to be a roomful of women. There is something distasteful about the accounts of all the enclosed, effeminized and effeminizing spaces described in the play. The various ladies' bedchambers and dressing rooms are oily and fetid with cosmetic fucuses, and Clerimont's rooms are the site of his trysts with his 'engle.' As Karen Newman points out, even the public places of the city seem to have been appropriated for female, consumerist activities, particularly for parading about in 'coach, and horses' (IV.vi.18) and for visiting merchants' shops.[34] The Collegiates Ladies have appropriated not only the china shops but also the Exchange for their discussions of the most private of feminine subjects, for example, 'those excellent receits ... to keepe [them] selues from bearing of children' (IV.iii.57–8). According to Tom Otter, his wife's toilette is a fit topic for conversation because her face is a construct of materials purchased all over London. From Mrs Otter's perspective, the city at large assaults her whenever she leaves the confines of her house dressed for some fine public occasion. She has nightmares about her clothes and other possessions being ruined by a malevolent, primarily outdoor urban world:

> I had a dreame last night too of the new pageant, and my lady Maioresse, which is alwaies very ominous to me. I told it my lady Havghty

t'other day; when her honour came hether to see some *China* stuffes: and shee expounded it, out of Artemidorvs, and I have found it since very true. It has done me many affronts. ... [A]ny thing I doe but dreame o' the city. It staynd me a damasque table-cloth, cost me eighteen pound at one time; and burnt me a blacke satten gowne, as I stood by the fire, at my ladie Centavres chamber in the colledge, another time. A third time, at the Lords masque, it dropt all my wire, and my ruffe with waxe-candle, that I could not goe vp to the banquet. A fourth time, as I was taking coach to goe to *Ware*, to meet a friend, it dash'd me a new sute all ouer (a crimson sattin doublet, and blacke veluet skirts) with a brewers horse, that I was faine to goe in and shift mee, and kept my chamber a leash of daies for the anguish of it. (III.ii.58-77)

Clerimont remarks, 'I would not dwell in the citie, and 'twere so fatall to mee' (III.ii.79-80). But, of course, he is a creature of the city, and, like Ben Jonson, he could no more fly from it than fly above it. Their concern is that their city, however terrifying to Mrs Otter, has been taken over by the monstrous regiment of women.

The architecture of Morose's house, the setting for most of the action, is laid out on the model of the closed and hence, in this play, feminized space. There is the gallery, the lobby, the study, the enclosed garden, the courtyard, and, above, the bedchamber. Each confined interior space is systematically taken over by the invading women and their co-conspirators. These feminized spaces are, as Lorraine Helms argues, appropriate to the restricted private theatre space available to the boy's company that first performed *Epicoene* in the refectory hall at Whitefriars.[35] Indeed, I would press her argument one step further, to say that what Jonson repeatedly registers in *Epicoene* is a deep concern that the theatre as an institution might be having a disastrously effeminizing effect on his entire city, that the 'children' it spawned were contributing to the cult of privacy and of the autonomous self, thereby undercutting traditional communal values that, for Jonson, identified a man reassuringly by his social position.[36]

The power of theatrical cross-dressing is elaborately thematized in *Epicoene* from its curious title term through a series of jests about sexual ambiguity to its final revelation. While in grammar the term 'epicene' means denoting either sex without change of gender, when applied to persons the term comes to mean 'effete' (L. *effetus*, worn out by childbirth). In Jonson's play, as in his culture, the term is applied not to postpartum women but rather to men whose virility is so exhausted as to render them effeminate. Jonson's title character (having not yet reached manhood), the socially and intellectually exhausted knights (John Daw and Amorous La Foole, who 'carry the feminine gender afore' them [V.i.31]), and the henpecked Tom Otter (the *'animal amphibium'* [I.iv.26]) all slide into the epicene category. But so too do the idle, frenchified, and apparently bisexual Clerimont and his two friends, Truewit and Dauphine Eugenie. The gallantry of the latter group brings them close to the tabooed sexuality of the Jacobean court, which in turn had allied itself with the licentious tricks of the London stage. Among others, Francis Osborne, a not altogether reliable seventeenth-century historian, explicitly links supposedly effeminizing same-sex love with both the King and the royally licensed theatres. In his *Secret History of the Court of James the First,* Osborne writes of James's ardent attentions to certain courtiers:

> The love the king shewed was as amorously convayed, as if he had mistaken their sex, and thought them ladies; which I have seen Somerset and Buckingham labour to resemble, in the effeminatenesse of their dressing ... [T]he kings kissing them after so lascivious a mode in publick, and upon the theatre, as it were, of the world, prompted many to imagine some things done in the tyringhouse, that exceed my expressions no lesse then they do my experience.[37]

Osborne's exposé of secret assignations (that, of course, far outrun his own properly heterosexual experience) moves coyly from a conditional misconstruction of events ('as if [James] had mistaken their sex') to a salacious joke ('kissing them ... upon the theatre'). However unpleasant we may find Osborne's voyeuristic view of history, the passage suggests that accusations that the stage was an effeminizing space were not confined to a handful of antitheatrical tracts. What goes on in the tiring house, that private space just off stage where boys dressed for their epicene parts, offers a particularly rich site for speculation. And Jonson, too, occasionally invites speculation that the secrets of *Epicoene's* art may not all be revealed on the Whitefriars stage.[38]

Having set up the central economic and social problems of his comedy with a pair of preliminary theatrical jests, the ones involving the Otters and Daw and La Foole, Jonson works through (but also apart from) his trickster, Truewit, to bring his play to its highly self-conscious, highly theatrical conclusion. First, Truewit directs the costuming of his actors:

> O, I'll make the deepest Diuine, and grauest Lawyer, out o' them two [i.e. Otter and Cutbeard] ... Clap but a ciuill gowne with a welt, o' the one; and a canonical cloake with sleeues, o' the other: and giue 'hem a few termes i' their mouthes, if there come not forth as able a Doctor, and compleat a Parson, for this turne, as may be wish'd, trust not my election. And, I hope, without wronging the dignitie of either profession, since they are but persons put on, and for mirths sake, to torment him [i.e. Morose]. (IV.vii.40-50)

These are to be the persons, the *dramatis personae*, of Truewit's play, and this speech is his apologetical prologue, explaining, as Peter Quince and, indeed, as Ben Jonson himself had on earlier occasions, that this is just theatrical fakery performed for mirth's sake, intending to offend no one. No one? Not even the secular and ecclesiastic authorities who, far from taking part in dramatic revelry, sought to spy out its secrets and to limit its popularity? Well, perhaps not, though Jonson seems at times to share an ironic, if not perverse, identification with his persecutors, much as Morose himself does.

As the penultimate scene of *Epicoene* gets under way, only the self-reflexive language of theatricality seems capable of serving Jonson's design. Truewit summons his actors and announces, 'I haue fitted my Diuine, & my Canonist, died their beards and all: the knaues doe not know themselues, they are so exalted, and alter'd. Preferment changes any man' (V.iii.2-5). But surely Truewit's creator knows better than to buy into this kind of *arriviste* thinking. Does Christopher Sly in the Induction to Shakespeare's *The Taming of the Shrew* change with his elevation to lordship, or does he remain the vulgar and violent lout that he was before he passed out? Much as Jonson's Whitefriars audience of young men living in hope of munificent patronage might have wanted to believe in the miracle of transformation by preferment within a stable, male-dominated social order, Jonson offers them little reason to expect it in *Epicoene*. Certainly Otter and Cutbeard remain very much their blathering and assaultive selves in their guises of Master Parson and Master Doctor. In the next scene these two will travesty the attempts of the judiciary to establish the terms of a legally binding marriage.[39] But in the preparatory, backstage scene Truewit focuses his attention elsewhere, on the standard three-doored set of much Roman and English comedy. He speaks first to Dauphine:

> Thou shalt keepe one dore, and I another, and then Clerimont in the midst, that he [Morose] may haue no meanes of escape from their cauilling, when they grow hot once. And then the women (as I haue giuen the bride her instructions) to breake in vpon him, i' the *l'enuoy.* O, 'twill be full and twanging! Away, fetch him. Come, master Doctor, and master Parson, looke to your parts now, and discharge 'hem brauely: you are well set forth, performe it as well. (V.iii.5–13)

Break a leg! he might well have said, in the fine tradition of theatre irony. One effect of the openly metadramatic language in the scene is to create a cozy sense of secret plots shared with an audience, both on stage and off, that no longer needs to remain outside the dramatic illusion. Like the cook at a public feast (the first Prologue, line 8), Jonson invites everyone to partake of the fare and the preparations. The scene suggests that there will be something to please all palates. What follows is indeed 'full and twanging' comedy, replete with absurd Latin legal jargon and seemingly endless *distinguos* from the tormentors, and near-escapes followed by further humiliations for the tormented. In a desperate attempt to halt the inquisition, Morose declares to the assembled company, 'I am no man, ladies ... Vtterly vn-abled in nature, by reason of *frigidity*, to performe the duties, or any the least office of a husband' (V.iv.44–7). When impotence proves insufficient grounds for divorce, on comes the brace of effeminate knights to testify to having shared the sexual favours of the bride. This too fails to do the trick, since the purported assignations are said to have occurred before Epicoene's marriage to Morose. Truewit's farce seems to lack an ending until Dauphine steps forward to remove Epicoene's wig and to declare an annulment on the basis of a palpable *error personae*, the joining of two men in marriage (V.iv.208).

With a single stroke, all the plot's insiders – including Jonson's audience – are made outsiders. At this moment the entire theatrical enterprise lurches slightly. The in-play director, Truewit, is made to look the fool along with the shamefaced knights who have exposed themselves as either liars or sodomites and the ladies who have taken a disguised man into their confidence. Even the triumphant Dauphine, the consummate trickster with his newly wangled £500 a year and his assured inheritance, emerges both as a mere emulator of his crony, Truewit, as well as the foolish suitor of *all* the Collegiate Ladies. Indeed, Truewit's earlier accusation that the

Collegiates can act only 'in aemulation one of another' (IV.vi.68) finds an uncomfortably close echo in the behaviour of all three gallants. However determined they have been to ridicule the supposed secrets of others – the myths of the maiden and the termagant wife;[40] the manly, boasting misrepresentations of Otter, Daw, and La Foole; the powers of the 'colledge' of masterless women who threaten the young men's dominance of London's public places – these city gents have proved themselves part of the problem that Jonson is addressing. Far from sharing the values of a unified community, each one has been plotting and fantasizing on his own behalf, excluding everyone else from his crumbling wit's commonwealth.[41]

Epicoene's revelation puts into focus the play's persistent concerns about the existence of a private, potent male self. That self draws its confirmation from legal, theological, and economic institutions and demands the suppression of all competitors, especially sexually ambiguous, effete, effeminized, cloistered, secret Others. The theatrical device of cross-dressing, which apparently relies on precisely drawn gender distinctions – Epicoene is *really* male and only appeared to be female because of his costume and wig – in fact propels Jonson's play into sociological and psychological gray areas of speculation and irresolution. Epicoene, both the character and the actor, exists in the highly secretive, liminal territory of pubescence or immediately pre-pubescence. Neither man nor boy, perhaps an 'engle' performing a woman's part in sex acts, Epicoene theatrically represents a gap in the social structures that legitimate the exercise and transfer of male prerogative and power. The young gentlemen in the Whitefriars audience could hardly have found Jonson's ending reassuring.

Surely Ian Donaldson is correct to insist about *Epicoene* that 'The idea of secrecy runs right through the play.'[42] It is also clear that the social force of secrets in the play is disintegrative. The real villains of the piece are those effeminized private spaces where the activities of sexual and economic unmanning take place. But the one secret that Jonson tries to exempt from criticism is his own private trick of last-minute discovery, the jest from which his audience has been completely excluded. Possibly the sole exception to Jonson's negative attitude toward both creators and violators of secrets is his own art of the theatre. The kind of small-room (if not drawing-room) comedy of manners that Jonson pioneered in *Epicoene* was to set the course for English stage comedy on into the

Restoration period and beyond. The confined theatrical spaces – bedrooms and closets, for example – and the homosocial motivations of generations of London stage fops replaced the characters and configurations of the Elizabethan theatre. The whispered secret and the hidden birthmark became the stock-in-trade of post-Jonsonian comedy in the wake of *Epicoene*, regardless of Jonson's frequently reiterated moral and intellectual revulsion from secrecy as a source of social control.

CHAPTER FIVE

The New Face of Secrecy in *The Alchemist*

Truewit's mock undertaking to preserve the secrets of the gossips' inner sanctum at the end of *Epicoene* shows Jonson once again reserving a prominent place for an attack on inside information gained by spying. While to some degree all theatre audiences are spies, eavesdropping on characters who are by convention unaware of their presence, Jonson doesn't foreground this fact in *Epicoene*. He relies instead on the quasi-public gossip of the Collegiate Ladies and the city gallants to reveal the secrets of face-painting, contraception, and promiscuity that characterize the trivialized world of the play. He never, for example, takes us into the boudoir for a cosmetic make-over the way he does at the beginning of act II of *Sejanus*. But *Epicoene*'s world of catty but studiously polite reporting gives way to a more aggressive, behind-the-scenes kind of conspiracy in *The Alchemist* (1610) and to a more intrusive, spy-like function for the audience.

The foundation of *The Alchemist* is the *arcana criminalis*, the cozening tactics of Jacobean con-artists.[1] Jonson's shady tricksters manipulate a discourse that suggests that they are in possession of special knowledge, powerful secrets that can make their followers wonderfully rich. Aspiring novitiates come to share these mysteries and the attendant riches, and in the process their secret longings are transformed into public humiliation. As in the plays we have been looking at, the self-protective function of secrecy is overtaken by the characters' urge to read all economic terms as though they were, on one hand, a secret code to be carefully guarded and, on the other, an evangelical message to be broadcast as widely as possible. The result is a crazily unstable epistemology that depends on exclusive information whose power requires its publication and whose publication entails its vitiation.

In dedicating *The Alchemist* to Mary, Lady Wroth, Jonson presents his play as one virtuous woman to another, scorning '*the ambitious Faces of the time: who, the more they paint, are the lesse themselves*' (lines 16–18). Certainly Jonson's was among the eager, ambitious faces at court at the time, but he excludes himself from the offending horde with his gender-specific reference to face-painting. The women from whom Jonson assiduously separates himself and Lady Wroth – who is, as he points out, a very Sidney for judgment – are imagined to have a unitary, essential self, one that can be craftily concealed. Some are more, some less, themselves, depending perhaps on the thickness of their foundation fucus. Inauthenticity is thus ascribed to women in a dedication to a very special, wholly authentic female patron. Jonson goes on to say that his printed text is '*forbidden to speake more; lest it talke*' (lines 15–16) as foolishly as female gossips.[2]

Among the list of persons in *The Alchemist* are only two women, one who scarcely has a voice and another whose voice rises above the most vociferous and powerful male voices in the play. The contrast between these two women, their faces and voices, can tell us much about the kind of comedy Jonson thought could profitably be written in 1610 and the kinds he knew could not.[3] To put the case for *The Alchemist* succinctly, the days of romantic comedy with its gentle ladies, fairies, queens, and *bona fide* fairy queens were dead and gone. The day of the hard-working, many-faced, multivoiced whore of city satire who could keep – or better yet propagate – a secret matrix of power was upon London.[4] Such women never act alone in Jonson's plays, however. They learn from their male mentors that knowledge is power only when it has been revealed. It was, after all, a man, Jeremy the butler, who did it and who flaunts the doing of it before his master, Lovewit, at the end of the play.

Dame Pliant, wooed by one man, promised in marriage to another, and lusted after by several others, speaks only nine lines in *The Alchemist*. Her most characteristic utterance is 'Ile doe as you will ha' me, brother' (IV.iv.36). This shiny-faced young widow is ready to abrogate her titled, landed power not only to her roaring-boy brother but to any man who will call her 'ladie' (IV.ii.55). By way of contrast, Dol Common will noisily arrogate to herself all the power that the alchemical, religious, literary, and criminal *arcana* at her disposal will allow. Behind her painted face and polysemic virtuosity of speech lie the ambitions of the New Woman, who will forcefully assert her power in the quest for the new, liquid assets of the city. As in *Volpone*, the conspiratorial, essentially financial intrigues of *The Alchemist* move not toward the social reconstruction and celebration of romantic comedy but toward collapse and retreat at the moment of comic revelation.

Dol spends much of her time trying to forestall the revelation of the secret enterprise based in Lovewit's London house. In the play's opening scene she attempts to restrain her brawling confederates, Subtle and Face, lest their 'precise neighbours' (I.i.164) should report their nefarious activities to the authorities. Not that she is any less deceitful or tyrannical than her male cohorts. She does not scruple to combine physical force with verbal persuasion:

> *She catcheth out Face his sword: and breakes Subtles glasse.*
> DOL. S'death, you abominable paire of stinkards,
> Leaue off your barking, and grow one againe,
> Or, by the light that shines, I'll cut your throats. (SD, I.i.115; 117-19)

There are at least two points at issue in this exchange. One turns on secrecy and publicity, helping to establish from the outset the kind of intrigue comedy we are watching. Another has to do with the woman's place in the cozening hierarchy. When she challenges Subtle with 'Doe not we / Sustaine our parts?' he answers, 'Yes, but they are not equall' (I.i.144-5). Subtle feels himself superior because in his mind he has quite sincerely invested the alchemical language of fermentation, cibation, and subtilization (his namesake) with the necessarily secret power of mystifying his dupes. But part of Dol Common's commonness is a strong strain of common sense that undercuts the claims of her self-important male cohort. For all his 'masculinity' as a poet, Jonson always finds effective ways to deflate male pomposity and posturing.

Secret knowledge and the power it is thought to confer in the worlds of *Sejanus*, *Volpone*, and *Epicoene* also lie at the heart of Jonson's representation of epistemological fraud in *The Alchemist*. A fervent exponent of what might now be called liberal humanism, Jonson was himself prepared at times, however, to assert the existence of a hidden, essential cause which provides the motive force behind all that we know. 'There is a more secret *Cause*,' he wrote in *Discoveries*, 'and the power of liberall studies lyes more hid, then that it can bee wrought out by profane wits' (*Disc.*, lines 168-70). This idea takes one distinctively Jonsonian form in his masques and another, equally forceful, one in the comedies of the middle period. In the masques, pretenders to the secrets of power are regularly routed at the moment of revelation, that instant when the scenic shell that has been obscuring the true and irresistible motive force behind Inigo Jones's wondrous machines opens to reveal regal power in its authentic, essential form.[5] In the middle comedies, the veil of worldly objects, whose texture lies so densely over these plays, is rent, sometimes with explosive force, to reveal not a single informing cause but an odd assortment of mutually contending causes, all of them rooted in the social and political economies of Jonson's London. Nowhere in his corpus did Jonson more deftly expose to full view the city's most extravagant (and profane) aspirations to find out the secret causes of happiness and large incomes than in *The Alchemist*.

Subtle's profane studies in the field of alchemy emerge as a shadowy reflection of the liberal studies to which Jonson devoted himself so assiduously. Subtle explains his method of alchemical exposition in a series of analogies.

> Was not all the knowledge
> Of the *Egyptians* writ in mystick *symboles*?
> Speake not the *Scriptures*, oft, in *parables*?
> Are not the choisest *fables* of the *Poets*,
> That were the fountaines, and first springs of wisedome,
> Wrapt in perplexed *allegories*? (II.iii.202–7)

On one hand, it may seem that the theory of language which Subtle so effectively sells to Mammon over Surly's protests in this scene is an essentially occlusive one. So long as his technical jargon mystifies his hearers, he can keep alive the promise of the Philosopher's Stone without actually having to produce anything but words. But his notion of language as perplexed and perplexing allegory is also an invitation to interpret what he says, to find out his secret meanings. Mammon is quick to accept the invitation. In his interpretation of one of the poets' choicest fables, Mammon imagines that Sisyphus suffers his everlasting punishment because he threatened to reveal the secret of the stone.

> Sisiphvs was damn'd
> To roule the ceaslesse stone, only, because
> He would haue made ours common. (II.iii.208–10)

From these lines, it would appear that the stone that Sisyphus is condemned ceaselessly to shove up the hill is not, as Alvin Kernan glosses it, the Philosopher's Stone (which Mammon distinguishes as *ours*, not *his*), but rather a common-garden-variety one, simply and always a burden.[6] I mention this because the distinction between the commonplace and the special is so prominent in the play. We hear of the distinction between the 'normal' neighbours and the colloquy of thieves, between the mass of the 'profane' and the handful of the elect, between everyday language and a variety of specialized, hieroglyphic ones, between common knowledge with its attendant modest aspirations and arcane knowledge that excites exotic dreams, transgressing the boundaries of common sense and common law.

The line of Mammon's quoted above, 'He would haue made ours common,' while announcing the punishment for publishing the secret code of the alchemists, also serves to cue the entrance of Dol Common, the common property of London whoremongers. Immediately following her silent passage through the scene, however, Face refers to her as 'a lords sister' (II.iii.222). He sets her apart from the common woman in the eyes of Mammon and Surly not only by her elevated social station but also by her imputed madness, caused by reading Hugh Broughton's millenarian tracts. This adds a touch of the abnormal, the exotic to Dol. Her amusingly rapid rise on the social ladder eventually carries her to the rank of Fairy Queen in act III. Here and elsewhere, Jonson plays with the distinction between the commonplace and the extraordinary through fables in which the one is linguistically transformed into the other.

In the highly popular literatures of cony-catching, puritan evangelizing, and alchemy, Jonson found forms of discourse that are self-contending in the sense that they promise to reveal what should not be revealed.[7] Each of these minor genres promises to expose the secret cause of things. Jonson was quick to exploit the often humorous contradictions inherent in forms of writing that claim to clarify but actually obscure their matter. While making and keeping secrets tend to divide those who can know from those who can't, revealing secrets to those deemed unfit to receive them merely creates confusion and lack of differentiation. The particular forms of differentiation or exclusion on which London society in the early seventeenth century was constructed included the secrets of merchant guilds, clerical training, patronage, attendance at court, and even an elaborate hierarchy of criminal types.[8] The indiscriminate publication of certain of these secrets in *The Alchemist* leads to comic misunderstanding and confusion. For instance, Jonson's puritan preachers, having dug through the cabalistic roots of their 'learning,' deny the difference between priest and laity yet insist on unfathomable distinctions between the elect and the damned.

Even when logical, social, and other forms of distinction are most thoroughly demolished for the characters in *The Alchemist*, the play retains its own cultural and comic logic. To take just one example of a débâcle with a purpose, in IV.v, Dol's babble, borrowed apparently at random from the puritan hysterics of Hugh Broughton, fuses chaotically with the simultaneously spoken lines of Face and Mammon, threatening to blot out all sense.

> And so we may arriue by *Talmud* skill,
> And profane *greeke*, to raise the building vp
> Of Helens house, against the *Ishmaelite*,
> King of *Thogarma*, and his *Habergions*
> Brimstony, blew, and fiery; and the force
> Of King Abaddon, and the Beast of *Cittim*:
> Which *Rabbi* David Kimchi, Onkelos,
> And Aben-Ezra doe interpret *Rome*. (IV.v.25-32)

But the choice of Dol's texts for this diatribe – *A Concent of Scripture* (1590) and *The Revelation of the Holy Apocalyps* (1610) – is by no means haphazard. Broughton represents for Jonson all that is wrong in the frantic resurgence of interest in reinterpreting biblical texts and had already come under attack in *Volpone* (II.ii.119). His technique for explicating scripture was, at once, prescriptive and obscurantist. His books claimed to present a clear and unitary account of biblical symbol and history. What they delivered instead was anti-Catholic propaganda and a literal-minded genealogist's impoverishing version of the Bible's poetry. Dol Common's lines carefully reproduce Broughton's authoritative-sounding rhetoric ('by *Talmud* skill,' etc.), prophetic fervour ('to raise the building vp ... against the *Ishmaelite*'), and incantatory invocation of exotic names. Not only has Jonson debunked the mesmerizing rhetoric of the zealous preacher by having Face and Mammon talk right through Dol's recitation, but he has extended his interrogation of religious discourse specifically to include those who would rewrite history in order to establish political power.

The Fifth Monarchists, whose apocalyptic interpretation of history Broughton documents in *A Concent of Scripture*, were just one of the marginal religious groups that, as recent historians have argued, had a far larger impact on the development of seventeenth-century political thought and action than is usually recognized.⁹ From Dol's fairly accurate review of the four 'monarchies' leading up to the Millennium, it appears that Jonson had done more than simply glance at Broughton's books.¹⁰ Contemporary Londoners were constantly being subjected to new accounts of the hidden forces behind the unfolding of human history. If the authors of these accounts were slightly unbalanced in Jonson's view, they also had at their disposal a potent and persuasive form of madness, a more or less rigorous discipline that threatened to enthral the common person with its new force. The charismatics had joined forces with the scholars to produce disciplined madness. Jonson captures the power of this odd combination of forces in *The Alchemist* when, as Dol's ravings reach their highest pitch, he has Subtle's alchemical laboratory explode off stage in a devastating parody of apocalyptic destruction that plunges Mammon's dream of the Philosopher's Stone once again into the obscure and inaccessible reaches of the human mind.

Just as explosions seem to have been a fairly regular feature of alchemical experimentation, obscurity was a trademark of alchemical discourse.¹¹ Alchemical writers regularly found themselves confronted with a paradox that seems to have amused Jonson greatly, the paradox of concealment and revelation. Roger Bacon, for example, keeps trying to explain how it is that he can 'deliuer ... great and hidden secret[s]' without violating the prohibitions religiously repeated by each member of the alchemical fraternity.¹² He takes as the starting point for his apologia for printing the unprintable no less an authority than Aristotle, who

> affirmeth in his booke of Secrets, that hee is a breaker of the celestiall seale that maketh the secrets of Art and Nature common. ... [H]ee impayreth the Maiestie of things, that diuulgeth mysteries. And they are no longer to bee tearmed Secrets, when the whole multitude is acquainted with them, if wee regard the probable diuision of the multitude, which euermore gainsay the learned. (75)

Never mind that Aristotle did not write the 'booke of Secrets.' Here, in relatively unmystifying terms, is the elitist distinction between the mindless 'common people' (Bacon's phrase) and the true understanders, a division of the readership to which Jonson has frequent recourse in his dedications and prologues.¹³

It can be argued, and indeed was as early as the seventeenth century, that Jonson himself appropriates the hermeneutic of secrecy through his scholarly obscurantism (see Dekker's critique of his welcoming verses for King James, above 8–9), his theatrical trickery (see my critique of *Epicoene*, above 81–3), and his demand in his prefaces for an audience of in-group 'understanders.' To insist that Jonson was single-mindedly averse to all secrets and in favour of open communications would be to construct him as a modern liberal advocate of free speech – which he decidedly was not. He would insist, however, that the understanding that he required of his interpreters was not of the arcane variety but was available to any educated person with even minimal intellectual agency. Those who were slaves to the various *arcana* of the day were fair game for his satiric pen. They could not expect to read his books as he intended them to be read.

Before the rapid spread of printing and the establishment of large public playhouses in England in the latter half of the sixteenth century, there were practical factors at work that automatically limited the size of the prospective audience for texts of whatever kind. Thereafter, writers sensitive to the vagaries of, if not a mass audience, at least relatively large and varied ones bid reluctant farewells to the books they are sending forth into the world to receive who knew what reception and construction.[14] In court circles, the habit of circulating one's literary efforts in manuscript to a restricted group of like-minded readers died hard.[15] This was a far safer readership than was encountered in the process of pre-publication censorship and the subsequent appropriations that any published text might suffer. Writers treating occult material were especially sensitive on this point. To stay with the example I have already used, Roger Bacon declares that 'he is worse then mad that publisheth any secret, vnlesse he conceale it from the multitude, and in such wise deliuer it, that euen the studious and learned shall hardly vnderstand it.'[16] What we are witnessing here is the institutionalization of a two-tiered system of readers, the multitude, who will skim the surface, and the select few, the initiates, who will be able to plumb the depths. The implication of Bacon's reflections on the alchemist's dilemma is that truly worthwhile texts – those that reveal the secret causes of things to those equipped to penetrate their symbols, figures of speech, riddles, and other such 'tricks of obscurity' (Bacon, 78) – will constitute an exclusive group and will be richly rewarded for their intellectual labours. Renaissance writers frequently likened the power of the secret knowledge generated and perpetuated by such laborious (and at times laboured) readings to the invaluable treasures arduously recovered from the gold mines of the New World and the archaeological excavations of the old. Extolling the virtue of hard work and careful trading, they write rapturously of the riches returned from the colonies to Spain, Italy, and England. By the same token, central to the imaginative recovery of ancient civilization was the physical labour of digging up and reconstructing the ruins of Rome.[17]

As with gold mines and Roman villas, so too with texts, ancient and modern. The deeper one dug into the material, or so the metaphoric suggestion ran, the greater the rewards. Within reason. And here Ben Jonson drew the line. He found laughable Roger Bacon's notion that the Jews expressly guarded their secrets by writing in 'consonants only' (Bacon, 76), a supposed code which Broughton proudly cracked by simply transcribing unvowelled Hebrew names into English in the preface to *A Concent of Scripture*, from which Dol Common quotes the lines,

> *a learned Linguist*
> *Shall see the antient vs'd communion*
> *Of vowells, and consonants –* (IV.v.18–20)

This was to find subtlety where none existed. Indeed, the whole notion of subtilization, so vital to alchemical discourse and laboratory procedure, provided Jonson not only with a suitable name for his alchemist but with the grounds of his critique of overly ingenious textual interpretation.[18] Jonson associates the rarefied air of scientific and religious speculation with the infamous incident in Parliament (ca. 1607) that occasioned those lines 'writ so subtly of the *fart.*'[19] Such subtlety flies *'in fumo,'* like the idle dreams spun out in Subtle's back-room laboratory (IV.v.58) and Lovewit's backhouse (III.v.78–81; V.iv.5–6).

The number of gags about flatulence, excrement, and anuses in *The Alchemist* is remarkable.[20] Bad smells and excremental visions emerge from every corner of Jonson's London – from the Houses of Parliament and the reformed pulpits, the pubs and open sewers, the printing houses and the royal presence chamber. Why does Jonson insist on dragging his audiences through all this muck? One answer – Edmund Wilson's in the classic essay 'Morose Ben Jonson' – is the psychological fixation of the large, untrained child in Jonson who found it clever to produce, accumulate, and display a sizable amount of disagreeable stuff that would serve to shock the adult world and give the lie to all its pointless proprieties.[21] Another possible answer is that there existed in Jonson's London a substantial alternative audience to the one he was striving to please in his court masques – a raw, vital, but largely suppressed society that craved the kind of stories available in such popular literary forms as ballads, cony-catching pamphlets, and, increasingly in the early seventeenth century, stage plays. This underworld made up as large a part of the symbolic geography of Jonson's London as Mary Le Bow or St Paul's, Whitehall or the Strand. The lines of significance on this new, alternative map of the city are the open sewers, the covered ditches, and the Pissing Conduit. To descend into this underworld was to offend, but equally to titillate, the world of perfumed popinjays at court. To accompany Jonson 'On the Famous Voyage' (composed ca. 1610) through London's stinking sewer system is to suspect that Jonson's transgressions of literary kind and bodily function in this poem and in *The Alchemist* must have some other purpose than to recommend by contraries a deodorized world of impeccable classical balance and proportion. There is, for Jonson, something worth seeing in the secret netherworlds of London, and only by entering the conspiracies behind the scenes can the theatre audience learn to outface the fiction embraced by the 'normal' world that none other exists. What was needed in order to make the point was an unusual setting within the familiar surroundings of early seventeenth-century London.

Establishing a conspiratorial sanctuary entails the mystification of a space, a place apart from the public, a place where secrets may be contained. Such a space must be limited, vacant, and indeterminate. The space selected by the conspiring *'venter tripartite'* is Lovewit's temporarily vacated London townhouse, before which and in which all the action of *The Alchemist* takes place. This is the most narrowly restricted of any of Jonson's settings. The inner sanctum is conveniently void of its normal life, and one might do worse than imagine the ghostly forms of sheet-shrouded furniture on stage for a modern production. Knaves and fools rush in to occupy this void, filling it with objects and activities, both real and imagined, that are invested with spurious meaning and value by the members of the conspiracy. The narrow hermeneutic constructed by this closed interpretive community cannot accommodate the intrusion of outsiders such as Surly (who is finally banished) and Lovewit (who co-opts all sense and the residual treasure). With the return of the interpretive norms of the suburban community – assertions of ownership, consultations with neighbours, appeals to the authorities – the conspirators can no longer legislate their own sense of things. They have, though, left their distinctive mark on the way we perceive the arbitrary business of assigning significance to human activities.

The conspiratorial act of investing space with the power to fulfil the desires of anyone gullible enough to be lured into the conspiracy bears a compelling resemblance to Jonson's own treatment of his audience and his theoretical space. In certain important ways the analogy is not exact, but it can reveal some of the ways that Jonson's play works as theatre. The nearly bare stage of the opening scene sketchily represents the doorway to a house. Before long, hints in the text begin to tie down time and place so as to locate the original audience at or near the scene of the crimes to be enacted on or about the dates specified. The year is 1610, the place Blackfriars, both in reality and in the fiction.[22] The sense of identification with the fictional setting must have been striking. The partly planned, partly improvised intrigues engineered by the tricksters are repeatedly likened to the playwright's invention and the actor's realization of it. Finally, the audience, seeking to be delighted and, perhaps, instructed, have much in common with those who present themselves at Lovewit's house to be rewarded with magic talismans, treated to glimpses of another world, and instructed in the fashions of the times. All the stage is a world, but the men and women in attendance are more than merely gulls. If they are taking Jonson's charge seriously, they are 'Iudging Spectators' (Prologue, 3), passing judgments on the activities portrayed in ways that Drugger, Dapper, Mammon, the puritans, and Kastril never do.

The activities of the first four acts are so rapid-fire and various as to mystify both Lovewit's neighbours and the gulls who enter the house in hopes of joining the exclusive club within. What they find is a *'labyrinth'* (II.iii.308) of indeterminate and impenetrable inner space. It's impossible for Dapper, for example, to tell precisely where the Fairy Queen is when the invisible Dol addresses him through a speaking tube (I.iv.4-5). Mammon and the religious fanatics, Tribulation and Ananias, find themselves barred from Subtle's inner sanctum, the alchemical laboratory where the subtilization of the Philosopher's Stone is supposedly going forward. When the loud noise off stage is heard in IV.v, the laboratory is, oddly, invested with still greater materiality. If it blew up, it must have been there.

Something has happened somewhere in this peculiar underworld warren, and Face is only too ready to interpret the event.

> O sir, we are defeated! all the *workes*
> Are flowne *in fumo*: euery glasse is burst.
> Fornace, and all rent downe! as if a bolt
> Of thunder had beene driuen through the house.
> *Retorts, Receiuers, Pellicanes, Bolt-heads,*
> All strooke in shiuers! (IV.v.57–62)

When Subtle collapses, '*as in a swoune,*' Face interprets that too, in a ploy reminiscent of Mosca's courtroom explication of Volpone's demon-exorcising faint. All of this action turns on the interpretation of the *invisibilia*, the physically absent and the spiritually hidden. And it all becomes grist for Mammon's 'voluptuous mind' (IV.v.74).

That quality of voluptuousness is a major creative force behind the mystification of space in *The Alchemist*. When Sir Epicure Mammon first appears at the start of act II, he relies heavily on the fantastic perspective used to enliven and mystify the travel books of Jonson's day.

> Come, sir. Now, you set your foot on shore
> In *nouo orbe*; Here's the rich *Peru*:
> And there within, sir, are the golden mines,
> Great Salomon's *Ophir*! He was sayling to 't,
> Three yeeres, but we have reach'd it in ten months. (II.i.1–5)

One arrives in this brave new world with the expectation of hidden riches to be mined from the depths of the mysterious place. Mammon is the best public relations man the confidence tricksters could have. He has made the alchemical dream of perfecting nature a lively part of his reality. He works in perfect concert with those who would fleece him, populating the void of Lovewit's house with his own visions. He has come to be initiated into the mytho-scientific conspiracy that will allow him to exclude, or at least to condescend to, all outsiders.

Initiating the gulls into the conspiracy constitutes a large part of the action of *The Alchemist*. These neophytes are encouraged to view the undifferentiated space in Lovewit's (or rather, as they think, Captain Face's) house as 'a world of ceremonies' (I.ii.144). They must prepare themselves intellectually and spiritually to receive whatever insights are to be vouchsafed them.[23] To be admitted into the confidence of those in charge, the visitors undergo ritualized tests of patience, poverty, and mortification of the flesh. Subtle tells Dapper that he must prepare himself to see the Fairy Queen by being 'bath'd, and fumigated, first' (I.ii.145). He continues,

> Sir, against one a clock, prepare your selfe.
> Till when you must be fasting; onely, take
> Three drops of vinegar, in, at your nose;
> Two at your mouth; and one, at either eare;
> Then, bath your fingers endes; and wash your eyes;
> To sharpen your fiue senses; and, cry *hum*,
> Thrise; and then *buz*, as often; and then, come. (I.ii.164-70)

The senses thus purged and heightened by symbolic gestures familiar to those seeking visionary experience, Dapper will be permitted to proceed to the next stage of the ritual in his quest for a magic charm for the gaming tables.[24] He must pay out a sizable sum of money, offering thereby to ingratiate himself with the supernatural powers and signalling his desire to divest himself of the things of this world so as to be prepared to glimpse another one. In III.iv Dapper offers up his Edward shillings, Harry sovereigns, and Elizabeth groats in a great paean to English coinage (III.iv.142-8). The parody of ritual divestiture and reinvestiture is complete with the detail of the clean shirt: 'You doe not know / What grace her *Grace* may doe you in cleane linnen' (I.ii.174-5). The solid middle-class juxtaposition of cleanliness and divinity confirms that for the (s)elect few there is a short, easy way from capitalism to the realm of the invisible.

The naturally fit instruments of their own undoing are Jonson's puritans, victims of their own religious doctrine and practice. They speak a specialized language that empowers them in something of the same way that the doctrine of election does: by excluding those whose speech has not been purged of Roman Catholic influence and other tokens of sin. They bring to the alchemist's house their own version of the dreamy economics of Dapper, Drugger, and Mammon. Inspiration is linked to aspiration in their lives through the agency of the *'beautifull* [inner] *light'* (III.i.46). They feel that the value of devout fervour generated totally from within defies judgment by external standards. This is where Jonson strikes hardest at his puritans. He repeatedly ridicules Tribulation and Ananias for their not-quite-innocent presumption of invulnerability. The often-repeated opposition to established forms provides, moreover, a built-in standard for judging the folly of their own jargon. *'Christ-masse'* will never do, says Ananias; the complete anti-papist must say '*Christ-tide.*' 'Coyning' of money by the brethren may excite scruples; it sounds a good deal like counterfeiting. So Subtle suggests the term 'casting,' and all is well. The Baconian dictum, which Jonson paraphrases in *Discoveries* – 'the study of words is the first distemper of Learning' – is amply illustrated by the sophistries of puritan erudition.

Puritan disdain for civil authority – 'We know no Magistrate' (III.ii.150) – combines with a lively sense of the cost of propagating the Cause to make Ananias and Tribulation two of Jonson's most eager empire builders. Unfettered by the restraints of legal and, now they hope, economic limitations, the puritans feel safe 'Against lords spirituall, or temporall, / That shall oppone' them (III.ii.50–1). Tribulation, especially, is filled with the confidence of the prosperous thief with an unassailable moral cover. Ananias is more defensive, and his mistrust of the world-at-large takes a form similar to Surly's censoriousness. His chief pleasure seems to be in the finality of God's judgments on the wicked – that is, on those who offend Ananias. His choric voice is raised above the tumult in two scenes of judgment, the first Surly's discomfiture in IV.vii and the second the assault on the locked door of Lovewit's house in V.iii. In both instances he refers to the offending persons as 'vnclene birds,' alluding to God's judgment on the debauched inhabitants of Babylon. The allusion is brief and in each case easily lost in the furious accompanying activity.[25] But it is worth considering for a moment because of the light it sheds on the mystification of words and judgments in the play. The passage from Revelation reads,

> And he cryed out mightely with a loude voyce, saying, It is fallen, it is fallen, Babylon ye great *citie*, & is become the habitation of deuils, and the holde of all fowle spirits, and a cage of euerie vncleane and hateful byrde ... and the marchants of the earth are waxed riche of the abundance of her pleasures. (Rev. 18:2–3)[26]

That Lovewit's house becomes 'the habitation of deuils' has been proposed in an ingenious essay by William Blissett.[27] Blissett argues that Dol allegorically represents the Flesh, Face the World, and Subtle the Devil. The reading is perhaps overly schematic, but it is suggestive. The wealth of the Babylonian merchants and 'the abundance of [the earth's] delicacies' certainly have counterparts in the aspirations of Drugger and Mammon, and there is something vaguely apocalyptic about the confusion that reigns at the moment of the great explosion. Though the witless enthusiast, Ananias, has perhaps hit upon an apt biblical analogue for the process of judgment in *The Alchemist*, his complicity in the construction of this particular version of Babylon locates him in the dock rather than on the bench.

The secular complement to the puritans' spiritual economy is the socially fashionable art of quarrelling and defending one's honour in the *'Duello'* (III.iv.25). To be initiated into these mysteries is Kastril's deepest desire, and to achieve it, he will contribute his wealthy, widowed sister, Dame Pliant, to the thriving sexual economy of the house. Face assures Kastril that Doctor Subtle has the technology, 'An instrument ... of his owne making,' to measure the danger level of any proposed quarrel. He can also prescribe 'rules, / To giue, and take the lie, by' (III.iv.25-37). Nor are his rules simply pugilistic. They are also grammatical, logical, and rhetorical.

> You must render causes, child,
> Your first, and second *Intentions*, know your *canons*,
> And your *diuisions, moodes, degrees*, and *differences*,
> Your *praedicaments, substance*, and *accident*,
> *Series externe*, and *interne*, with their *causes*
> *Efficient, materiall, formall, finall*,
> And ha' your *elements* perfect – (IV.ii.22-8)

Subtle's instruction is in the basic stuff of language – division and difference. And like a good semanticist, he views difference as infinite, meaning as indeterminate, and the entire instructional endeavour as play. From the point of view of the characters, the result is the opposite of demystification: Subtle spins linguistic charms that dazzle his slow-witted fellow conspirators.

The mystification of the word is nowhere more evident than in Subtle's pictorial deconstruction of Abel Drugger's name as he designs a shingle for the tobacco shop:

> I will haue his name
> Form'd in some mystick character; whose *radij*,
> Striking the senses of the passers by,
> Shall, by the vertuall influence, breed affections,
> That may result vpon the partie ownes it:
> As thus – ... He first shall haue a bell, that's Abel;
> And, by it, standing one, whose name is Dee,
> In a rugg gowne; there's *D.* and *Rug*, that's Drvg:

And, right anenst him, a Dog snarling *Er*;
There's Drvgger, Abel Drvgger. That's his signe.
And here's now *mysterie*, and *hieroglyphick*! (II.vi.14-24)

To which Face chimes in, 'Abel, thou art made.' And made he is – constructed of phonetic signs devoid of sense, at least any advertising sense. Drugger is willing to be entirely rebuilt in hopes that he will thrive better in a world of hieroglyphics than in a world of ordinary signifying. What is made obscure in this process becomes his secret to share and to withhold from his customers. For once, he will be an insider, knowing that fine gallants with fashionably heavy spurs will be drawn to his shop by the magnet concealed under his threshold (I.iii.69-71).

There are, however, no secrets from the audience. Jonson had tried that trick in *Epicoene* with only partial success. In *The Alchemist* we hear all the strategy sessions and are privy to each new mystification of the word, whether in palmistry or chemistry, underworld cant or otherworldly incantation.[28] When Surly appears in act IV disguised as a Spaniard, Face and Subtle amuse themselves by poking fun at the foreigner who they imagine has no English.

SVR. *Sennores, beso las manos, à vuestras mercedes.*
SVB. Would you had stoup'd a little, and kist our *anos*. (IV.iii.21-2)[29]

It's crude but effective; and it's all Jonson needs to provide the measure of ignorance and arrogance in the learned doctor who assumes that anyone without the basic language of the conspiracy (English in this case) deserves to be mocked and submitted to the universal body language of the nearest available prostitute. Surly, there to spy out the tricks of Subtle's trade, has the perfect cover of apparent non-comprehension. He is allowed to overhear all the stratagems, not, as in the case of Dapper and Drugger, just carefully selected lines. To the foreigner, the language of Subtle and Face is apparently *all* a mystery, not just isolated pockets of incomprehensible jargon.

Without fully understanding each other's motives, the new members of the conspiracy pull together in act IV to drive out Surly, who tries to reveal all the secrets of the game at once. Such a radical form of demystification is not acceptable to those like Kastril and Ananias whose dreams are heavily invested in the specialties of the house – quarrelling and counterfeiting. Surly is driven away by a noisy assault on his popish fashion of dress and his duplicity in disguising himself in the first place. When the revelation of knavery depends on spying, as in this case, the line between the authentic and the inauthentic becomes so thoroughly blurred that there is little hope of undoing the mystifications of the charlatan's language. As Alvin Kernan argues, Surly conforms to the type of the satirist-satirized. Part of his function is to reveal the folly of underestimating the seriousness of conspiratorial threats to the community of good sense.[30]

Surly spends most of his time on stage grumbling, objecting, railing at, and bullying the weaker characters. Though he properly diagnoses the cozenage in progress, his manner and judgments are so crude as to make him come off very badly. His treatment of Dame Pliant is particularly high-handed and offensive. Putting aside his Spanish don's disguise, Surly tells the young widow,

> Lady, you see into what hands, you are falne;
> Mongst what a nest of villaines! ...
> I am a gentleman, come here disguis'd,
> Onely to find the knaueries of this *Citadell*,
> And where I might haue wrong'd your honor, and haue not,
> I claime some interest in your loue. (IV.vi.1-11)

Surly's reforming zeal in exposing Subtle, Face, and Dol is never anything but self-interested. Far from wishing to shield his friend Mammon from the crooks, for example, Surly seems to delight in Mammon's disappointment over the ruined alchemical equipment.[31] When we see Surly tormenting Mammon by mocking his shattered illusions, he is about as endearing as anyone who says, 'I told you so.' Though set apart from the play's foolish talkers by his genuinely churlish disposition, Surly is the dupe of his own brand of cant. Ironically he is driven away by the very people he claimed to be helping. His final criticism is, however, directed toward himself; it points up the curious mixture of folly and perception that makes up the censorious man: 'Must I needs cheat my selfe / With that same foolish vice of honestie!' (V.v.83-4). Like Othello pronouncing himself an 'honorable murderer,' Surly is not notable for his sound judgment.

Lovewit's house has become more than a den of thieves and whores. Its converts, newly initiated into the extravagance of the mind and human desires, are themselves as knavishly motivated as the original trio of tricksters. This is the turn of the 'voluptuous mind' that propounds the ultimate obfuscation of the play, the mystification of desire itself. Merely wanting money, sex, and power is the sordid objective of Volpone's *captatores*. Sublimating these desires – that is, masking them while feeding them – is the business of Jonson's alchemist. The elevation, extension, and refinement of human desire is parodied by the process of transforming impure nature into the Philosopher's Stone, which in turn can bring to golden perfection all base metals. The process is purely linguistic and depends entirely upon the ironic gap between signifier and signified. Dapper's vast imagined winnings far exceed both his initial modest request for a 'familiar' to improve his luck in some low-stakes gambling ventures and the twenty nobles he actually hands over to Face. In this case big talk leads to small losses, while in Mammon's case, verbal refinements keep blundering into crass actualities. His erotic vision may include the vaporization of the body, but it also entails husbands pimping for their wives.

>   Then my glasses,
> Cut in more subtill angles, to disperse,
> And multiply the figures, as I walke
> Naked betweene my *succubae*. My mists
> I'll haue of perfume, vapor'd 'bout the roome,
> To loose our selues in; and my baths, like pits
> To fall into: from whence, we will come forth,
> And rowle vs drie in gossamour, and roses.
> (Is it [i.e. the Philosopher's Stone] arriu'd at *ruby*?) – Where I spie
> A wealthy citizen, or rich lawyer,
> Haue a sublim'd pure wife, vnto that fellow
> I'll send a thousand pound, to be my cuckold. (II.ii.45–56)

For all the obscuring mists, sunken baths, and gossamer towels, Mammon's sexual imagination consistently turns from the rarefied to the sordid. A woman becomes desirable because her chastity can be sullied and her wealthy husband can be financially outdone.

Mammon's fantasies go on and on, rising to the heights of his stunning verbal invention, then plummeting back to earth with a dull thud. The purpose of this vacillation seems to be the prolongation of desire. There can be no instant gratification of desire in this play, much of which is concerned with spinning out men's hopes, protracting them in time as well as in space. As the contemporary case of the alchemist Edward Kelley (who is mentioned at IV.i.90) suggests, protraction was a standard part of the alchemist's program. After waiting through years of promises, the Emperor Rudolph II finally threw Kelley in prison in 1593 and again in 1595 to encourage him to produce some tangible results from the Stone.[32] These things couldn't, it seems, be rushed. The golden dream was always a dream deferred.

Timing is as vital to conspiracy as to alchemy. The over-eager dupes begin to arrive before their appointed hour, and there is a frantic scramble to retime the next trick, to keep the would-be initiates apart, and to postpone the catastrophe of revelation. Dapper is surprised to learn that he will not be able to take his 'familiar' away with him after his initial interview, but he is told the time is not yet auspicious. He has a *long* wait for the Fairy Queen in the privy, gagged with stale gingerbread and nearly overcome by the stench. Such stalling tactics will not, however, work on the Spanish don, who, according to Face, 'know[s] / All the delays' (IV.iii.56-7). The Brethren are somewhat more patient: when Tribulation asks 'how long time ... must the *Saints* expect, yet?' for the *magisterium*, he seems to accept the answer of fifteen days. Finally, time, specifically plague time, runs out, and Lovewit appears at his door – before the full fruits of the conspiracy can be gathered in and the thoroughly mystified desires of each initiate exploited. In Jonson's puritans the conscience fails to do the work of judgment but instead runs instead to wild, uncheckable fantasy. These characters seldom consult external authority in making choices, and there is no appeal from the court of their conscience.[33] While others can be put in the wrong by its dictates, no one can challenge its justification of a personal desire. When Dapper decides, for example, that he requires a more powerful lucky charm for his gaming exploits, Face, acting as intermediary between him and Subtle, pretends to be scandalized in conscience by the larger request:

> FAC. Why, this changes quite the case!
> Do' you thinke, that I dare moue him? DAP. If you please, sir,
> All's one to him, I see. FAC. What! for that money?
> I cannot with my conscience. Nor should you
> Make the request, me thinkes. DAP. No, sir, I meane
> To adde consideration. FAC. Why, then, sir,
> I'll trie. (I.ii.92-8)

Conscience, which should judge and restrain, becomes simply another form of chicanery put up for sale to the highest bidder. The behaviour is altogether arbitrary and the altered case resolved simply by upping the payment. Even less reliable is the conscience of Jonson's puritans. A subsequent case, the one involving counterfeit coinage, requires careful distinctions, but the outcome of the appeal to the consciences of the puritan brethren is never in doubt as Tribulation, Ananias, and Subtle discuss the case.

> TRI. I, but stay,
> This act of coyning, is it lawfull? ANA. Lawfull?
> We know no Magistrate. Or, if we did,
> This's forraine coyne. SVB. It is no coyning, sir.
> It is but casting. TRI. Ha? you distinguish well.
> Casting of money may be lawfull. ANA. 'Tis, sir.
> TRI. Truely, I take it so. SVB. There is no scruple,
> Sir to be made of it; beleeue Ananias:
> This case of conscience he is studied in.
> TRI. I'll make a question of it, to the *Brethren*.
> ANA. The *Brethren* shall approue it lawfull, doubt not. (III.ii.148-58)

And approve it they do, silencing moral and legal questions before they can become public. The conscience, then, emerges as a prime agent for suppressing truth in the play.

Catering to human desires on such an individual basis makes the chore of the tricksters at once easy and complicated. Their victims are so eager that little subtlety is required of them, yet the situations change so fast that new stratagems are constantly being called for. Improvisation comes to be the name of their game. No single plan will serve the alchemical conspirators in the way it could the political conspirators of *Sejanus* and *Catiline*. It might be argued that the most impressive achievement of *The Alchemist* is not, as Paul Goodman argues, its careful plotting, but the subtly negotiated and improvised status transactions, as a recent actor-critic calls them, between established and aspiring conspirators.[34] In his book, *Impro: Improvisation and the Theatre*, Keith Johnstone, a long-time instructor at the Royal Court Theatre, describes what it means to *play* status:

> Status is a confusing term unless it's understood as something one *does*. You may be low in social status, but play high, and vice versa. For example:
>
> TRAMP: 'Ere! Where are you going?
> DUCHESS: I'm sorry, I didn't quite catch ...
> TRAMP: Are you deaf as well as blind?
>
> Audiences enjoy a contrast between the status played and the social status. We always like it when a tramp is mistaken for the boss, or the

boss for a tramp. Hence plays like *The Inspector General*. Chaplin liked
to play the person at the bottom of the hierarchy and then lower
everyone.[35]

What is unusual about the status transactions in *The Alchemist* is
that they occur within the boundaries of an extended conspiracy
and without regard for the rank and rules of the larger society outside.
As we have seen, any desire can be legitimized by the individual
conscience, and only the constantly shifting status of each character
determines the outcome of the various contests for power. Each
of these contests appears to be improvised (or, from Jonson's point
of view, should appear to be improvised) when the trickster's prepared
script breaks down.

Status transactions between and among the tricksters and their
marks, which is to say between senior and junior conspirators, become
exponentially more complex as the number of characters in
the scene increases. Johnstone's sequence of the tramp and the duchess
is rudimentary comedy compared to the following encounter
between Subtle, the self-elevated spiritual adviser, and the two puritans,
the parson and his subordinate deacon. Subtle opens the exchange
in the position of superior status, as ecstatic creator of the
Philosopher's Stone:

> SVB. O, but the *stone*, all's idle to it! nothing!
> The art of *Angels*, Natures miracle,
> The *diuine secret*, that doth flye in clouds,
> From *east* to *west*: and whose tradition
> Is not from men, but spirits. ANA. I hate *Traditions*:
> I do not trust them – TRI. Peace. ANA. They are *Popish*, all.
> I will not peace. I will not – TRI. Ananias.
> ANA. Please the prophane, to grieue the godly: I may not.
> SVB. Well, Ananias, thou shalt ouer-come.
> TRI. It is an ignorant zeale, that haunts him, sir.
> But truely, else, a very faithful *Brother*,
> A botcher: and a man, by reuelation,
> That hath a competent knowledge of the truth.
> SVB. Has he a competent summe, there, i' the bagg,
> To buy the goods, within? (III.ii.102–16)

Ananias's flat-footed counter-assertion of individual authority, 'I
hate *Traditions*,' threatens to upset the arrangements by which Tribulation
believes the gold-making power of the Stone will benefit

him and his evangelical cause. The offending term 'tradition' apparently carries only its neutral Latin sense of 'transfer' in Subtle's phrase, but since Ananias would be offended by that too, Tribulation simply snaps at his outspoken inferior, telling him to hold his peace. When Ananias refuses with, 'I will not peace,' Subtle forestalls the impasse that is bound to ensue ('You will!' 'I won't!') with a concessive but condescending reassurance that once again places him on top of the pecking order: 'Well, Ananias, thou shalt ouer-come.' In a bid for higher status, Tribulation joins in Subtle's condescension, even as he excuses his subordinate's 'ignorant zeale.' But Subtle, who will allow no one to set or co-opt the terms of his discourse, shifts from Tribulation's phrase 'competent knowledge of the truth' to a business-like concern for the 'competent summe ... in the bagg.' Ananias has dropped out of the competition altogether when he is referred to in the third person, as though he were not even present. Subtle and Tribulation have, that is, forged a conspiratorial alliance to exclude the third party and get on with their business transaction.

If Ananias is the loser in this bit of dialogue, he is, at least in his own eyes, triumphant in both previous and subsequent scenes. Within conspiracies, status is always being rearranged to suit fresh contingencies. More than in *Volpone*, the improvisational nature of these arrangements tends to dissipate any sequential patterning of events in the play. The changes might be rung indefinitely, had not Jonson built in from the beginning the condition of ending the mutual nourishment of gulls and knaves. When Lovewit appears at the front door, his indisputable status as owner and master has seemed to many readers to shift the dynamics of conspiracy. I would argue, however, that instead, Jonson extends his study of the conspiratorial habit of mind to include the respectable and legitimate within the terms of the criminalized other. Lovewit, that is, gives us more of the same, establishing a fresh conspiracy with Face-Jeremy to replace the *'indenture tripartite.'*

When Lovewit tries to get a straight story from his neighbours about what has happened at his house during his absence, he gets instead what sounds to him a garbled and contradictory account of all sorts of visitors arriving at all hours of the day and night. This factual account is, oddly, too accurate to be convincing, and the newly clean-shaven Jeremy the butler is able easily to outface the spying neighbours, who become less and less sure of what they have seen in this house of theatrical and alchemical deceptions over

The New Face of Secrecy in *The Alchemist*

the previous three months. Such testimony would scarcely hold up in a court of law, and Lovewit shrewdly accepts Jeremy's partial confessions and agrees to forgive him. The master will keep the hardware collected in the cellar and also the young widow. Simply because he is master, Lovewit would seem to have all status and prerogative on his side, but the servant's status-enhancing secret is that it was he who summoned his master, not vice versa. As Jeremy-Face puts it to his former co-conspirators,

> The right is, my master
> Knowes all, has pardon'd me, and he will keepe 'hem.
> Doctor, 'tis true (you looke) for all your figures:
> I sent for him, indeed. Wherefore, good partners,
> Both hee, and shee, be satisfied: for, here
> Determines the *indenture tripartite*,
> Twixt Svtble, Dol, and Face. All I can doe
> Is to helpe you ouer the wall, o' the back-side;
> Or lend you a sheet, to saue your veluet gowne, Dol.
> Here will be officers, presently; bethinke you,
> Of some course sodainely to scape the dock:
> For thether you'll come else. Harke you, thunder. (V.iv.126-37)

The thunder is not a sign of divine retribution, as it is in many Renaissance plays. Instead, it is the knocking of law enforcement officers who will finally enforce no laws. What has been described is not 'the right' in moral terms but simply the way things are. Moral order is neither assumed nor vindicated in *The Alchemist*. The commonwealth of tricksters has been dissolved for the time being and their empire temporarily reduced to rubble. The world 'ouer the wall, o' the back-side' has, however, its share of would-be conspirators and new locations to begin business again.

From Lovewit's final speech, a kind of epilogue, we can reasonably conclude that a love of wit is no proof of moral superiority in this play.

> That master
> That has receiu'd such happinesse by a seruant,
> In such a widdow, and with so much wealth,
> Were very vngratefull, if he would not be
> A little indulgent to that seruants wit,
> And helpe his fortune, though with some small straine
> Of his owne candor. Therefore, gentlemen,

> And kind Spectators, if I haue out-stript
> An old mans grauitie, or strict canon, thinke
> What a yong wife, and a good braine may doe:
> Stretch ages truth sometimes, and crack it too. (V.v.146-56)

Lovewit has the trickster's quick eye for easy profit and glib tongue for self-justification. His readiness to put 'some small strain' on his candour, to 'stretch ages truth,' has the familiar false casuistical ring of the puritan's conscience-salving phrases. But unlike the puritans, Lovewit is careful always to keep the law on his side. He makes no moral judgments, except to call into question his own honesty. Instead, he completes the robbery of Mammon, the puritans, Surly, and the others which had been initiated by Subtle, Face, and Dol. In this way he enters into the action if not quite the spirit of the gulling holiday. The difference between his trickery and Subtle's is that he uses established laws and social pressures of the community to do the work of Subtle's perverse, jargon-rich imagination. Lovewit is the cheater of everyday, the encyclopedia salesman in the ghetto; Subtle is the cheat of holiday, the barker for the greatest, tawdriest show on earth – human folly.

Jonson's conspiratorial mode of representing folly effects such issues as gender, genre, comic morality, and the view of authority in the middle plays. One of the features that most clearly marks the genre of Jonsonian satiric comedy is the constantly collapsing, periodically reconstituted relationship between characters who claim power through special knowledge (those characters usually designated as knaves) and those who aspire to be initiated into this secret source of power (generally called dupes).

A corollary of this distinguishing mark of the comedies is Jonson's paradoxical formulation of aspiration and act, secret longing and public proclamation of supposedly hidden 'truths.' One effect of his paradoxes is to test severely the stereotypes of virtuous innocent and experienced villain on which many comic subgenres rest. Jonson's dupes are, in fact, would-be con men, his tricksters *de facto* dupes. Those who share in the most secret intrigues are compelled to publish their activities in order to attract a paying audience or mark for their scam. Eventually the secret leaks out, and the power it had momentarily conferred is dissipated. This radical instability is not accidental but basic to the form of satiric comedy as Jonson knits, ravels, and reknits it.

Jonson's tragedies too, we should recall, problematize the expected relationship between villain and victim, perpetrator and dupe, legitimate authority and enemy of the commonwealth. Behind Tiberius's façade of caring for the Roman state in *Sejanus*, for example, Jonson revealed a strategy more insidious than anything a Macro or a Sejanus, or, for that matter, a Subtle or Face, could perpetrate. The power that we sometimes imagine to accrue to those with specialized knowledge regularly proves either specious or feeble when set against the everyday cheats whose power is validated by self-perpetuating governmental structures. What appears to be a desperate crisis in the history of Western civilization, Catiline's conspiracy to end all civil order, dwindles to dwarfish proportions compared with the officially licensed suppression of information about still more threatening conspiracies in Jonson's last tragedy, to which we turn next.

CHAPTER SIX

Catiline's Conspiracy and the Problem of Containment

Jean de Marconville's *Treatise of the Good and Evell Tounge* (ca. 1592) relates the instructive tale of 'little *Papyrius*,' who, according to the custom of inviting boys of up to seventeen years of age to attend the Roman senate to learn the ropes, had been present for a particularly sensitive debate and was sworn to secrecy about it. Later, being hard pressed by his mother to reveal the subject of the debate, he made up the story ('practised a prettie policie') that the proposal under discussion had been 'that euery man should hereafter haue two wiues.' Early the next morning, the married women of Rome turned out in force to demonstrate before the senate house, and eventually little Papyrius was commended by the senators for having so ingeniously diverted his mother and the other gossips from the true topic of their deliberations.[1]

The fall-out from Papyrius's lie was easily contained, indeed enjoyed by the authorities. In the jargon of today's politics, it had 'deniability.' Bigamy was not on the agenda on the day in question, and the women of Rome were silly to think it would have been. The confidence of the senate had been protected through a harmless ruse. After all, the thinking would go, this deception was practised only on prying, loose-tongued women, and in the context of much Renaissance writing, such a practice, like lying to the infidel, was acceptable. Men, even boys, had, by all means, to guard state secrets. Still, there are some residual uneasy feelings about all this. Lying to one's mother just doesn't feel right, and the fact that the lie receives the imprimatur of the state doesn't make it any better. The story sits rather uncomfortably in Marconville's treatise on God's punishment of perjurers.

Some of the same sense of uneasiness dogs the political morality of *Catiline His Conspiracy* (1611). Institutionalized deception is rife in the tragedy, and the moral taint spread by rumours is never completely contained. Women, moreover, play a highly questionable part in the generation and discovery of the conspiracy. Catiline's wife, Aurelia, arranges sexual entertainments for the conspirators; Fulvia wheedles the plot out of her adulterous lover and snitches to Cicero; Sempronia, an aging society lady, argues that women 'could make / As honorable spies' for the state as any male ambassador (IV.717-19). Rome is a veritable rumour mill, and even the noblest Romans of them all – Cicero and Cato – cannot escape the irrepressible whisperings of sedition. Indeed, suspicions of deep-rooted corruption in Rome's institutions radically destabilize the latter half of Jonson's tragedy.

Evidently aware that he had a problem in this area, Jonson set to work his much beloved Chorus to reassure his audience that the leaders of Rome are above suspicion and reproach.

> So, in our censure of the state,
>   We still doe wander;
> And make the carefull magistrate
>   The marke of slander.
> What age is this, where honest men,
>   Plac'd at the helme,
> A sea of some foule mouth, or pen,
>   Shall ouer-whelme?
> And call their diligence, deceipt;
>   Their vertue, vice;
> Their watchfulnesse, but lying in wait;
>   And bloud, the price. (IV.875-86)

In attempting to quell the persistent 'censure of the state,' begun by Catiline but ably continued by Caesar and Crassus, the Chorus never denies the techniques of espionage employed by the Consul Cicero. Rather it contends that these methods have been misnamed: deceit for diligence, vice for virtue, lying in wait for watchfulness. The last of these seems a distinction without a difference, not so much because blood is the price extracted from Catiline and his band of malcontents, but because, as we shall see, Cicero deliberately suppresses all charges against equally dangerous enemies of Rome. Against this inequitable application of the law Jonson poises the assertion of the Chorus, which is performing the function assigned it by Horace in the *Ars Poetica*. The Chorus, according to Horace, must defend the public peace, uphold the laws, and cover up faults in the system. Jonson translates the relevant passage this way:

> It [the chorus] still must favour good men, and to these
> Be wonne a friend; it must both sway, and bend
> The angry, and love those that feare to offend.
> Praise the spare diet, wholsome justice, lawes,
> Peace, and the open ports, that peace doth cause.
> Hide faults, pray to the Gods, and wish aloud
> Fortune would love the poore, and leave the proud.[2]

What is most challenging about *Catiline*, in my view, is that there is so much in the play that subverts this official line and reveals depths of political understanding seldom ascribed to Jonson.

What does Cicero, in particular, do to undercut his own worthy action in prosecuting the traitor Catiline and delivering Rome from a particularly vicious plot to attack its walls, set fire to its buildings, and overthrow its government? Mainly he sets up an elaborate system of spies and counterspies, offering substantial rewards to any conspirator who will turn informer. Such a procedure to ensure national security is perhaps not in itself culpable, but in this case it adds fuel to the seditious fire that Cicero is attempting to extinguish.[3] While the rewards for informers are mentioned briefly in Jonson's chief source, Sallust's *The Conspiracy of Catiline* ('if anyone should give information as to the plot which had been made against the state, he should, if a slave, be rewarded with his freedom and a hundred thousand sesterces, and if a free man, with immunity for complicity therein, and two hundred thousand sesterces'),[4] Jonson gives them considerably more prominence. For example, when enlisting Curius to carry out surveillance of the conspiracy, Cicero exclaims,

> What thankes, what titles, what rewards the *Senate*
> Will heape vpon you, certaine, for your seruice? (III.401-2)

Subsequently Caesar will voice his disapproval of remunerating Curius for pointing the finger in his direction:

> Was not that Curivs your spie, that had
> Reward decreed vnto him, the last *Senate*,

Catiline's Conspiracy and Containment 133

> With Fvlvia, vpon your priuate motion?
> CIC. Yes. CAES. But, he has not that reward, yet?
> CIC. No.
>   Let not this trouble you, Caesar, none beleeues it.
> CAES. It shall not, if that he haue no reward.
> But if he haue, sure I shall thinke my selfe
> Very vntimely, and vnsafely honest,
> Where such, as he is, may haue pay t'accuse me. (V.356-64)

Caesar has good reason to feel uncomfortable in the circumstances, but it is easy for him to discredit the bribe-taking Curius, even when he is telling the truth.[5] The very actions of the authorities make truth an enormously unstable commodity in this play.

When Fulvia first comes to reveal the secret conspiracy in act III, Cicero makes several slips of the tongue that tend to cast doubt on his integrity and wisdom. Jonson may not have viewed these slips as damaging to his hero, but they nonetheless contribute to a pattern of bias and manipulation that lends some credence to accusations levelled against Cicero by his enemies. Comparing Catiline's proposed attack on the city with the horrors perpetrated under Marius and Sylla, Cicero appears callous, shrugging off too much that is repugnant.

> Would not the barbarous deeds haue beene beleeu'd,
> Of Marivs, and Sylla, by our children,
> Without this fact had rise forth greater, for them?
> All, that they did, was pietie, to this!
> They, yet, but murdred kinsfolke, brothers, parents,
> Rauish'd the virgins, and, perhaps, some matrons. (III.270-5)

To be sure, he is speaking with heavy irony here when he calls the earlier deeds 'pietie,' but there is also something crude about the way he casually tosses 'some matrons' into the batch of ravished virgins. The 'perhaps' is particularly symptomatic of his indifference. His crudeness finds an ample sounding-board in the person of Fulvia, who describes the secrets she has just revealed to Cicero as though they were bad gas to be vented.

>   I was all
> A vapor, when 'twas told me: and I long'd
> To vent it any where. 'Twas such a secret,
> I thought, it would haue burnt me vp.
> ... CIC. You haue discharg'd it, safely. (III.289-95)

The image of informing as flatulence is, of course, unflattering to both parties involved. Shortly thereafter Cicero commends the unscrupulous Fulvia for her service to the state.

> Here is a lady, that hath got the start,
> In pietie, of vs all; and, for whose vertue,
> I could almost turne louer, againe: but that
> Terentia would be iealous. What an honor
> Hath shee atchieued to her selfe! What voices,
> Titles, and loud applauses will pursue her,
> Through euery street! (III.341–7)

And on and on. Cicero's deceitful praise of Fulvia may very well strike the audience as unnecessarily fulsome and his joking reference to his wife's imagined jealousy as simply fatuous. The only relevant jealousy is what Fulvia feels for her rival Sempronia:

> Come, doe you thinke, I'ld walke in any plot,
> Where madame Sempronia should take place of me,
> And Fvlvia come i'the *rere*, or o'the *by*? (III.375–7)

This petty competition is Fulvia's real motive for going to the authorities with her information. Though Cicero is not deceived about her motives, his mock deification of her lowers state intelligence to the level of personal back-biting.

The basic fact of Jonson's play is that Cicero is defending the institutions of Roman civilization against the onslaughts of a man whose 'incests, murders, [and] rapes' the ghost of Sylla gleefully recites as the play opens. Chief among these threatened institutions is the family. As Anne Barton formulates the matter, 'All the conspirators are associated with the perversion or violation of ordinary domestic ties,' while 'Cicero upholds the normalities of family life.'[6] The generalization rightly directs our attention to a significant standard of value in the play and to the pervasive analogy between the politics of empire and of the household, which Barton identifies as tragic and comic respectively. Equally important, it permits us to see more clearly the occasional lapses from positive familial attitudes that characterize Cicero and his dilemma.

In the midst of discovering the conspiracy, Cicero repeatedly expresses his concern for the commonality. In particular he views Rome as 'our common mother' (III.366). But there is another, contrasting sense of commonness abroad in the scene. Cicero reveals in soliloquy his true estimation of Rome's saviour, Fulvia: he calls her 'a base / And common strumpet' (III.450-1).⁷ The two senses of 'common' come together in a comic but revealing grammatical slip by the other informer, Curius. Two women have been present in the preceding dialogue (nurturing Rome and lascivious Fulvia), and Curius catches himself with an ambiguous referent for his feminine pronoun:

> Most noble *Consul*, I am yours, and hers;
> I mean my countries. (III.407-8)

More accurately, he has been Fulvia's – that is, her sexual and political tool (cf. II.321-62), and now he is to become the common property of another manipulative woman, Rome, the spy-master (-mistress).

Cicero encourages Curius to rejoin the conspirators to be his eyes and ears, to fight insurgency with counterinsurgency.

> Keepe still your former face: and mixe againe
> With these lost spirits. Runne all their mazes with 'hem:
> For such are treasons. Find their windings out,
> And subtle turnings, watch their snaky wayes,
> Through brakes, and hedges, into woods of darkenesse,
> Where they are faine to creepe vpon their brests
> In paths ne're trod by men, but wolues, and panthers.
> ... Ile see, that *Rome*
> Shall proue a thankefull, and a bounteous mother:
> Be secret as the night. (III.414-32)

The imagery of serpentine indirection that lends such a sinister undertone here to Cicero's recruitment of a secret agent corresponds closely with that used repeatedly early in the reign of King James to describe political intrigues in London. In 1604, for example, Lodowick Lloyd, who served as 'Sergeant-at-Armes' (*DNB*) to both Elizabeth and James, published the following account of the workings of sedition, basing his observations partly on recent political developments:

> It was euer the wonted practice of policy among the seditious and factious people, to taunt Magistrates, or to speake some whispering speech against a prince, to feele and to heare, who will ioyne with them to moue sedition. These be the Vipers that bite men priuily: these be the domesticall Serpents, the secret brue-bates of Commonwealths, in whom there is no fayth found, nor othes to be beleeued, as *Aristophanes* sayth.⁸

Cicero is certainly the butt of a good deal of 'whispering speech' in *Catiline*, and we need to investigate more closely the accusations that he used his rhetorical skills to make both the threat of conspiracy and his achievement in subduing it seem greater than they actually were. Also worth further consideration is Lloyd's emphasis on the 'domesticall' nature of sedition and the secrecy employed by 'brue-bates,' a 'brew-bate' being 'one who stirs up quarreling or dissension' (*OED*). Finally, the matter of oaths plays a theatrically important part in Jonson's treatment of Catiline's conspiracy in a scene that requires some explanation.

From the outset, the Roman senators and citizenry have been suspicious of Cicero's eloquence. There is a sense that he may be more impressive in word than matter. Drawing on this suspicion, Caesar tries, with some success, to convince Catulus that all the reports of conspiracy have benefited Cicero but not Rome.

> Reports? Doe you beleeue 'hem Catvlvs,
> Why, he [Cicero] do's make, and breed 'hem for the people;
> T'endeare his seruice to 'hem. Doe you not tast
> An art, that is so common? Popular men,
> They must create strange monsters, and then quell 'hem;
> To make their artes seeme something. Would you haue
> Such an Hercvlean actor in the scene,
> And not his Hydra? They must sweat no lesse
> To fit their properties, then t'expresse their parts. (III.93–101)

Again, Caesar invokes the negative connotations of 'common,' turning Cicero's popularity against him. The most negative kind of popularity he can think of is that associated with an 'actor in the scene,' and he casts Cicero as what Eugene Waith has called a Herculean hero, a stagy miracle-worker but also an outlaw that bears watching.[9] Since Cicero is himself already the master spy, Caesar and his seditious companions, Crassus, Catulus, and Antonius, resolve to 'watch the watcher' (III.108). In this play of conspiracies, everyone watches everyone else.

The spying and whispering trickle down to the smallest arena of political exercise depicted in the play, the domestic household. The first scene between Curius and Fulvia provides an instructively parodic analogy with the power struggles that, on a higher level, engage the Roman senate.[10] Curius, having been rebuffed initially by his mistress, accuses her of feigning a greater threat of discovery by her husband than is actually present, much as Caesar had hinted that Cicero was inventing a conspiracy in order to control it. He recalls occasions on which she let him in through a window when the front door would have done as well, presumably to create a *frisson* of imminent discovery. He goes on to recount her tricks in a way that reduces their secret affair to a bedroom farce:

> And, then, being a-bed with you,
> To haue your well taught wayter, here, come running,
> And cry, her lord, and hide me without cause,
> Crush'd in a chest, or thrust vp in a chimney.
> When he, tame crow, was winking at his farme;
> Or, had he beene here, and present, would haue kept
> Both eyes, and beake seal'd vp, for sixe *sesterces*. (II.261-7)

The intrigue has far exceeded the need for secrecy, and Curius knows he has been made to play the fool. The irate lover is, however, outdone by his still more irate mistress. When he tries to force himself on her, she melodramatically draws a knife, and they then both draw parallels with the Rape of Lucrece. The entire literary charade falters momentarily until Fulvia decides to seduce Curius in order to learn whatever secret he is harbouring. The scene undercuts the seriousness of the threat to the empire's security, much as the oath-swearing scene in act I had done.

When the conspirators swear themselves to secrecy, they do so in a ceremony that feels more literary than genuinely terrifying in its Senecanism. Darkness settles over the place, a groan is heard from underground, and a fiery light appears. Catiline proposes a toast in human blood, but the thunder he summons is apparently not forthcoming.

> I'haue kill'd a slaue,
> And of his bloud caus'd to be mixt with wine.
> Fill euery man his bowle. There cannot be
> A fitter drinke, to make this *sanction* in.
> Here, I beginne the sacrament to all.
> O, for a clap of thunder, now, as loud,
> As to be heard through-out the vniuerse,
> To tell the world the fact, and to applaud it.
> Be firme, my hand; not shed a drop: but powre
> Fiercenesse into me, with it, and fell thirst
> Of more, and more, till *Rome* be left as bloud-lesse,
> As euer her feares made her, or the sword. (I.483-94)

As in *The Alchemist*, where the cozeners' desire for publicity contradicts their need for privacy, Catiline's urge to 'tell the world' would break the faith of the conspirators. But in Lodowick Lloyd's words, 'there is no fayth found [here], no othe to be beleeued.' Not only can the takers of such an oath not be trusted (cf. Curius's subsequent treachery), but the devilish 'sacrament' is so melodramatic as to appear incredible.

The case is not quite so easy as this, however. While the leap from conspiratorial rhetoric to underworld groans may seem prodigious to modern audiences, in Jonson's day certain writers were insisting that a connection existed, even at the level of etymology, between conspiracy and communion with the devil. In a pious refutation of exorcists and other magicians, Jonson's contemporary James Mason is apparently fighting a rearguard action to distinguish the kind of adjuration or exaction of an oath that Catiline pursues from both *con*juration and conspiracy.

> So dothe the Latine word *adiuro* come of *iusiurandum* which betokeneth the same thing. As for English terme we haue none (that I know) that can in all points expresse the greeke, or latine word, wherefore we are constrained to make an English word of the Latine, saying (we *adiure*) for the common vsuall word of coniuring in our language, cannot well stand with the sense of this place: Neither doe I know how it hath crept into our tongue in these matters, seeing that it signifieth rather (*conspiring*) when diuerse haue conspired, and as it were sworne together to doe any act.[11]

All these terms – adjure, conjure, and conspire – were evidently synonymous in common usage. Thus, at the level of language, a strong link was forged between sedition and devil-worship in the anglicized version of Roman political moralizing. Sensationalist traditions of stage tragedy and theorizing about governmental stability existed, then, in a reciprocal relationship. On one hand, Elizabethan Seneca and the Shakespeare of *Titus Andronicus* had made familiar such lines as Jonson's, 'The day goes back ... As at Atrevs feast!' (I.313–14) and directions like '*A grone of many people is heard vnder ground*' (SD, I.316). On the other, the works of Cicero, the Italian *discorsi*, and English diatribes against popish conspiracy (among other texts) provided a political context for the denunciation of sedition. Both kinds of discourse entertained extreme gestures, and Jonson, for all his critical utterances preaching restraint, indulged this extremism in *Catiline*.

The inversion of sacramental language in the oath-taking scene is just one instance of the way that Roman institutions are twisted out of shape and turned against the state in this play. Even as Jonson is dramatizing the salvation of these institutions, he is highlighting their deformities and nurturing strongly interrogatory attitudes about the foundations on which his own humanism rests. The role of family histories, for example, is not quite what one would anticipate in this tragedy. Cicero is the self-originating, rootless hero of early Marlovian tragedy, not the noble Aeneas rescuing his father and the household gods on his back. He is a 'new fellow' (I.501), a 'meere vpstart, / That has no pedigree, no house, no coate, / No ensignes of a family' (II.119-21), 'a burgesse sonne of *Arpinum*' (IV.480). Family tradition is all on the side of the dissipated Catiline, who upbraids the senate for ignoring his distinguished ancestry:

> But I hope,
> This *Senate* is more graue, then to giue credit
> Rashly to all he [Cicero] vomits, 'gainst a man
> Of our owne order, a *Patrician*;
> And one, whose ancestors haue more deseru'd
> Of *Rome*, then this mans eloquence could vtter,
> Turn'd the best way: as still, it is the worst. (IV.465-71)

Opposing eloquence to ancestry may have been a source of some pleasure to Jonson, whose rhetorical reputation far outdistanced the line of his ancestors. Still, there has long been a suspicion that there is too much of a good thing in the oratorical elevation of Jonson's language in *Catiline*, especially in act IV, which closely renders Cicero's first oration against Catiline, delivered 7 November 63 BC. When he published his play, Jonson fumed at the 'Reader in Ordinarie' for '*dislik*[*ing*] *the Oration of Cicero, in regard you read some pieces of it, at Schoole, and vnderstand them not yet.*'

Cicero's oration is brilliant by any standard, and, when grandly delivered in the manner of the Renaissance stage, could have been riveting. It is also remarkable for its political subtlety. Its implicit accusations are as damning as its explicit ones, its innuendo as effective as its evidence. The 'private' or 'secret' vices of Catiline become the ground of the public attack mounted by Cicero, whose most telling strategy is the broadly suggestive rhetorical question:

> What domesticke note
> Of priuate filthinesse, but is burnt in

> Into thy life? What close, and secret shame,
> But is growne one, with thy knowne infamy?
> What lust was euer absent from thine eyes?
> What leud fact from thy hands? what wickednesse
> From thy whole body? where's that youth drawne in
> Within thy nets, or catch'd vp with thy baits,
> Before whose rage, thou hast not borne a sword,
> And to whose lusts thou hast not held a torch? (IV.316–25)

These largely sexual sins are made to seem more disgusting when hinted at than when named, as they were in Sylla's earlier tasteless iteration. Cicero's reticence in identifying his enemy's vices reveals more than it conceals when he balks at describing Catiline's marriage to his own sister.

> Thy latter nuptialls I let passe in silence;
> Where sinnes incredible, on sinnes, were heap't:
> Which I not name, lest, in a ciuill state,
> So monstrous facts should either appeare to be,
> Or not to be reueng'd. (IV.326–30)

It would appear that such violations of taboo (filicide as well as incest) must go unspoken if civilization is to be preserved from civil disorder. This cultural assumption raises the issue of silence and secrecy and their role in Cicero's Rome. It is another aspect of the covert state surveillance that Cicero promises to continue:

> I haue those eyes, and eares, shall still keepe guard,
> And spiall on thee, as they haue euer done,
> And thou not feele it. What, then, canst thou hope? (IV.232–4)

The question is a chilling one.[12]

Jonson makes fear a prominent part of the conclusion of his tragedy. All the intrusive intelligence-gathering done by the state bears fruit in the fourth-act accusations against Catiline and the fifth-act removal of the co-conspirators to the place where they will be executed by strangulation. In each case, though, the actions are not so much dramatized as narrated, one by way of a familiar classical oration, the other by off-stage action that is merely alluded to. A nuntius relates the final battle in which Catiline, surrounded, fights to his death. It appears that Jonson wished to retain as much authorial control as possible over the history he was presenting on stage, and he used various narrative strategies to do so. As in the case of Jonson's *Sejanus*, enclosing dramatic characters in stories is one way to control their destinies.[13] Thus, Cicero textualizes Catiline in his oration, permitting him little opportunity to react to the story the Consul is telling the senators. Replacing the villain-hero, Catiline, with the more conventional hero, Cicero, in the final acts of the play goes some way toward enforcing moral, as well as dramatic, closure.[14] But there is simply too much happening in the play to be so neatly contained by the form of classical tragedy. The whisperings about a political leader who manipulates events and sets citizens to spying on each other are too insistent to be ignored. Indeed, one recent critic speaks of Cicero's 'essential resemblance to Catiline in his political opportunism.'[15] The official attempt to cover up Crassus's and Caesar's part in the conspiracy is too cynical and inept to win an audience over or to permit a strong sense of dramatic closure.[16] The elements that will not be contained by the form of the play, secrets that will not be hushed up, provide a wicked undertow to the Ciceronian tide that sweeps the play toward Rome's salvation.

A perennial objection to readings that take account of the political undertow of seventeenth-century texts is that the patronage and censorship systems of the period would discourage authors from challenging state authority. In the case of Jonson this type of critical assumption gains support from the fact that he was strenuously seeking courtly patrons and patronesses as well as royal assent for his efforts at masque-making. If, as we have seen in the case of *Sejanus*, parallels between ancient Rome and Jacobean London were an expected feature of the drama, how could Jonson dare to include destabilizing elements in his representations of an exemplary Roman polity saved from insidious conspiracy? The answer to this question is not simply to show that Jonson was often personally a dissenter from authority, but to argue that his conception and practice of the poet's profession required that his art express its power over its political materials even as it acknowledged its dependency on those in power. In *Catiline*, both consul and conspirators derive enormous powers from secrecy. Jonson's considerable achievement is in making both sides compelling and, in some larger movement of history, self-cancelling. As Annabel Patterson puts it, assuming 'a sharp divide between ruling class and opposition, between writers who legitimate and writers who subvert ... will fail to deal with Jonson.'[17] While Patterson is tracing the careful negotiations of praise and power in Jonson's lyric poems, something of the kind must also be borne in mind when studying his treatment of politically sensitive issues on the stage. Censors and patrons could be unpleasant when displeased but could also be valuable protectors of the outspoken artist who understood the hermeneutic codes of praise and blame.

The final act of *Catiline* is a particularly good example of a text that simultaneously legitimates and subverts authority. It provides ample evidence that Jonson was able to treat the sensitive issue of sedition without espousing either the overthrow of governments or their infallibility. The sense of threat, both to Rome and to her enemies, is enormous in the closing speeches of the play. The loyal Roman general Marcus Petreius narrates Catiline's bloody end. Trapped between two advancing legions, Catiline chooses to attack Petreius, thereby sealing his own fate but also holding the fate of Rome precariously in the balance.

> It pleas'd *Fate*,
> To make vs th'obiect of his desperate choise,
> Wherein the danger almost paiz'd the honor:
> And as he riss', the day grew black with him;
> And *Fate* descended neerer to the earth,
> As if shee meant, to hide the name of things,
> Vnder her wings, and make the world her quarrie. (V.631-7)

Just as Catiline had threatened to burn and raze the entire city, here Fate threatens to flatten all distinctions, 'to hide the name of things.' Without the differentiations that language permits, the order of things would be shaken to its very foundations: diligence would be named deceit; virtue, vice; watchfulness, lying in wait (Chorus, IV.883-6). Though Petreius is victorious, Catiline and the conspiratorial threat he represents die very hard, if at all:

> So Catiline, at the sight of *Rome* in vs,
> Became his tombe: yet did his looke retayne
> Some of his fiercenesse, and his hands still mou'd,
> As if he labour'd, yet, to graspe the state,
> With those rebellious parts. (V.684-8)

Rebellion continues to twitch in the state, despite what Cicero calls 'all my labours, / My watchings, and my dangers' (V.694-5). Subsequent history proved that such vigilance was not adequate to protect Ciceronian, republican Rome from the advance of Caesarian, imperial Rome. As Jonson knew from his own political world, once the whispers of conspiracy and of counter-espionage come to dominate the state, the state apparatus functions mercilessly. 'The mercifull *Prince*,' he wrote, 'needs no Emissaries, Spies, Intelligencers, to intrap true Subjects. ... They have nothing in their brests, that they need a Cipher for' (*Disc.*, lines 1191-6).

However admirable the discretion of little Papyrius may seem in the story from Jean de Marconville with which I began this chapter, there is a quite different face to concealment in Jonson's drama. The page-boy whom Catiline singles out for threats and abuse immediately following the oath of confederacy in act I is as much a part of the negotiation of power in Rome as was Marconville's boy. Joining Catiline in this distasteful exchange is the aptly named Bestia:

> CAT. Why, now's the businesse safe, and each man strengthned.
> (*He spies one of his boyes not answere* –)
> Sirrah, what aile you? PAG. Nothing. BES. Somewhat modest.
> CAT. Slaue, I will strike your soule out, with my foot,
> Let me but find you againe with such a face:
> You whelp – BES. Nay, Lvcivs. CAT. Are you coying it,
> When I command you to be free, and generall
> To all? BES. You'll be obseru'd. CAT. Arise, and shew
> But any least auersion i' your looke
> To him that bourds you next, and your throat opens. (I.504-12)

In the wake of a perverted 'sacrament' intended to make the conspiracy 'safe' through secrecy, Jonson calls our attention to the private, sexual implications of what is going on in Rome. Catiline flies into a rage when one of his catamites, employed especially to cater to his fellow conspirators (I.171-2), makes a sour face at the proceedings. The boy should be open, 'free, and generall / To all,' not closed, coy, or private. Should he close his body off 'To him that bourds' him next, Catiline will open his throat from ear to ear.[18] The boy's behaviour will be closely 'obseru'd.' Indeed, according to the stage direction, Catiline 'spies' him out. Here in small is the image of Rome struggling with the conflict of open versus covert action. Even as Catiline exhorts the servant boy to openness, he swears the conspirators to close silence. Neither conspirators nor senators finally choose openness, and from this situation Jonson constructs the occasion for the series of dramatic revelations that constitutes his plot.

The text of Jonson's *Catiline*, like the political institutions whose preservation it records, is unable to control or to contain all the secret senses it generates. However unequivocal Cicero's final lines about the primacy of the conscience (V.697–702), another small voice continues its 'whispering speech against the prince.' To deny either speaking voice a hearing is to reduce the tragic impact of *Catiline His Conspiracy*.

CHAPTER SEVEN

State-Decipherers and Politique Picklockes: Interpretation as Self-Replication
in *Bartholomew Fair*

Before *Bartholomew Fair* gets under way, three playhouse employees wander on to the stage, discussing the play at hand. The way that Jonson teases his audience about the (im)possibility of interpretation in the course of this conversation can serve as a model of the problems that any conscientious reader of his plays must face. At first the stagehands offer criticism and then read out a series of 'Articles,' prepared by the author, limiting the audience's right to exercise its critical judgments on this particular play. This mock-legal contract assumes that none but the most 'solemnly ridiculous' interpreter in the audience would ransack Jonson's play-text in search of hidden meanings. The covenant between author and audience stipulates, in part:

> It is finally agreed, by the foresaid hearers, and *spectators*, that they neyther in themselues conceale, nor suffer by them to be concealed any *State-decipherer*, nor politique *Picklocke* of the *Scene*, so solemnly ridiculous, as to search out, who was meant by the *Gingerbread-woman*, who by the *Hobby-horse-man*, who by the *Costard-monger*, nay, who by their *Wares*. Or that will pretend to affirme (on his owne *inspired ignorance*) what *Mirror of Magistrates* is meant by the *Iustice*, what *great Lady* by the *Pigge-woman*, what *conceal'd States-man*, by the *Seller* of Mouse-*trappes*, and so of the rest. But that such person, or persons so found, be left discouered to the mercy of the *Author*, as a forfeiture to the *Stage*, and your laughter, aforesaid. (Induction, 135–48)

This is Jonson, the libertarian in his own cause, rounding smartly on the would-be code-cracking interpreter. The only secret identity 'concealed' in the text, he implies, is the (mis)reader himself, whom

Jonson will expose to the audience's derogatory laughter. The more general implication is that any of us viewing Jonson's texts as lockboxes and ourselves as burglars plundering them for topical meanings do so at our own risk.[1]

The problem of interpretation that Jonson broaches playfully in his Induction has as its source the urge to ground readings of literary texts in something 'real,' that is, non-fictional. For a reader uncertain about how to 'take' a text, there is something comfortingly familiar and reassuring about an allusion to a recognizable, historical event. The benchmark for orienting such readings can then be a solid 'fact' rather than an unstable idea. Searching for, and hence often finding, well-known statesmen in a *drame-à-clef* is simply one version, a particularly egregious one for Jonson, of the play-consumer's need to know where he or she is and to feel superior to the text in question.

Authors have always been hard on scandal-snooping interpreters, even as they lured them on with titillating clues. Such interpreters are accused of being aesthetically reductivist and politically dangerous. Jonson himself certainly had trouble with this kind of reader from *The Isle of Dogs* and *Eastward Ho* to *Sejanus* and *The Devil Is an Asse*, however tightly he wrapped himself in the by then well-known cloak of innocent universalizing.

> *What broad reproofes haue I vs'd? Where haue I beene particular? Where personall? except to a mimick, cheater, bawd, or buffon, creatures (for their insolencies) worthy to be tax'd? ... I know, that nothing can bee so innocently writ, or carryed, but may be made obnoxious to construction; mary, whil'st I beare mine innocence about mee, I feare it not. Application, is now, growne a trade with many; and there are, that professe to haue a key for the decyphering of euery thing.*[2]

The Psalmist's cadences in the sentence about bearing his innocence through the valley of shadowy misconstructionists yet fearing no evil puts Jonson's case for plain, pure, old-fashioned entertainments in the strongest possible terms. The terms he chooses are certainly not, however, ideologically unalloyed or unallied. He stands with the godly, the prophetic, and the scriptural as he concedes that even the word of God *'may be made obnoxious to construction.'* Just imagine what *de*construction can do to this kind of innocent authorial posturing! Would it be churlish to suggest that Jonson eggs on the very kind of interpreters he inveighs against when he says that he is never personal, *except* ... ? Readers who don't like being toyed with this way don't like Jonson; the rest of us enjoy the challenge.

Jonson himself more than halfway acknowledges what the post-structuralists have been at some pains to tell us in recent years: no text is universally true or ideologically innocent. A strong element of cultural production in all texts renders dubious even the most light-hearted authorial disclaimers of topicality, but such references are notoriously tricky to read. As Theodore Leinwand has shown us, what gets represented on the London stage in the age of Jonson is not 'a bundle of flesh-and-blood particulars' but 'the ways Londoners typed one another.'[3] And this is just one of the complications that arise when we try to construe the theatrical re-invention of any event, person, or set of attitudes apprehended via other modes of representation by the audience of the day.

Any resemblance in the plays of Jonson to persons either living or dead, contrary to the old libel-proofing demur, was probably intended (if he thought of it) and almost certainly relevant to the act of interpretation whether he thought of it or not.[4] His work, especially such a carefully localized play as *Bartholomew Fair*, invites topical, that is, 'placed' readings. The fair in Smithfield, going back nearly half a millennium, produced associations in the minds of Jonson's audience whether he wanted them or not, and he is not likely to have chosen that specific setting had he not wanted to play with, and against, those resonances.

His play, in turn, furnished the stuff from which subsequent textual reconstructions of the fair would be built. The author of the anonymous 1641 pamphlet called *Bartholomew Faire, or variety of fancies ... with the severall enormityes and misdemeanours, which are there seene and acted* almost certainly draws on material 'seene and acted' not on the fairgrounds but on the Jonsonian stage. The resemblance between the 'precise puritan' who attacks puppet motions in the pamphlet and Zeal-of-the-Land Busy in act V of Jonson's play is too close to be accidental, as is the similarity between the third robbery of Cokes (in IV.ii) and the 'cheating costermongers' of the pamphlet, 'who have a trick now and then to throw downe a basket of refuge peares, which prove cloake peares to those that shall loose their hats or cloaks in striving who shall gather fastest.'[5] My point is that Ben Jonson's pleas for an autonomous, non-interpretable art form notwithstanding, interpretations and reconstructions simply will proliferate.

Nor is Jonson's purpose in forbidding interpretation itself free from interpretation. He presents his attacks on ignorant and wilful misconstructions of his dramatic texts as an invigorating game. If to prohibit interpretation were obviously pointless, then to play out the follies of hieroglyphic deciphering for five acts, as he does in *Bartholomew Fair*, might just provide an amusing challenge for the playwright whose abuse of his audience had been fairly constant for the past fifteen years.[6] While Shakespeare might quip that one would have to be an ass to set about expounding Bottom's dream, he accepted interpretations silently and never, for example, represented an entire cast of London citizens greedily sniffing their way toward the unsavoury misconstruction of a supposed hidden truth, as Jonson did in *Bartholomew Fair*.

What Jonson's characters seek in *Bartholomew Fair* is licence to pursue their own individual desires, some authorizing words that will liberate them from the bothersome task of defending themselves before a censorious world. Like the 'solemnly ridiculous' interpreter of the Induction, his characters assume that there is some secret power in the text of such a licence. Cokes's carefully guarded marriage license is a modest example of the kind. Justice Overdo's warrant, desperately sought by the madman Trouble-all, is a more extravagant version. And what Knockem Jordan calls the 'Oracle of the Pigs head' (III.ii.71) – in fact a cut-down beer bottle that serves as urinal for all the female characters in the vicinity of Ursula's booth – is an obscene travesty of the quest for enabling authority at the fair.[7] Other texts and sources of prophetic utterance are also outrageously misconstrued: a selection of biblical texts, the ballad of a pickpocket, and a pair of classical tales translated into a puppet-play script. Imagining the unitary source of meaning to reside in some transcendent, translucent text, Jonson's characters regularly misinterpret the welter of experience around them. The warning is salutary.

In addition to the ur-texts that his characters use as lenses to distort the world around them, there are other sorts of intermediary texts through which Jonson encourages his audience to read his play. These include cony-catching pamphlets, duke-in-disguise plays, and letters by prominent public officials. The cumulative effect of all these mediating texts is to create a highly self-reflexive, non-naturalistic representation of a corner of seventeenth-century London, a representation that satirically mocks and baffles efforts at interpretation.[8]

The pursuit of an authority to justify what is pure self-indulgence in *Bartholomew Fair* differs significantly from the appeal to the authority of the state that we saw as central to *Catiline*. Rather than emphasizing a single and ultimately corrupting common good administered by an acknowledged master of oratory, as he did in that play, Jonson here mockingly represents myriad conflicting authorities that are produced, reproduced, or twisted beyond recognition by a barely controllable, pleasure-seeking London citizenry. As authority figures proliferate, the social structure becomes increasingly unstable. Communal bonds are stretched beyond their limits. Character groupings that originally constituted extended families splinter upon impact with the fair.[9] Neither Rabbi Busy nor the scolding Humphrey Waspe is able to retain control of the fair-goers in his charge. Failing on a grander scale, Justice Overdo attends more closely to the image he is projecting than to the abuses he proposes to ferret out. What emerges from all this is a complex critique of both the would-be licensing authorities and the wilful fools who invoke them in their own behalf. As R.B. Parker argues, 'the play exposes law and authority as merely further forms of aggression.'[10]

The general bias among the characters in *Bartholomew Fair* is that the most reliable and powerful authorities are not the nearby, voluble ones but the remote, silent ones, the secret authorizers of action. No one is content with the authority at hand but must seek another, more mysterious one. Although events in the play are often plain to the most commonsensical observer, Jonson's characters tirelessly pursue more arcane interpretations of what has happened around them. Appearances are forever being rejected in favour of subtle extrapolations from the obvious. Here, for example, is one of Justice Overdo's obtuse readings of the character of the cutpurse, Edgworth, and his balladeering accomplice, Nightingale:

> I cannot beget a *Proiect*, with all my politicall braine, yet; my *Proiect* is how to fetch off this proper young man, from his debaucht company: I haue followed him all the *Fayre* ouer, and still I finde him with this songster: And I begin shrewdly to suspect their familiarity; and the young man of a terrible taint, *Poetry*! with which idle disease, if he be infected, there's no hope of him, in a state-course. *Actum est*, of him for a common-wealths-man: if hee goe to't in *Rime*, once. (III.v.1-9)

Edgworth, of course, cares less about people's poetry and politics than about what is in their pockets. He has already carried off several foists in plain view of the audience while Overdo just barely misses seeing what has happened. While the blind Justice, like Knowell in *Every Man In His Humour*, suspects that a potential 'commonwealths-man' will be lost to the ravages of poesie, Edgworth has given no indication of caring to be anything but adept at his trade. Only by straining his imperfect observations through his anti-poetic and pro-civic prejudices can Overdo so thoroughly misjudge the petty thief. These are the fruits of 'projecting' one's own values onto the scene with such a 'politicall braine.' What Jonson has epitomized here is interpretation as self-replication. This satiric strategy is an extension of Jonson's familiar way of implicating any critic who complained of having been put into one of his plays. Such a complaint, Jonson maintained, was tantamount to forging an identification with such fools or knaves, quite apart from the author's professedly innocent intentions. Such critics found themselves accused of creating the world in their own image, much as Overdo himself does. And Overdo thereby denies in practice what he acknowledges in precept: '*Non te quaesiueris extra*' (IV.vi.100-1), a tag from Persius's *Satire 1*, meaning roughly, 'Do not try to find yourself outside yourself.' The least *introspective of soliloquists and the clumsiest of spies, Overdo does just this in his repeated self-projections.

Jonson's crooks, the fair people, are masters of insinuating themselves into throngs – and indeed, into the hearts of Overdo, Bartholomew Cokes, and those audiences who romanticize and applaud their exuberant lawlessness. His frustrated reformers are equally good at insinuating themselves into the accounts of the enormities they imagine they have discovered. In attempting to penetrate deceptive appearances to get at underlying truths, they instead perpetrate the ultimate deception of the self. That is, their perceptions are so shaped by what Overdo calls a '*proiect*' or premeditated scheme that the result is simply deeper and deeper self-absorption. The exploration of this form of folly, which had been implicit in Jonson's drama since the beginning of his career, involves the playwright in a literary technique that we have come to associate primarily with first-person prose fiction, namely characters' self-narration. Its chief mechanism in drama is the soliloquy.

We tend to think that Shakespeare is the English Renaissance master of the soliloquy and that tragedy is the genre most congenial to such extended acts of self-presentation, particularly by villains such as Iago but also by disaffected heroes like Hamlet and Lear. Karen Newman has explored the ways that Shakespeare also uses soliloquy in the comedies to create convincingly 'real' dialogue within the minds of individual characters.[11] Jonson does something different from Shakespeare with his solitary speakers, however. Their mode is oratorical, not personal. They deliberately project into the public arena a self whose self-deceptions, though palpable, they are blind to. Alone on stage, they declaim about projects that are in fact elaborate projections of a constructed nonce-self, one that believes itself somehow capable of accessing truths unavailable to the everyday self. Overdo sets in motion such a nonce-self with full-blown pomposity at his first appearance. He circumscribes his maiden soliloquy – or rather solitary oration – with the symbols of public authority. He begins, 'Well, in Iustice name, and the Kings; and for the common-wealth!' and concludes, 'And as I began, so I'll end: in Iustice name, and the Kings; and for the Common-wealth' (II.i.1-49). Proclaiming his new-made public self, dubbed Mad Arthur o' Bradley, Overdo protects his secret self, the undercover agent. By doing his own spying, he cuts out the unreliable intelligence-gathering middlemen and -women on whom Cicero was forced to rely so heavily in *Catiline*. Overdo outlines the curious situation of 'all men in authority,' those 'publike persons' who 'heare with other mens eares ... see with other mens eyes.'

> This wee are subiect to, that liue in high place, all our intelligence is idle, and most of our intelligencers, knaues: and by your leaue, our selues, thought little better, if not errant fooles, for beleeuing 'hem. I *Adam Ouerdoo*, am resolu'd therefore, to spare spy-money hereafter, and make mine owne discoueries. (II.i.36-41)

This is a telling admission. The final phrase, 'mine owne discoueries,' like so many of the inadvertent justice's public pronouncements, rushes off in several directions at once. By generating his own 'intelligence,' he will replicate his own folly, discovering only himself in the world around him and shaping that world to his own fanciful specifications. By act III, having delivered himself of a long speech against bottle-ale and tobacco (II.vi.1-90) that provides a cover for Edgworth to steal Cokes's first purse, thereby incurring Waspe's wrath, Overdo resolves in another declamatory soliloquy that he 'will make no man orations, shall draw on these tragicall conclusions':

> To see what bad euents may peepe out o' the taile of good purposes! the care I had of that ciuil yong man, I tooke fancy to this morning,

(and haue not left it yet) drew me to that exhortation, which drew the company, indeede, which drew the cut-purse; which drew the money; which drew my brother *Cokes* his losse; which drew on *Wasp's* anger; which drew on my beating: a pretty gradation!

(III.iii.13–20)

He finally decides that this is not a wholly regrettable pattern of events because it will make such a good story around the dinner table. The story has 'a publike good designe' (25–6) both in the sense of intending to prosecute public wrongdoing and in the sense of being based on the sound rhetorical principle of 'gradation.' As soon as Overdo concludes his monologue with the Justice-King-Commonwealth formula, Winwife, who has been standing aside listening with Quarlous, says, 'What doe's he talke to himselfe, and act so seriously?' (42–3). With these words, any vestige of the convention of soliloquy as directly perceived interior thought flies out the window. Instead, the audience finds itself eavesdropping on an incompetent law officer who talks to himself. Overdo's thoroughgoing self-deception, not the fair's rather commonplace misdemeanours, seems to be Jonson's satiric target. The deepest form of folly would appear to be the quasi-official acts of misreading that are daily perpetrated on the world, both on and off the stage. Jonson demonstrates that none of these authoritative statements addresses 'the times deformitie' with the kind of self-awareness – the essential ironic distance – that characterizes his own plays.

The necessity for such distance is driven home by the elaborate intertextuality with which Jonson has carefully encoded *Bartholomew Fair*. I refer specifically to the Lord Mayor's account of spying out 'enormities' in London and to a series of cony-catching pamphlets to which Jonson also alludes.[12] These texts are not so much sources, in the sense that Tacitus was for *Sejanus* or Sallust for *Catiline*, as they are analogous accounts of the seamy side of contemporary London that had gained some currency and credibility as objective descriptions of how things really were. Jonson's reworking of this material reveals the misleadingly covert fictionality of such texts. In particular, Jonson cuts through the moral cant used in these sensational and self-serving exposés. In most cases the moral justification for acts of official spying as well as for publishing so-called rogue pamphlets was to warn an innocent citizenry against sharp dealers and to publish ringing denunciations of their duplicity. This is how Robert Greene explains his motives in the Epistle Dedicatorie to his *Second Part of Conny-Catching* (1591):

> Thus Gentlemen I haue discouered in briefe, what I meane to prosecute at large: though not eloquently, yet so effectually, that if you be not altogether carelesse, it may redownd to your commoditie: forewarned, forearmed: burnt children dread the fire, and such as neither counsaile, nor other mens harmes, may make to beware, are worthie to liue long, and still by the losse. But hoping these secrets I haue set abroach, and my labours I haue taken in searching out those base villanies, shall not be onely taken with thankes, but applied with care: I take my leaue with this farewell. God either confound, or conuert such base minded Cooseners.[13]

The camaraderie that Greene tries to foster with his audience by rehearsing humble folk adages and sharing secrets is similar to the conspiratorial soliloquies that Overdo shares with his. In each case, the secrets seem either false or not worth knowing, and the moralizing seems ineptly tacked on to what is really happening in the text.

In the process of summarizing the achievements of his undercover investigations in the first half of the play, Justice Overdo inadvertently gives the lie to the widely accepted Renaissance practice of spying: 'To see,' he moans, 'what bad euents may peepe out o' the taile of good purposes!' One of the most infamous of the official spies of the period was a particular Lord Mayor of London, not, as thought for much of this century, Sir Thomas Hayes, but rather one Thomas Middleton, not the playwright.[14] Middleton may have taken his cue for engaging in clandestine escapades in 1603-4 and again in 1614 from George Whetstone's *A Mirour for Magestrates of Cyties* (1584), a volume to which Jonson alludes twice in *Bartholomew Fair*. Whetstone describes the magistrate's desire to peer into each dark corner with his own eyes (a concern elaborately proclaimed by Overdo, as we have seen) in something like the oxymoronic terms of Milton's 'darkness visible': 'Your sightes are not invisible, and (therfore) necessarie, that you haue visible Lightes, in obscure Corners. A Physition, can not see euery secrete griefe, but vpon Reuealement, may applie a curable Medicine for a hidden Discease.'[15] More pertinent to our present concerns than the possible adumbration of a Miltonic phrase is Shakespeare's 'duke of dark corners' in *Measure for Measure* and the other duke-in-disguise plays by such dramatists as John Marston and Thomas Middleton. Plays of this kind invariably are more concerned with satirizing the blindness of authority than with the corruption of the politically powerless. Whetstone's medical metaphor for unseen but curable social ills finds its way into much of the satiric drama of the Jacobean age, Jonson's being no exception. Nothing is so consistently ridiculed in these texts as the ways that practitioners of medicine, religion, and the law ignorantly poke and probe into the secret parts of the body politic.

Each of the visitors to Jonson's fair either seeks or asserts socially approved, authoritative interpretations of their world. As Gabriele Bernhard Jackson has argued, the process of interpretation in Jonson's plays is often synonymous with evaluation or judgment.[16] Weaknesses of judgment are repeatedly exposed in *Bartholomew Fair* when actions that are approved one minute are condemned the next by the same character, depending on how he or she chooses to construe the unstated intention behind an action or a text. The process is instructively analogous to the perplexed search for authorial intention which Jonson keeps reproblematizing in his own text. As author of a popular entertainment, for example, he negotiates an agreement with his audience in the Induction, but he also admits that he himself requires another kind of licence, namely that of the Master of the Revels, Sir George Buc. Buc or one of his agents would likely have previewed *Bartholomew Fair* before it was played at court.[17]

As others have noted, there is widespread concern among the characters in *Bartholomew Fair* about obtaining various forms of permission from the prevailing authorities.[18] Dame Purecraft, Grace Wellborn, Quarlous, and Winwife all require the permission of a madman to marry, for instance. A marriage licence bearing Justice Overdo's seal passes from hand to hand and is eventually tampered with so that it ratifies a marriage that the Justice knows nothing about. The most desperate and voluble pursuit of an official licence is Troubleall's repeated demand that characters show Overdo's warrant for anything they do. Troubleall himself will not change his shirt or relieve himself without such warrant. At one point the loyal members of the King's watch are interrupted by Troubleall in the act of stocking a miscreant, Overdo in his Mad Arthur disguise: 'If you haue Iustice *Ouerdoo's* warrant, 'tis well: you are safe; that is the warrant of warrants. I'le not giue this button, for any mans warrant else' (IV.i.19–21). But everyone at the fair knows that Troubleall was driven mad long ago by one of Overdo's miscarriages of justice. The 'warrant of warrants' in *Bartholomew Fair* is not, finally, a legal document nor even the published Word of God (the puritan zealots notwithstanding) but rather the boisterous fiction that Jonson creates, a fiction that both includes and transcends all these rival claims to authority. It is the master playwright, speaking for the city fathers, who licenses this fair.

The play is characterized by the noise and confusion of one authority figure cannoning off another. A suitable image of this contention, at the low end of the scale of rational discourse, is the game of vapours in which the inebriated participants rival one another's claims to authority through the simple expedient of flat contradiction.[19] Here are Knockem, Val Cutting, Humphrey Waspe, and Captain Whit at it full-tilt:

> KNO. He is i' the right, and do's vtter a sufficient vapour.
> CVT. Nay, it is no sufficient vapour, neither, I deny that.
> KNO. Then it is a sweet vapour.
> CVT. It may be a sweet vapour.
> WAS. Nay, it is no sweet vapour, neither, Sir, it stinkes, and I'le stand to't.
> WHI. Yes, I tinke it dosh shtinke, Captaine. All vapour dosh shtinke.
> WAS. Nay, then, it do's not stink, Sir, and it shall not stinke.
> CVT. By your leaue, it may, Sir.
> WAS. I, by my leaue, it may stinke, I know that. (IV.iv.54-65)

The disputants move with wondrous dispatch from questions of right to questions of smell. And over all this babble of voices presides the final anti-authority of all, Ate, Goddess of Chaos, in the guise of Ursula the Pig Woman. As R.B. Parker points out, extending the work of Jackson Cope on the subject, the figure of *Discordia* is usually represented in Renaissance emblem books holding a firebrand in one hand (compare Ursula's entrance at II.v.59) and a sheaf of legal papers in the other as an image of the folly and tumult that characterize the pursuit of authority at law.[20] Staged iconography, then, combines with Jonson's spoof of actual magisterial spying and his satiric language of misinterpretation occasioned by unrestrained self-projection to produce a richly vital image of Londoners on a busman's holiday.

As the fair is a natural setting for a holiday celebration, critics of *Bartholomew Fair* have been attracted to the interpretive frame of festival provided by the work of Barber, Bakhtin, Weimann, Bristol, and others.[21] The first thing to notice in any such study is that

Jonson's characters carry along all of their everyday determinations as they enter the fair. While Overdo holds fast to his magistrate's mentality and misses the genuine 'enormities' that swirl around him, Busy locks his experience and that of his followers into his own unyieldingly biblical interpretive frame. His readings of the fair are nothing if not overdetermined. He is one of the hypocritical brethren whose imagined purity bubbles up from some hidden source within and finds subsequent justification in literal interpretations of scriptural texts. Jonson does not depict this approach to knowledge sympathetically. As David Norbrook observes, Jonson was 'suspicious of claims to inner purity: any attempt to achieve absolute purity in a fallen world seemed to him potentially hypocritical.'[22] As we saw in the case of Ananias and Tribulation Wholesome in *The Alchemist*, Jonson delighted in mocking the puritans' arrogance in rejecting church tradition in favour of their own inner promptings and idiosyncratic readings of Scripture while remaining impervious to any external scrutiny. He pursues these problems to their logical *reductio* in the figure of Zeal-of-the-Land Busy.

Busy is a hypocrite in the commonplace sense of one who, without conviction, merely impersonates socially approved behaviours (Gr. *hypokrites*, a stage actor) and also in the deeper sense of being taken in by his own zealous acts of interpretation, falling victim to self-deceit.[23] We need to understand both aspects of Busy's hypocrisy to grasp the basic anti-institutional impulse that Jonson sees as characteristic of the puritan and that he uses to balance out Overdo's civic and legal interventions at the fair.

The year following the first performance of *Bartholomew Fair*, Daniel Dyke published a small volume that may shed some light on the kinds of deception that Jonson attributes to 'Rabbi' Busy. Dyke called his book *The Mystery of Selfe-Deceiuing*, but he carefully set it apart from other books on the art of deception such as the rogue pamphlets and stage plays that, as we have already seen, found their way into Jonson's creative process. Dyke warns that

> Indeed oftentimes the discoueries of cousenages, and deceits in the world make many, before honestly ignorant, to turne couseners and deceiuers. But heere needes no such feare, for heere we are taught no new deceit or cousening trickes, which yet wee practise not; but rather are conuinced of that cousenage, with which we deceiue our owne soules, and yet will not be borne downe to be guilty of imposture. This point is worthy our best wits, and knowledge. That heathen Philosopher neuer thoughtns [sic] himselfe to begin to know Philosophy, till hee began to know him-

selfe. But surely wee neuer begin to know Diuinitie *or* Religion, *till wee come to know our selues: our selues we cannot know, till wee know our hearts.] but, our hearts are deceitfull aboue all things, who can know them?*[24]

The real problem, according to Dyke, is to know thyself, not to recognize the impostures of others. Jonson dealt with both matters, though his critics have less frequently noted his engagement with the former, more philosophical problem. He pursues the question of secret, inner knowledge in very different directions from those puritan moralists and polemicists, interpreters of the human heart like Daniel Dyke, whom he parades so ridiculously on the stage. Chief among these reformers in *Bartholomew Fair* is Rabbi Busy.

Besotted by the glories of his own rhetoric, Busy claims the sanctions of religious law for what is actually an indulgence of appetite. He is a 'notable hypocriticall vermine,' whose disdain for all traditional wisdom places him, as Quarlous says, in a state of *'Originall ignorance'* (I.iii.146). This last phrase, glancing at the origins of sin itself, pushes Jonson's satiric anatomy of self-absorption beyond the level of Cokes's unawareness and Overdo's unconscious self-projection to embrace wilful self-deception. Busy does not shrug off the law as others in the play do; rather, he adjusts it to fit particular circumstances. When Win Littlewit feigns a pregnant longing for roast pig, Busy supplies the authoritative moral rationale for his puritan sister to indulge her appetite for the forbidden meat. Win, he claims, is not succumbing to the lust of the flesh but rather following the law of her nature that requires nourishment. He is left, however, with one scruple concerning the profane place where the pig feast is to occur. Puritans were notorious for their scrupulous care about the trappings and location of rituals, but in the present case the scruple quickly vanishes beneath a 'vaile' of religious appearances. Busy concludes, 'the place is not much, not very much, we may be religious in midst of the prophane, so it [the pig] be eaten with a reformed mouth, with *sobriety*, and humblenesse' (I.vi.72-4). For Busy, reformation of the mouth means, in practical terms, wholesale parroting of biblical phraseology and a glib justification for devouring great quantities of Ursula's roast pork.

Busy has been acting as a casuist, resolving a case of moral doubt in problematic circumstances by the exercise of reason. Unlike the legitimate casuists of the sixteenth and seventeenth centuries, who attempted to help their congregations and readers to resolve troubled consciences, he is a hypocritical Houdini of the conscience, engineering dazzling escapes from impossibly tight spots where he is squeezed between moral law and unenlightened self-interest. Jonson, by emphasizing the humorous discontinuity between precept and practice in Busy's casuistry, may well be satirizing such noted puritan casuists as William Ames and William Perkins, who, he seems to suggest, manipulate their immediate circumstances to fit conveniently into the ever-widening gap between moral principle and raw appetite.[25] Busy is a memorable master of keeping his principles flexible, his belly and purse full, and his holy image bright. He is most grand when being most sincerely the hypocrite, that is, when he is doing what he most enjoys, namely, exhorting the wicked to play the game of life by his rules. His authority is, of course, the Word of God, as in the following tirade against Lanthorn Leatherhead's dolls and hobby-horses: 'Peace, with thy Apocryphall wares, thou prophane Publican: thy *Bells*, thy *Dragons*, and thy *Tobie's Dogges*. Thy Hobby-horse is an Idoll, a very Idoll, a feirce and rancke Idoll: And thou, the *Nabuchadnezzar*, the proud *Nebuchadnezzar* of the *Faire*, that set'st it vp, for children to fall downe to, and worship' (III.vi.54-9). Busy lifts from the Bible not only its prose rhythms and its proscription against idols but even, shortly after this passage, the role of Christ cleansing the temple when he pulls down Joan Trash's 'Idolatrous Groue of Images' made of gingerbread (III.vi.98).

Busy regularly appropriates reconstructed biblical texts as a way to distance the authority of his much-advertised spiritual purity from the capitalistic distribution of sin at the fair. He rails against the 'merchandize of *Babylon*' (III.vi.91-2) sold at the 'shop of *Satan*' (III.ii.42) partly because these petty Smithfield shopkeepers are cutting in on his own trade in rich widows. The puritan financial conspiracy that parallels that of the hustling and thieving carni-people who work the crowds at the fair is, by Dame Purecraft's admission, a far more lucrative proposition. Having been denounced by Quarlous as 'part of the society of *Canters*, Outlawes to order and *Discipline*, and the onely priuiledg'd *Church-robbers* of *Christendome*' (V.ii.44-6), Purecraft confesses her part in the great puritan deception in order to retain the 'madman' she loves:

> I must vncover my selfe vnto him, or I shall neuer enioy him, for all the *cunning mens* promises. Good Sir, heare mee, I am worth sixe thousand pound, my loue to you, is become my racke, I'll tell you all, and the truth: since you hate the hypocrisie of the party-coloured

> brotherhood. These seuen yeeres, I haue beene a wilfull holy widdow, onely to draw feasts, and gifts from my intangled suitors: I am also by office, an assisting *sister* of the *Deacons*, and a deuourer, in stead of a distributer of the alms. I am a speciall maker of marriages for our decayed *Brethren*, with our rich *widdowes*; for a third part of their wealth, when they are marryed, for the reliefe of the poore *elect*: as also our poore handsome yong Virgins, with our wealthy Batchelors, or Widdowers; to make them steale from their husbands, when I haue confirmed them in the faith, and got all put into their custodies. And if I ha' not my bargaine, they may sooner turne a scolding drab, into a silent *Minister*, then make me leaue pronouncing *reprobation*, and *damnation* vnto them. Our elder, *Zeale-of-the-land*, would haue had me, but I know him to be the capitall Knaue of the land, by making himselfe rich, by being made *Feoffee* in trust to deceased *Brethren*, and coozning their *heyres*, by swearing the absolute gift of their inheritance. (V.ii.48-70)

Entangling suitors and arranging rich marriages provide access to substantial sums of inherited money in the realm. While Ursula's band of pedlars, petty crooks, and prostitutes draw off the occasional purse from a Bartholomew Cokes, it is the men and women of the Church who have access to family fortunes. Borrowing the authoritative rhetoric of the Bible and claiming the unchallengeable interpretive gifts of the inner light, Jonson's puritans exploit the richest area of social and economic vulnerability, that is, human sexuality. Their 'poore handsome yong Virgins' are the surest way to lure 'wealthy Batchelors, or Widdowers' into the faith and into a legal trap once their property has been transferred into the custody of those carefully controlled women (lines 60-3). The capital gains from trading on the unscrutinized inner truth of the puritan sisters and brothers line the pockets of 'the capitall Knaue of the land,' Rabbi Busy.

Having heard Dame Purecraft's detailed revelations, Quarlous – like that other careful guardian of public order and his own interests, Cicero in *Catiline* – decides to respect the confidence and not to rock his own boat. Self-consciously he joins the conspiracy of churchmen, confiding in soliloquy:

> It is money that I want, why should I not marry the money, when 'tis offer'd mee? I haue a *License* and all, it is but razing out one name, and putting in another. There's no playing with a man's fortune! I am resolu'd! I were truly mad, an' I would not! well, come your wayes,

follow mee, an' you will be mad, I'll shew you a warrant!
(V.ii.80-6)

If this be madness, yet there's money in it. Quarlous need only tamper with one small bit of text and his friend Winwife will be provided with a licence for a sizable marriage settlement. The economy of sexuality, then, extends well beyond the recruitment of prostitutes by the bawd, Captain Whit. When Quarlous accepts a wife for the profits from a religious confidence racket, he, like Lovewit in *The Alchemist*, loses whatever moral authority had accrued to him as a perceptive interpreter of the play's action.

Because Quarlous's complicit silence can be bought for £6,000 and an unscrupulous widow, Busy's authority remains unchallenged, at least for the moment. The challenge, when it comes, strikes with the full force of comic improbability. Busy bursts in on the Littlewit-Leatherhead puppet show to denounce this 'prophanation,' this 'beame in the eye, in the eye of the brethren' (V.v.2, 8-9). Spreading his net to include 'your *Stage-players*, *Rimers*, and *Morrise-dancers*' (V.v.10-11), Busy invokes the biblical injunction against worshiping idols as he attacks the puppet Dionisius (V.v.54). Such a vocation, Busy insists, is profane. The puppet, seconded by Lanthorne Leatherhead, the puppeteer, retorts that it is not; Busy that it is, and so on, replicating the back-and-forth contention of the game of vapours in a pseudo-theological mode. Busy's 'base noyse' (76) substitutes for reasoned analysis as they discuss a fine point of doctrine:

> BVS. Yet, I say, his *Calling*, his Profession is prophane, it is prophane, *Idoll*.
> PVP D. *It is not prophane!*
> LAN. It is not prophane, he sayes.
> BVS. It is prophane.
> PVP. *It is not prophane.*
> BVS. It is prophane.
> PVP. *It is not prophane.*
> LAN. Well said, confute him with *not*, still. You cannot beare him downe with your base noyse, Sir. (V.v.67-76)

This scene provoked a shrewd comment from Jonson's friend John Selden in his volume *Table-Talk*:

> Disputes in Religion will never be ended, because there wants a Measure by which the Business would be decided: The Puritan would be judged by the Word of God: If he would speak clearly, he

means himself, but he is ashamed to say so; and he would have me believe him before the whole Church, that has read the Word of God as well as he. One says one thing, and another another; and there is, I say, no Measure to end the Controversie. 'Tis just as if Two Men were at Bowls, and both judg'd by the Eye: One says 'tis his Cast, the other says 'tis my Cast; and having no Measure, the Difference is Eternal. Ben Johnson Satyrically express'd the vain Disputes of Divines by *Inigo Lanthorne*, disputing with his puppet in a *Bartholomew Fair*. It is so; It is not so: It is so, It is not so, crying thus one to another a quarter of an Hour together.[26]

Selden's argument that for the puritan the sole measure of interpretive accuracy is the self, the inner revelation set against the traditions of 'a whole Church,' neatly formulates Jonson's satiric strategy for exposing foolish acts of interpreting or 'measuring' texts. The eye beholds what the eye projects, and the text under scrutiny disappears from view altogether. The revealed Word becomes the concealed power of textual construction, in this case the killjoy's determination to emerge victorious from the dispute.

When he fails to win the first round, Busy falls back on the well-tried biblical prohibition against transvestitism to sustain what Jonas Barish calls his 'anti-theatrical prejudice.'[27] 'My maine argument against you,' cries Busy, 'is, that you are an *abomination*: for the Male, among you, putteth on the apparell of the *Female*, and the *Female* of the *Male*' (V.v.98-100). Lifting up his garment to expose – or, rather, to fail to expose – himself, Puppet Dionisius successfully confutes the biblical literalist. The moment is a stunning parody of Revelation in which the secret that is shown forth proves to be precisely nothing. What is 'read' as counter to the injunction from Deuteronomy 22:5 is the anatomically incorrect body of a nonperson, a manikin or impersonator. Not the body of the text but the body *as* text absurdly carries the day. In the process, Jonson satirically diminishes both puritan interpretationists and the members of the Lady Elizabeth's Men.

Parallel and equally mindless quests for an authorizing text engage Quarlous and Winwife as they compete for the hand of Grace Wellborn. The first crucial piece of writing to impinge on this action is Justice Overdo's marriage licence authorizing the union of Grace, whose marriage rights he has purchased from the Court of Wards (III.v.273-4), and Bartholomew Cokes, his wife's brother. The licence is locked away in a black box in the possession of Cokes's irascible tutor, Humphrey Waspe, but Grace's new-found pair of suitors employ Edgworth as picklock to bring them the licence, leaving Waspe the box 'to play with' (III.v.253). It is then a simple matter of 'scraping out *Cokes* his name' (IV.iii.106) and replacing it with either Quarlous's or Winwife's, and the rights to Grace will be transferred to that man. But just which one it is to be will be determined by a bizarre lottery engineered by Grace herself, the results being kept secret until some later time.

The mechanics of Grace's marriage lottery require the creation of yet another text, this one consisting of just two secretly coded names, selected from the corpus of romance literature by Quarlous and Winwife. A neutral observer will select the lucky name.

> GRA. I saw one of you buy a paire of tables, e'en now.
> WIN-W. Yes, heere they be, and maiden ones too, vnwritten in.
> GRA. The fitter for what they may be imployed in. You shall write either of you, heere, a word, or a name, what you like best; but of two, or three syllables at most: and the next person that comes this way (because *Destiny* has a high hand in businesse of this nature) I'le demand, which of the two words, he, or she doth approue; and according to that sentence, fixe my resolution, and affection, without change.
> QVAR. Agreed, my word is conceiued already.
> WIN-W. And mine shall not be long creating after.
> GRA. But you shall promise, Gentlemen, not to be curious to know, which of you it is, is taken; but giue me leaue to conceale that till you haue brought me, either home, or where I may safely tender my selfe. (IV.iii.45–61)

Having the name chosen finally by the madman, Troubleall, and postponing the announcement of the lucky man's name are parts of an elaborate travesty Jonson has concocted, based on the romantic poetics of secrecy that had gained such high favour in the reign of Queen Elizabeth. The arts of secrecy are suggested partly by the sexualizing of the act of writing in this passage. These 'maiden' tables (46) on which words will be 'conceived' (56) by a male pen must, like the widow's own non-virginal sexuality, be concealed from public view until she 'may safely tender [her]selfe' (61).

In courtly circles the documents containing and preserving the young lady's purity would not have been a judge's licence or a name scribbled on a cheap pair of tables but rather a sheaf of manuscript sonnets. The poetic strategies devised by the sonneteer to blazon forth the estimable inner self of the beloved, in fact, work in precisely the opposite way to Jonson's text. As Patricia Fumerton has argued, sonneteers who followed Sir Philip Sidney's lead '"represent" their private loves through conventional artifice that keeps them hidden.'[28] Such poems and the selves they sought to capture and protect were, in at least some cases, further distanced from public scrutiny by being secured in locked boxes in the inmost chambers of great ladies' residences. Thomas Nashe, responding to a very different impulse, namely to publish and to dramatize these images of women, says in the preface to a pirated 1591 edition of Sidney's sonnets that such poems may remain 'oftentimes imprisoned in Ladyes casks' unless an enterprising publisher employs 'some priuate penne (in steed of a picklock) to procure his violent enlargement.'[29] It may be argued that Jonson chose to demystify those qualities of inwardness in *Bartholomew Fair* for the popular playhouse audience, and, by royal request, for the court.[30] In doing so, what he reveals is vulgarity and, finally, vacuity. Like the salacious riddles, mysterious anagrams, and sonnets written by and for the Collegiate Ladies in *Epicoene*, the written texts in *Bartholomew Fair* reveal only inadequacies in the discourse of love. Such clever lock-picking at the supposed secrets of the text is the ultimate interpretive presumption in Jonson's eyes. It will reveal nothing but a deformed self, projected by what one of the fairmen calls 'your prying cat-eyed-citizen' (IV.v.52).

Marrying for love, a dream cherished by citizens of middling condition and fostered by numerous stage representations, takes a severe knock in *Bartholomew Fair* when the barter for brides emerges as an extension of Captain Whit's brisk trade in female flesh, his tireless recruiting of prostitutes. In the grand finale of revelations in V.vi, one after another of the disguised and hypocritical interpreters of the play's actions is confounded – to use Busy's earlier term from the puppet debate – by the ubiquity of the sexual trade at the fair. Both John Littlewit's and Justice Overdo's wives have, in their alcoholic haze, been recruited for the profession. After Win-the-Fight Littlewit is discovered in this fashion, Overdo advises her chagrined husband to remain as silent as Harpocrates, god of silence (V.vi.48), in an attempt to contain the damage done to reputations by his own prying. His ongoing – and false – revelations of enormities are rudely interrupted when Mrs Overdo throws up noisily in the middle of his big scene and, dropping her prostitute's disguise, calls out for her husband's aid. This is Quarlous's cue to take over the part of remover of disguises, unifier of plots, corrector of false suppositions, and discoverer of hidden truths. None of these functions of closure escapes Jonson's fine ironic touch, however. No one knows better than Quarlous, for instance, that the '*Innocent young man*' whom Overdo has 'tane such care of, all this day, is a *Cutpurse*' (75-6), because Quarlous has employed Edgworth in just that capacity. When Quarlous triumphantly produces the stolen licence and thanks Overdo for the gift of a wife, we know the document to be a forgery. When he announces the winner of the lottery for Grace's hand, we know that he is violating the 'article' that would have kept that madcap business private. 'I thank you Sr.' he tells Overdo, 'for the gift of your *Ward*, Mrs. *Grace*: look you, here is your hand & seale, by the way. Mr. *Win-wife*, giue you ioy, you are *Palemon*, you are possest o' the Gentlewoman, but she must pay me value, here's warrant for it' (V.vi.81-5). Reminders of Quarlous's venality in various conspiracies keep surfacing along with the revelations with which he mocks others. As George Rowe has argued, Jonson systematically collapses the distinction between the witty urban gallant and the objects of his derision – the country bumpkin, the pretender to wit, and the unsavoury denizens of the fair.[31] When Quarlous finally invites Overdo to 'compare our *discoueries*; and drowne the memory of all enormity in your bigg'st bowle at home' (V.vi.99-100), the audience is well aware that such discoveries contain more enlightened self-interest than moral truth.

Jonson's chief mockers of authority, the fair people, establish early in the play that the judge will be judged while the profitable deceit goes along unexposed. The irony of justice being blinded by self-promoting lawlessness is most humorously represented in the scene (III.v) in which Nightingale sings his ballad, '*A caueat against cutpurses*,' while Edgworth filches Cokes's second purse, and the hapless judge misses what is going on under his nose. The text of the ballad, with its strong ties to Robert Greene's discovery of thievish tricks in the cony-catching pamphlets, like the embedded texts discussed earlier, conspicuously fails to reveal the theft now in progress. In the following account, Greene introduces the motif of the ballad-maker who warns his audience of cutpurses even as the cutpurse who is 'compacted together' with him works the crowd.

> A roging mate, & such another with him, were there got upon a

stal singing of balets which belike was som prety toy, for very many gathered about to heare it, & divers buying, as their affections served, drew to their purses & paid the singers for them. The slye mate and his fellowes, who were dispersed among them that stoode to heare the songes: well noted where everie man that bought, put up his purse againe, and to such as would not buy, counterfeit warning was sundrie times given by the rogue and his associate, to beware of the cut pursse, and looke to their pursses, which made them often feel where their pursses were, either in sleeve, hose, or at girdle, to know whether they were safe or no. Thus the craftie copesmates were acquainted with what they most desired, and as they were scattered, by shouldring, thrusting, feigning to let fall something, and other wilie tricks fit for their purpose: heere one lost his purse, there another had his pocket pickt, and to say all in briefe, and at one instant, upon the complaint of one or two that sawe their pursses were gone, eight more in the same companie, found themselves in like predicament.[32]

The balladeer's brazen self-narration, which closely parallels Autolycus's story to the Clown in *The Winter's Tale* (IV.iii.87-100), exposes the limits of ordinary interpretation. Accepting the conventions of third-person narration, the on-stage audience assumes that Greene's singers, like Shakespeare's Autolycus and Jonson's Nightingale, must be describing some other action with other players, not the present events, which would normally have identified the narrator-in-the-story with the first-person-singular speaker. Speaking in defiance of the convention, these tricksters delight in denouncing fraud even as they perpetrate it. Nightingale goes so far as to decry the corruption at the very seat of authority in the realm, that is, among the pleaders at Westminster (III.v.89). His next verse tells of a pickpocket's jest involving a judge on the bench, a jest attributed to Sir Thomas More in the play bearing his name:[33]

> *Nay, once from the Seat*
> *Of Iudgement so great,*
> *A Iudge there did lose a faire pouch of veluete.* (III.v.102-4)

And moving a step closer still to an actuality unperceived or unbelieved by his hearers, Nightingale lists among the occasions of purse-lifting, '*At* Court, *& in* Christmas, *before the Kings face*' (III.v.126). Though not exactly at Christmas, this song was indeed sung before the King and his assembled court. The ironies are multiplied exponentially in Jonson's text as Cokes, Overdo, Quarlous, and Winwife add commentaries on the text of the ballad and the actions of the cutpurse.

Edgworth's theft of Cokes's purse, then, does not go undetected, but, having spotted the action, Quarlous and Winwife choose to remain silent and to use the pickpocket's skills to their own advantage. As the conspiracy spreads, the texture of life at the fair comes more and more to resemble the deceits of every day. In these circumstances, what C.L. Barber calls 'clarification through release' is denied us because the banal world of day-to-day cheats is absorbed so completely into the holiday world which, in a festive comedy, would be expected to provide an alternative or liberating perspective.[34] The common mode of discourse in *Bartholomew Fair* is the secret whose sense escapes everyone on stage. The intention of all the characters seems to be obfuscation, not communication.

If the visitors to the fair feel a compulsion to mystify the commonplace with the cant of fundamentalist religion (Busy), state spying (Overdo), and literary quibbles (Littlewit), those who count on the fair for their livelihood go even further in using specialized language to disguise their outlawed activities. Extremely simple codes are established between the fair people, often by borrowing a set of terms from some innocent realm of discourse and applying it to their particular covert activity. Ursula, for example, identifies prostitutes as edible fowl (IV.v.14-19). The arbitrary change in the conventionally accepted signifiers is part of the subversive charm and linguistic creativity that one senses in Jonson's behind-the-scenes operators. Jordan Knockem, the horse trader, transferring his equine terminology to Mrs Littlewit, reduces her to marketable flesh.

> Is't not pitty, my delicate darke chestnut here, with the fine leane head, large fore-head, round eyes, euen mouth, sharpe eares, long necke, thinne crest, close withers, plaine backe, deepe sides, short fillets, and full flankes: with a round belly, a plumpe buttocke, large thighes, knit knees, streight legges, short pasternes, smooth hoofes, and short heeles; should lead a dull honest womans life, that might liue the life of a Lady? (IV.v.21-8)

The loss of distinction between what Knockem calls 'dull honest' women and 'Lady'-prostitutes, between honest London merchants and the carni-folk, between civil authorities and the local madman, precipitates a series of violent encounters. The unwritten laws of territory and of specialized discourse have been violated, and everyone's response is anger. Alice, the rampant 'Punque of Turnball,' pummels Mrs Overdo soundly for invading her turf:

> ALE. A mischiefe on you, they are such as you are, that vndoe vs, and take our trade from vs, with your tuft-taffata hanches.
> KNO. How now, *Alice*!
> ALE. The poore common whores can ha' no traffique, for the priuy rich ones; your caps and hoods of veluet, call away our customers, and lick the fat from vs. (IV.v.65-71)

Respectable women are doing what common punks should do, but doing it in secret, privily. The already scandalous Alice would precipitate further scandal by unmasking the middle-class hooker-for-a-day, but Knockem and Whit suppress the revelation, ejecting Alice with 'A kick ... in the parting vapour' (IV.v.84-5). The confusions will persist for another act before the various secret confederacies collapse.

Those violent confusions become further compounded in the final act as the characters assemble to witness the Littlewit-Leatherhead puppet play that conflates and updates two recently re-revived classical romance tales into a farcical brawl over a bankside wench. The exotic jostles against the familiar in ways that deny the universality of aesthetic experience even while trying to transcend time and place. Leatherhead collapses Jerusalem, Nineveh, Sodom, and Gomorrah all into the city of Norwich in his account of puppet plays that combine Bible stories 'with the rising o' the prentises; and pulling downe the bawdy houses there, vpon *Shroue-Tuesday*' (V.i.7-11). Undiscriminating crowds evidently loved these modernizations of old tales, but the biggest hit of all seems to have been 'the *Gunpowderplot*,' which Leatherhead calls a real 'get-penny' (12) and which was the local favourite of Sir Politic Would-bee, as we have seen.[35] Ironically, in *Bartholomew Fair*, with its completely English setting, Jonson makes clear that few home-truths can be expected from such 'home-borne proiects' as these (14).

Jonson's embedded travesty of Richard Edwardes's *Damon and Pithias* and Christopher Marlowe's *Hero and Leander* is definitive proof that, as a tool of the satirist, familiarity breeds nothing but contempt. In the Littlewit-Leatherhead version, the delicately poised suggestiveness of Ovidian bucolic-erotic verse is rendered into thumpingly vulgar London street slang. Only a playgoer as witless as Bartholomew Cokes could extract subtle delights from lines like, '*Kisse my* hole here' (V.iv.134); 'A Pimpe and a Scabbe? / I say between you, you haue both but one Drabbe' (247–8); and 'Kisse the whore o' the arse' (339). Here, if ever, is an art of the surface: what you hear is all you get. There are no hidden meanings. Nor can there be any satisfactory closure, no final revelations, not only because Busy stops the show, but because the dramatic text in question has no supposes and no subtext. The implications should be clear for the 'politique Picklocke[s]' of Jonson's scene: anyone who would 'go about t' expound' this play is as much an ass as Bully Bottom or Bartholomew Cokes.

While Jonson saw as a satirizable folly his audiences' desire to reinterpret everything they saw and heard in the theatre, he also admitted that one particular interpreter had the power to set the limits of his art and entertainment: King James. Jonson acknowledges the King's special status as construer of meaning in an epilogue written for the court performance of *Bartholomew Fair*:

> *Your* Maiesty *hath seene the* Play, *and you*
> *can best allow it from your eare, and view.*
> *You know the scope of* Writers, *and what store*
> *of* leaue *is giuen them, if they take not more,*
> *And turne it into* licence: *you can tell*
> *if we have vs'd that* leaue *you gaue vs, well:*
> *Or whether wee to rage, or licence breake,*
> *or be* prophane, *or make* prophane *men speake?*
> *This is your power to iudge (great Sir) and not*
> *the enuy of a few. Which if wee haue got,*
> *Wee value lesse what their dislike can bring,*
> *if it so happy be, t' haue pleas'd the King.*

Being granted royal allowance meant that Jonson received both permission and payment from the King. This combination entails both a subject's obligation under the licensing power and the artist's dependence on the generosity and right-readings of his patron. When 'leaue' turns to 'licence,' an allowable limit has been breached, at least in the view of one all-important interpreter. The King's 'view' is worth more than all the critical readings produced by 'prophane' and envious spectators. For one special performance, the possible lines of interpretation all met in one spot, the seat of royalty.[36]

We have no record of how James received *Bartholomew Fair*. The play's boisterousness, rough language, sexual farce, and anti-puritan satire were well within the scope of his tastes. The mockery of foolish laws, blind justice, and official snooping was evidently mild enough for James to include it within the acceptable bounds of the playwright's licence. But, as Jonson points out in his epilogue, licence is an ambiguous concept. It affords certification by a legitimately constituted authority, but it also denotes disorderly 'rage' (licentiousness) that transgresses the bounds of official sanction.[37] *Bartholomew Fair* ranges freely along that boundary, poking fun at the reasons that people desire licence in both senses.

When characters in the play exceed the limits of the law, they generally encounter a world of innocent-looking people who are actually just waiting to fleece them. Part of Jonson's satire takes as its butt those like Cokes and Littlewit who desire to escape the incarceration of everyday rules. Another part exposes the secret tricks of those like Busy, Edgworth, and Purecraft, who live on the criminal and theological fringes of society, ready to prey on those who would dabble in the freedom promised beyond legal allowances. Still a third part mocks the law itself when it tries to patrol its own borders and to penetrate the outlaw camp. Overdo's ridiculous faith in his powers to interpret appearances and to reveal duplicity does more to confuse than to stabilize interpretations of the law in *Bartholomew Fair*.

As a maker of plays working under the licensing authority of the Master of the Revels and ultimately of the King, Jonson managed in this case not to offend with his revelations about London life. That is, he managed to conceal, in a paradoxically conspicuous manner, certain unflattering truths about the ineptitude of actual civic authorities, the rapaciousness of certain ecclesiastical ones, and the probable conclusion that Chaos, in the person of an obese old woman, Ate-Ursula, was the order of the day in some parts of the city. Every act of concealment being an invitation to discovery, Jonson seems to encourage his audience to interpret his comic fiction in the light of contemporary reality and vice versa. As we have seen, the author of at least one subsequent pamphlet imitated rather closely the shape that Jonson gave to the fair at Smithfield. It is the shape of concealment and revelation, both artfully partial. Titillated and intrigued by what is shown and what suppressed, the audience is lured into precisely the active role of interpreter that Jonson mocks so strenuously in the Induction to his play. As Janet Clare rightly points out, there is 'more than an element of disingenuousness in such protestations, since the avowals of innocence and assaults upon "picklocks" of the scene are part of a dual strategy, designed to repel the attentions of the censor while simultaneously exciting the interest of the initiated spectator in decoding those apparently forbidden meanings.'[38]

There is a persistent strain in language theory from the creators of the hieroglyphics in Egypt to the author of *The Genesis of Secrecy: On the Interpretation of Narrative*, Frank Kermode, that sees language as concealing meaning from all but the initiated. While Jonson's sometime collaborator, George Chapman, was enthralled with this theory of writing and reading, Jonson himself was highly critical of giving any self-proclaimed initiate a licence to delve into texts, there to find authorization for his own preoccupations. Everything mined from such readings was as corrupting as the gold and silver that men were busily ripping from the earth's bosom during the great age of exploration and exploitation, a kind of Mammon's '*nouo orbe*' of textual exploration (*The Alchemist*, II.i.2). 'Wee search, and digge for the evill that is hidden,' Jonson records among his *Discoveries* (lines 1381-2), and that bad currency drives out the true coin of poetry ('Epistle to Elizabeth Covntesse of Rvtland,' *The Forrest*, XII, 18-30). Meanings that lie hidden beneath the surface of texts and need to be mined are as dangerous to the satirist as they are essential to him. Accepting the world at face value is a gull's game, poking around in its secret services a knave's. And the case is still more complicated than this, because the gulls occasionally try their eye at snooping and the knaves prove to be imperfect readers at best.

Midway through *Bartholomew Fair*, Quarlous urges Grace Wellborn to consult someone well read in legal texts, 'some crafty fellow, some picklocke o' the Law' (III.v.278-9), to help her to free herself from Overdo's guardianship.[39] Subsequently, as we have seen, he hires a thief to pick the lock on the box containing Grace's marriage licence and, armed with the authority of this text, alters her marital future. While her freedom from a life with the simpleton Bartholomew Cokes seems a desirable comic outcome, the underhand methods and mercenary motives of achieving this end deny that there is any significant difference between incompetence within the law and fraud outside it. Every text incorporated into Jonson's play is misappropriated in some way or other, from Overdo's warrant to Lord Mayor Middleton's letter to Christopher Marlowe's epyllion. Each case involves wilful misreading of the kind that Jonson taunts his audiences for replicating in their treatment of his play. As in all great satire, the joke is on the misreaders. There are no authorized readings, only misreadings which, taken in the proper spirit, both instruct and entertain.

Conclusion

Nothing reveals so much about a culture as the secrets it keeps – or, rather, doesn't keep. But it is never an easy matter to see what has been systematically hidden from view – the rarest medicinal herbs in tribal cultures, the madwomen in the attic, the nuclear wastes in our oceans. One of the most engrossing chapters in the history of World War II involves the use of early computers to generate and, subsequently, to crack Nazi Germany's military codes. What was revealed in the process were not just the local strategies of an enormous army but some basic lessons about how power is communicated in a highly technological age. To take an example somewhat closer to the present study, a volume of literary criticism published in the mid-1960s called *The Other Victorians* caused a considerable stir at the time.[1] Perhaps this was because it provided an academically respectable peephole into the secret world of Victorian pornography, but it also opened up a number of engrossing questions about cultural otherness and about what are legitimate texts for study. The book revealed as much about the age in which it was written – the period of the so-called Sexual Revolution – as about the age it took as its subject. Some of the questions it raised concerned institutional censorship (a hot topic in the United States in those pre-Freedom of Information Act days, when an FBI file was considered an academic credential), but the secrets it revealed moved well beyond censorship into the area of redefining public and private discourses by redrawing the boundaries that determine what may be known, when, and by whom. Setting these boundaries has often been seen as the prerogative of power, but if that is so, it is a power extraordinarily vulnerable to accident.

A point that I have been at pains to stress in this study of Ben Jonson's art of secrecy is the large part played by inadvertence in any power structure based on manipulating secret information. Just as the army intelligence officer is as likely to stumble over valuable information as to walk purposefully to it, so too an artist working in a medium as flexible as Renaissance drama, even an artist as deliberate as Jonson, frequently finds the best laid plans of concealment and revelation suddenly slipping out of control. Politically sensitive issues keep creeping into the play-text, and views attributable to the author and/or the actors keep slipping out. Within the fictional intrigues of the play, the most brilliant moments occur when some unforeseen circumstance causes the characters to improvise madly to keep the game going. The multivocality of the living, spoken language of the theatre continually exceeds prescription. The resulting supplementary postscripts keep cutting the ground away from the social and personal barriers constructed to separate various realms of experience. As a case in point, Jonson was an extremely public poet (compared with such contemporaries as George Herbert, Thomas Middleton, or even William Shakespeare), but in plays like *Sejanus*, *Volpone*, and *Epicoene*, he forges connections between what goes on behind closed doors (in the most private domestic settings) and the transactions of public life (in the senate house, the marketplace, and the theatre). The line between the private fantasies of Sir Politique Would-bee, Sir Epicure Mammon, and Bartholomew Cokes, on the one hand, and such public concerns as state paranoia, community morality, and holiday entertainment, on the other, repeatedly blur. The secrets of the one bleed into the other, and revelations occur at the most awkward moments.

Jonson's art of secrecy generates its own peculiar set of problems and contradictions, including, but not confined to, the workings of inadvertence within carefully regulated forms. During the period 1603–14 Jonson produced six play-texts (and a seventh, collaborative effort that I have not discussed, in addition to masques and poems) in consort with three acting companies and six printers. In the process he revealed to full metatheatrical view a great many of the secrets of his trade or *mystère*, but others he kept well concealed. At the same time that he distrusted the exclusivity of the *arcana*, he also sought to construct a coterie audience of initiates for his plays. He decried state secrecy, yet he defended his monarch's and his own privilege not to be open to direct questioning by inferiors.

Conclusion

And while he repeatedly defied the largely invisible censoring hand of the Master of the Revels, he came very close to holding that office himself. He managed through all this to maintain a kind of poise that has led his critics to associate his name with artistic integrity. Just how he achieved this cannot be immediately apparent. When it came to the topic of secrecy, for example, he was ruthless and abrasive in his accusations of hidden corruption and his attacks on folly masquerading as wisdom.

More than the 'humour' plays or the 'dotages,' Jonson's middle plays relentlessly uncover the ways that people devise covertly to exploit one another. His characters display an edge of nastiness that emerges only occasionally in Shakespeare's plays and only in a melodramatically exaggerated form in the tragedies of the later Jacobean period. Rapaciousness strikes few characters in Jonson as unusual or even undesirable. It is an everyday quality that is treated as though it doesn't exist until it becomes so outrageous that it causes a highly visible scene. Then a judgment of some kind is pronounced – often irrationally, venally, inaccurately – and the society of the play returns to its undercover forms of nastiness.

Plays like *Sejanus*, *The Alchemist*, and even the apparently more gentle but perhaps even more vicious because more trivializing *Epicoene* are stark examples of Sissela Bok's thesis that 'secrecy is central to every form of injury to human beings.'[2] Characters such as Tiberius, Subtle, and Dauphine use secrets for self-empowerment by threatening others with what is kept from them. Though his characters hope that secrets can protect them from their enemies and from the unwanted incursions of more general forms of cultural absorption, Jonson represents largely the injury done by the various forms of the *arcana*. The remarks that Captain Otter makes behind his wife's back, however wittily expressed, are as cruel in their way as the tricks played on Dapper in the privy, and the conspiracy to disinherit Bonario is as damaging on a small scale as a conspiracy to overrun Rome is on a large one. In Jonson's plays, no government is genuinely strengthened, no profit made, and no family cemented by secrecy, however artfully practised. Neither comic nor tragic outcomes draw positively on the fruits of clandestine behaviour, as they sometimes do in Shakespeare's plays. The pattern is continuous through the drama of Jonson's mid-career.

He first seriously turned his satiric talents to an anatomy of conspiracy in *Sejanus*. Tiberius, the ominous absent presence just beyond the reach of the horde of incompetent aspirants to power, is master of the secretive mode. His political strength lies in his inscrutability, as Dio Cassius suggests with his report that Tiberius became furious if anyone understood him.³ This is to rely on the *arcana imperii* with a vengeance, and vengeance is precisely the motive behind the deadly letter of ambiguous praise and condemnation with which Tiberius secures the downfall of Sejanus in the senate. The wilful misconstruction of texts that had earlier led to Cordus's disgrace prepares the reader of Jonson's play for the fatal instability of that masterfully written letter. In *Sejanus* – unlike Jonson's other extant tragedy, *Catiline* – the real source of power finally remains cloaked and safely removed from all the political manoeuvring, while would-be reformers and rash conspirators perish.

Volpone is less skilful than Tiberius in handling the conspiracies that function as the dramatic mimesis of his secret desires. When he takes Mosca into his confidence, Volpone unwisely shares with him his desires for sexual and gustatory luxury and his contempt for the authority of the Venetian state. With Mosca plotting fulltime on his own behalf, conspiracy confounds conspiracy, making a mockery of people's attempts to mystify their desires and the state's attempts to obscure the basis of its authority. Sir Politique's accounts of conveying state secrets in hollow toothpicks and his withdrawal into a huge tortoise shell after burning his spy reports are close echoes of Mosca's and Volpone's efforts to defraud individuals and to destabilize the social structure by drawing others into a series of conspiracies that is finally self-consuming. In the trial scene, Mosca violates the code of silence that protects secrets, and the state exacts stiff penalties.

Although the state recedes from view in Jonson's next play, secrecy and silence do not. The conspiracy of silence in *Epicoene* centres on homosocial desire at the level of the family and the neighbourhood rather than the state. A triumvirate of young London aristocrats try to impress one another with their schemes to mock their social and intellectual inferiors and to secure Morose's inheritance for one of their group. They attempt this by constructing a woman to Morose's specifications, a silent woman. The silence of Epicoene is then associated with a broad range of secrets that the young men attribute to women generally – the arts of cosmetic disguise, recipes for contraceptives, concealed lusts, and other cultish conspiracies against man-kind. In terms of the mechanisms of Jonson's plot, however, these imputed secrets pale next to the covert designs of

Truewit, Clerimont, and Dauphine as they trick and torment the Otters, Daw and La Foole, the Collegiate Ladies, and Morose. The assault of the aristocratic young men on the personal identities of these feminine and effeminate Others and the private spaces to which they retreat is analogous but not identical to Jonson's own apparent hostility toward the purportedly effeminizing enclosed space of the Whitefriars theatre. While Truewit's scheme to transfer a rural shaming ritual, the charivari, to the city setting fails to provide an effective solution to Dauphine's economic problems, Dauphine and, in an analogous way, Jonson create a stunning ending for the comedy by keeping the secret of Epicoene's male identity to the last possible moment. Though Jonson may well have alienated his first audiences by tying the dramaturgy of *Epicoene* to a secret that excluded them, he managed to create a type of comedy of manners, verbal wit, consumerism, homosocial intrigue, and intimate theatrical space that provided a model for subsequent generations of playwrights.

The Alchemist reveals secrets of social behaviour that were often safely cordoned off from the kind of aristocratic private life that Jonson exposed to view in *Epicoene*, namely criminal conspiracies, religious hypocrisy, and scientific quackery. It is amusing, but not particularly threatening, to be reminded of the tawdry secret desires that lie mysteriously beneath the surface of these societally marginal activities. Indeed, there is something positively attractive about the virtuosity of Jonson's master charlatans - Lovewit, Tribulation Wholesome, Subtle, Face, and the others. Their conspiracies, unlike Volpone's, will doubtless continue to flourish long after they are discovered and displaced on the Jonsonian stage. Although the incompetent conspiracies of the dupes, like those in *Volpone*, self-destruct, the emergence of the crafty Lovewit as a stabilizing authority figure at the end of this play is no more reassuring than that of the triumphant Cicero in *Catiline* or the venal Quarlous in *Bartholomew Fair*. The secret source of power, an exclusively male preserve in Jonson, remains undisturbed.

The preservation of the Roman republic under the watchful eye of the master counterspy, Cicero, is particularly disturbing. As we have seen, in this play an aristocratic conspiracy against the body politic is successfully met by an official counter-conspiracy. Catiline's private desires for both political and sexual hegemony are less carefully dissembled, less discreetly removed from the public view than those of Tiberius in *Sejanus*. As in that play, the opposition between political leader and political aspirant is forever being blurred in *Catiline*. The criticisms whispered against Cicero take their toll. Some of the mud sticks to the polished surface of his masterful rhetoric. As he employs Catiline's own conspirators against him, Cicero permits Caesar and his powerful, seditious companions to remain undisturbed. His counter-conspiratorial cynicism taints the idealism of his public speeches. While he is no Volpone or Subtle, Cicero, perhaps without Jonson's full knowledge, busily undercuts the very authority that he and the state rely upon, the *arcana imperii*. Jonson's appropriation of the historical Cicero's splendid orations seems in some sense to have been a misappropriation, the kind of 'wresting' from their original context to which critics subjected Jonson's own texts.

The mischievous misinterpretation of texts is a prominent and highly self-reflexive concern of the last of Jonson's middle plays, *Bartholomew Fair*. The primary flaw of such misreadings is the projection of the would-be interpreter into the text at hand. What passes as a discovery of another's secret or hidden meaning is mainly a fatuous and self-serving interpretation of the reader himself. In this way, even holy scripture can appear *'obnoxious to construction'* (*Volpone*, Epistle, line 63). To this layer of comic misunderstanding is added the obfuscation of a variety of special-interest jargons: the mystifying cant of puritans, state spies, literati, and underworld slangsters. The language of *Bartholomew Fair* is as riddled with secret motives and meanings as that of *Sejanus*, the first of Jonson's middle plays. The characters imperfectly conceal their identities only to have them imperfectly revealed. The emphasis is as much on the imperfection of the procedure as on the doing and undoing of secrets. Zeal-of-the-Land Busy is not just the foiled fool he admits to being after his encounter with Leatherhead and his puppets. He is also several other kinds of hypocrite. No witty Justice Clement such as sorted out the single-minded characters of *Every Man In His Humour* can be counted on to adjudicate the wrongs inspired by multiple conspiracies in *Bartholomew Fair*.

The secret arts of language that so annoyed Jonson supplied a sufficient challenge for his fine-edged satiric wit. The duplicity of the linguistic medium itself sometimes seems to undo what Jonson's texts are doing: the glib, self-serving remarks uttered by his urban gallants in *Epicoene* keep undercutting their authority as satiric presenters of the Amorous La Fooles and Jack Daws of their world;

Conclusion

the smooth surface of Cicero's oratory in *Catiline* keeps cracking to reveal a substructure of crass political expediency. The effect is not to weaken the plays but to demand more and more careful readings of Jonson's difficult texts.

For Jonson the art of secrecy provided a resilient set of plot conventions for both intrigue comedies and political tragedies. Second, it opened the way to represent two prominent secret societies of his day – the court and the city of London – to themselves, sometimes with considerable danger to himself. Finally, it allowed him to offer a blistering critique of the art of reading, or rather misreading texts – that is, of penetrating good sense to arrive at bad.

However ubiquitous the idea of secrecy in the plotting, characterizations, ideas, and interpretive strategies contained in Jonson's plays, I don't pretend to have discovered any kind of pass-key to this complex figure's art. At the outset I quoted Michel Foucault's warning that in the business of interpreting texts there is no 'timeless essential secret.'[4] I do not take Foucault to mean that there are no puzzles about Jonson's play-texts and how they were produced. I certainly have not been able to figure out, for example, how Jonson managed to escape more serious punishment for his early literary indiscretions. Nor do I understand what private attitudes toward women, religion, or learning lay concealed behind the public pronouncements of this highly professional writer. His relations with his wife remain a complete mystery to me, as does the empathy he felt with the puritan ideals that he so vigorously assaulted in his comedies, and the gift he had for appropriating both the polished Latin phrases of the ancient poets and the obscenities of the London street vendor to his own use.

If I have hit upon a few nonce truths in relation to the theatrical, sexual, and political hermeneutics of secrecy in Jonson's fine middle plays, I will be well satisfied. As Frank Kermode says, 'we glimpse the secrecy through the meshes of the text.'[5] But what we see in the interstices is often not a clearly vouchsafed revelation but a complicated, leading question, in this case, the question of why, after all our attempts to be understanders, Ben Jonson continues to puzzle us.

Notes

Introduction

1 G. R. Elton, *Policy and Police: The Enforcement of the Reformation in the Age of Thomas Cromwell*, 327 and 342.
2 For a general review of covert exercises in the period see Martin Hume, *Treason and Plot* and Lacey Baldwin Smith, *Treason in Tudor England: Politics and Paranoia*. Smith's totalizing theological thesis is that individual traitors were treated, quite apart from specific political contexts, as perpetrators of the original sin of rebelliousness. He says, for example,
   With no sense of change, except as retrogression, and no concept of destiny or direction, except in terms of the fate reserved for individual men and women whose struggles for good and evil might indeed bring about the collapse of kingdoms, and with every device at society's command designed to nip treason in the bud even before it had taken cognitive shape, the traitor stood as a kind of Judas, a social and cosmic pariah, inwardly tormented and driven on by evil but necessary as the only instrument through which God and his providential change could operate and, at the same time, perversely responsible for his crimes and richly deserving of his horrible end. (140-1)
The most recent study of the subject, one I have not been able to consult, is John Michael Archer's *Sovereignty and Intelligence: Spying and Court Culture in English Renaissance Writing*.
   On the intelligence activities of Walsingham see Conyers Read's three-volume work, *Mr. Secretary Walsingham and the Policy of Queen Elizabeth*, esp. 2:340-433 and 3:1-70. The Gowrie Conspiracy was originally detailed in John Ruthven's *The Earle of Gowries Conspiracie against the Kings Maiestie of Scotland*, a volume that went through eight editions in 1600

and 1603. Andrew Lang's *James VI and the Gowrie Mystery* (1902) remains the fullest account of these bizarre events. The Gunpowder Plot is considered in some detail in connection with the subplot of *Volpone* in chapter 3 below.

3 See Richard A. Burt, '"Licensed by Authority": Ben Jonson and the Politics of the Early Stuart Theater,' esp. 549–50. This material is reworked in his *Licensed by Authority: Ben Jonson and the Discourses of Censorship*. This excellent book was published only after I had completed the major part of my own work. Drawing in part on Richard Dutton's detailed study of the workings of patronage politics in the office of the Master of the Revels, Burt argues convincingly that there was more mutual respect and shared economic advantage than antagonism between Jonson and his censors (who were, after all, also licensers or 'allowers'). See Richard Dutton, *Mastering the Revels: The Regulation and Censorship of English Renaissance Drama*, and 'Ben Jonson and the Master of the Revels.' Also see Leah S. Marcus, *The Politics of Mirth: Jonson, Herrick, Milton, Marvell, and the Defense of Old Holiday Pastimes*, 24–63; Philip J. Finkelpearl, '"The Comedians' Liberty": Censorship of the Jacobean Stage Reconsidered'; and Albert H. Tricomi, *Anticourt Drama in England, 1603–1642*.

4 For an account of Jonson's Catholicism, its origins and implications, see David Riggs, *Ben Jonson: A Life*, 50–3 and HSS 1:19, 37–43, and 65–9.

5 It is sufficient here to mention a few of the more influential monographs in this by now familiar debate: E.M.W. Tillyard, *The Elizabethan World Picture*; Jonathan Dollimore, *Radical Tragedy: Religion, Ideology and Power in the Drama of Shakespeare and His Contemporaries*; Catherine Belsey, *The Subject of Tragedy: Identity and Difference in Renaissance Drama*; Michael D. Bristol, *Carnival and Theater: Plebeian Culture and the Structure of Authority in Renaissance England*; Stephen Greenblatt, *Shakespearean Negotiations: The Circulation of Social Energy in Renaissance England*.

6 On the oppositional relationship between theatre and court, especially within the genres of topical satire and political tragedy, see Albert H. Tricomi's provocative study, *Anticourt Drama in England, 1603–1642*.

7 *Sejanus*, 'To the Readers' (1605 quarto). HSS, 4:351.

8 Richard C. Newton observes that the printed text, in its complete form and with clearly announced authorship, gave Jonson a feeling of being able to control the way his works were interpreted. See Newton's '"Ben./Jonson": The Poet in the Poems.' As George E. Rowe points out, however, it is difficult to maintain such a naïve view of textual interpretation in the wake of postmodern theory (*Distinguishing Jonson: Imitation, Rivalry, and the Direction of a Dramatic Career*, 49).

9 Carlo Ginzburg, 'High and Low: The Theme of Forbidden Knowledge in the Sixteenth and Seventeenth Centuries.'
10 *Basilikon Doron*, in *The Political Works of James I*, 14.
11 For example, when a legal handbook by John Cowell entitled *The Interpreter, or Booke containing the signification of words* (London, 1607) that dealt (approvingly) with the royal right to make laws apart from Parliament was brought to James's attention in 1610, he let it be known through his Lord Treasurer, Robert Cecil, that 'the King will not have this thing brought into question.' See *Proceedings of Parliament 1610*, 1:29.
12 Thomas Dekker, *Dramatic Works*, 2:254–5.
13 See Orgel's *The Jonsonian Masque* and *The Illusion of Power*; Gordon's 'Rolls and Mysteries' (1965), rpt. in *The Renaissance Imagination*; and Goldberg's *James I and the Politics of Literature: Jonson, Shakespeare, Donne, and Their Contemporaries*, chapter 2, 'State Secrets.'
14 Lois Potter, *Secret Rites and Secret Writing: Royalist Literature, 1641–1660*, xiv.
15 For convenient accounts of the varieties of repression and suppression visited on each of these plays (except *Catiline*) see Janet Clare's *'Art Made Tongue-Tied by Authority': Elizabethan and Jacobean Dramatic Censorship*. A type of *de facto* censorship not commented on by Clare was the official closing of the theatres, sometimes for months at a time, especially during the middle years of Jonson's career, to prevent the spread of disease. See Leeds Barroll, *Politics, Plague, and Shakespeare's Theater: The Stuart Years*.
16 Richard Burt, *Licensed by Authority: Ben Jonson and the Discourses of Censorship*, x.
17 Perhaps this sureness of theatrical judgment, combined with his experience of political/theatrical preferences at court, led to Jonson's being awarded the reversion of the Mastership of the Revels in 1621, a post for which he appeared ill suited during his censor-troubled early career and which he never, after all, occupied. See Dutton, 'Ben Jonson and the Master of the Revels,' 80.
18 There is a seventh play written during this period, *Eastward Ho* (1605), which I have chosen not to discuss at length because it is a collaborative effort involving Jonson, George Chapman, and John Marston. C.H. Herford and Percy Simpson explain the anomalous position of the play in the Jonson corpus:

> *Eastward Ho* stands apart from the canon of Jonson's works. He was only part author of the play; his share in it is disputable and can be traced only by that most fallacious of tests, the internal evidence of style. Further, he did not supervise the printing of the Quarto, though he may have been consulted, or he may have intervened, to

ensure that the allusions which provoked the King's anger were omitted from the text. But the play will not require consideration in the critical survey of Jonson's acknowledged work. (HSS, 4:503)
19 Anne Barton, *Ben Jonson, Dramatist*, 90 and 94.
20 John Webster, *The Duchess of Malfi*, V.ii.244-5.
21 Michel Foucault, 'Nietzsche, Genealogy, History,' 142.

Chapter One

1 Reginald Scot, *The Discoverie of Witchcraft*, 77-8.
2 Compare the *Malleus maleficarum* (pt. 2, qu. 1, ch. 7). The intertextual strategies deployed by Scot in this case are similar to those that Stephen Greenblatt finds linking Samuel Harsnett's *Declaration of Egregious Popish Impostures* and *King Lear*, namely 'evacuation,' or the emptying out of a text's cultural value. See Greenblatt, 'Shakespeare and the Exorcists' in *Shakespearean Negotiations: The Circulation of Social Energy in Renaissance England*, 94-128. A difficulty that Greenblatt's theory does not fully address is that the anterior text can never be completely 'emptied,' and its ideology may even be given new cultural currency by the subsequent act of appropriation.
3 Keith Thomas, *Religion and the Decline of Magic*, 568. It should be noted that Thomas offers this point concessively, preferring to argue that *maleficium* (injury), whether sexual or other, was secondary to the heresy of devil-worship among the charges brought against English witches in this period (438). Still, he would not deny that witchcraft was gender-specific and that it was supposed to have been carried out under a veil of secrecy.
4 According to Madelon Gohlke, anxiety about possible effeminization afflicts most of the prominent male characters in Shakespeare: 'Male resistance ... stems from fears of occupying a position of weakness, taking in essence a "feminine" posture in relation to a powerful woman.' See Gohlke's '"I wooed thee with my sword": Shakespeare's Tragic Paradigms,' 155. Later feminist critics have echoed and expanded this point. See also the discussion of theatrical effeminization in chapter 4 below.
5 Sissela Bok, *Secrets: On the Ethics of Concealment and Revelation*, 26.
6 James Fernandez, foreword to Beryl L. Bellman's *The Language of Secrecy: Symbols and Metaphors in Poro Ritual*, viii.
7 See Gail Kern Paster, 'Leaky Vessels: The Incontinent Woman of City Comedy,' rpt. in her book, *The Body Embarrassed: Drama and the Discipline of*

Shame in Early Modern England, 23–63, and Geoffrey Whitney's emblem of a woman holding a sieve in *A Choice of Emblemes*, 12.
8 Fernandez in Bellman, viii. In the essay that he contributed to his collection entitled *Secrecy: A Cross-Cultural Perspective*, Stanton Tefft elaborates on this notion of social orders: 'Some secret associations pursue goals that are hostile to the central values and institutions of the political community. Such secret associations are alienative ones. Other secret organizations support or at least are in close accord with the dominant values of the community. These are conformative secret orders' (52). Tefft's definition of secrecy as 'the mandatory or voluntary, but calculated, concealment of information, activities, or relationships' (320) covers only some of the examples that I will cite from Renaissance drama.
9 On the impact of revealing the *arcana naturae* by these writers, see Peter French, *John Dee: The World of an Elizabethan Magus*, 81, and Frances Yates, 'The Hermetic Tradition in Renaissance Science,' 263–4.
10 The most important of the censorship studies are discussed in my Introduction and will figure in my subsequent discussions of individual plays.

Certain secrets concerned with political power have been teased out of these texts by such new historicist critics as Stephen Greenblatt, Leah Marcus, Louis Montrose, Stephen Orgel, Leonard Tennenhouse, and Don E. Wayne. For specific works, see my list of Works Cited. Though their approach has been frequently and cogently criticized, their creative application of the Foucaultian notion of the bi-directional interplay between text and society has produced some first-rate work. Richard Burt has recently applied discourse theory to the relationship of social and textual authority in ways that avoid some of the problems of the new historicism. In *Licensed by Authority*, Burt quite properly argues that the relationship of the licensing authorities to Renaissance plays varied a great deal from one circumstance to another, that the early Stuart courts were extremely inconsistent in what they tolerated, and that, far from always defending the *status quo*, the systems of licensing could and did encourage change.

In the discipline of sociology, Tefft's work on conflict theory (49–63) establishes that secrecy, like censorship, works variously to promote differentiation, exclusion, and the power arrangements that lead to social change.
11 Frank Whigham, 'Sexual and Social Mobility in *The Duchess of Malfi*,' 174. Erasmus's colloquy, *Of the Yong Man and the Evill Disposed Woman*, puts an

ironic spin on the privacy of ladies' boudoirs: one Sophronius, a 'handsome beardling,' accompanies the whore Lucres to her bedroom, a 'place aparte from all compayne' and eventually into a 'place yet more secret and privie,' the closet where she keeps her 'jewels and array.' But even there, Lucres tells him, they are not out of sight of God and his angels. This prompts Sophronius, recently reformed by reading Erasmus's translation of the New Testament, to deliver a sermon on the secret evils of lust. This 'secret place,' like the one that cost Gloucester his eyes in *King Lear*, is closely related to the whore's most private parts. The discourse of these privacies is the province of secret lovers, preaching friars, and gossiping women.

In her book *Gossip*, Patricia Meyer Spacks points out that, although fictional prose has gained considerable authority in the twentieth century, its conversational counterpart, 'gossip – more volatile, more secret, more ostentatiously female – has for several centuries been the object of fierce efforts toward suppression' (263). Spacks brilliantly defends gossip as a form of discourse well suited to exploring human experience and as a central strategy in narrative fiction. I am grateful to Lissa Paul of the University of New Brunswick for recommending this book to me.

12 Alan Nelson explains this scheme of staging admirably in 'Some Configurations of Staging in Medieval English Drama,' in *Medieval English Drama: Essays Critical and Contextual*. For the particular examples I cite, see the Fleury *Slaughter of the Innocents* and the Wakefield *Noah* in David Bevington, *Medieval Drama*, 69–71 and 300–1. The terms *loci* and *platea* have been applied with variable success to the Renaissance stage by Robert Weimann in *Shakespeare and the Popular Tradition in the Theater: Studies in the Social Dimension of Dramatic Form and Function*, and Michael E. Mooney in *Shakespeare's Dramatic Transactions*.

13 See the introduction to George Walton Williams's Regents Renaissance Drama edition of Middleton and Rowley's *The Changeling*, ix.

14 A particularly striking contrast to the basically 'open' staging of the Elizabethan era is the use of space in Milton's *Samson Agonistes*. Samson, who 'Gave up [his] fort of silence to a Woman' (line 236), finds his physical world shrunk to the limits of his outstretched arm. Early in the play Milton establishes the thematic link between the secret revelation that cost Samson his eyes and the confinement of spatial extension that now characterizes his 'intimate impulse' (line 223) and the indeterminate 'rousing motions' (line 1382) that lead to the final implosion of his world, its collapse in on itself at the moment of disaster. I quote from John Milton, *Complete Poems and Major Prose*, ed. Merritt Y. Hughes.

15 Jacques Derrida, 'The Law of Genre,' 217–18.
16 John Gordon Sweeney, III, *Jonson and the Psychology of the Public Theater*, 3–16.
17 Anthony Dawson, 'Giving the Finger: Puns and Transgression in *The Changeling*.'
18 For example, Mark Rose presents a careful analysis of Shakespeare's way of arranging public and private scenes into a series of triptychs in *Richard II*. See *Shakespearean Design*, 143–5.
19 From another, expressly male point of view, that of Thomas Fuller writing in *The Holy State* (Cambridge, 1642), Brutus is well advised to safeguard his *arcana imperii*, since the good husband is one who keeps his wife '*in the wholsome ignorance of unnecessary secrets*,' especially 'weighty Counsels, too heavy for the weaker sex to bear' (9).
20 Jonathan Goldberg, 'Shakespearean Inscriptions: The Voicing of Power,' 128.
21 For the earliest occurrence of the proverb in Shakespeare's work, see *Titus Andronicus*, IV.ii.144. There is some evidence that not even one person can keep his own secrets. A case in point is Vendice, Tourneur's indiscreet revenger, who feels compelled to boast of his undiscovered villainies after all his accomplices are dead, only to find himself condemned out of his own mouth.
22 There is a terrible irony about the Queen's feeling oppressed by self-imposed (or is it state-imposed?) silence, since pressing, sometimes to death, with enormous weights was a favourite method for extracting secrets from recalcitrant prisoners.
23 As Phyllis Rackin has forcefully demonstrated, within Renaissance historiography 'women represented a constant source of anxiety, for ... no man could truly know that he was the father of the boy who was destined to inherit his name and property.' See her essay, 'Genealogical Anxiety and Female Authority: The Return of the Repressed in Shakespeare's Histories,' 324. This essay is also incorporated into chapter 4 of Rackin's superb book, *Stages of History: Shakespeare's English Chronicles*.
24 D.A. Miller, 'Secret Subjects, Open Secrets,' 19. In a similar vein, Stanton Tefft, drawing his conclusions from sociological observation, explains that 'Through regulated control and disclosure of information, individuals as well as groups may exert some control over their environments by making it difficult for outsiders, whether competitors, rivals, or enemies, to predict their actions and take counteraction against them' (*Secrecy*, 321).
25 Frank Kermode, *The Genesis of Secrecy: On the Interpretation of Narrative*, 144.

Chapter Two

1 Anne Barton, *Ben Jonson, Dramatist*, 92–105.
2 Richard Bancroft, *Daungerous Positions and Proceedings, published and practised within this iland of Brytaine*, 3 and 7.
3 Jonson told Drummond that 'Northampton was his mortall enimie,' by whom he was 'called befor ye Councell for his Sejanus & accused both of popperie and treason' (*Conversations*, lines 325–7; HSS, 1:141). His speedy exoneration from the charges may owe as much to his politic evasions and his connections at court as to his innocence.
4 In *James I and the Politics of Literature*, Jonathan Goldberg remarks that 'confederacy ... is everywhere a principle of political organization' in Tiberius's Rome. 'No place,' he continues, 'is free of spies, and the eyes of the court extend even into the secrets that never are allowed expression' (181). The inexpressible secrets in this and in many other Jacobean plays are, according to Goldberg, reflections of James's struggle to contain republicanism with his own form of absolutism. The critic's exclusive focus on this issue sometimes unnecessarily limits his analysis of the literature of the period.
5 These are lines 407–60 of act III. See *Conversations*, line 602 (HSS, 1:149).
6 Goldberg says in a lengthy footnote that 'Femininity in these plays [*Sejanus* and *Catiline*] seems to be for Jonson a root image of betrayal of the body; beneath the female counsel and female political argument lurks the hidden form of passion, the ghost that moves inside these corrupt and painted bodies' (*James I*, 281 n23). Given the way that male doctors, spouses, and politicians harass and politicians assault innocent as well as corrupt female bodies, I find it difficult to conclude that women are any more radically betrayers for Jonson in *Sejanus* than are men. Women are more marginalized than vilified in the play. I will return to the gender question in the final section of this chapter.
7 As Jongsook Lee says, 'Tiberius's art of tyranny through deceptive public rhetoric and misinterpretation of others' language reaches its fine pitch of psychological torture in his offstage performance in act 5,' that is, in his letter to the senate. See *Ben Jonson's Poesis: A Literary Dialectic of Ideal and History*, 23.
8 George E. Rowe, *Distinguishing Jonson: Imitation, Rivalry, and the Direction of a Dramatic Career*, 97.
9 *Dio's Roman History*, 7:213.
10 See Michel Foucault, *Discipline and Punish: The Birth of the Prison*, chapter 2, 'The Spectacle of the Scaffold.'

11 Francis Barker, *The Tremulous Private Body: Essays on Subjection*.
12 That battle scars continued to be a powerful form of political testimonial into the seventeenth century is suggested by a letter from Ralph Winwood to Robert Cecil, dated Paris, 7 July 1602, in which he reports that the Duke de Biron, threatened with torture if he refused to reveal the names of his fellow conspirators, '*unbraced his Doblet and shewed his Breast covered with Scarrs; and asked, what part of his Body they could put to Torment which had not already sufficiently been torn for their Safetie, and the Service of his Countrey.*' See *Memorials of Affairs of State in the Reigns of Q. Elizabeth and K. James I* (London, 1725), 1:423.
13 Edward Forset, *A Comparative Discourse of the Bodies Natural and Politique* (London, 1606), 'To the Reader,' sig. ¶iiiv.
14 William Hazlitt, *Lectures Chiefly on the Dramatic Literature of the Age of Elizabeth*, 167.
15 Barbara DeLuna changes the spin on the favourite indoor sport of personality paralleling in *Sejanus* when she asks, 'Did Jonson ... intend to shadow forth [the disgraced Earl of] Essex in the much-abused and heroic Silius [rather than] in the bloody and hypocritical Sejanus himself?' See B.N. DeLuna, *Jonson's Romish Plot: A Study of 'Catiline' and Its Historical Context*, 8. In his edition of *Sejanus*, Philip J. Ayers maintains that possible parallels with the two-year-old Essex rebellion were less likely to have excited Northampton's ire than the clearer connection with the just weeks-old treason trial of Sir Walter Ralegh (Revels Plays, 16-22). For a fuller account of the historical parallels between the third-act trial of Caius Silius and Ralegh's legal railroading by Sir Edward Coke, see Ayers's 'Jonson, Northampton, and the Treason in *Sejanus*,' Albert H. Tricomi argues in *Anticourt Drama in England, 1603-1642*, 72-9, that the significant historical parallel is between the suffocation of the republican spirit under the absolutism of Tiberius and that under King James.

The critical practice in which DeLuna, Ayers, and Tricomi are engaged would have been familiar to Jonson under the label of 'application' (i.e. drawing parallels between different historical situations and personages, one remote, the other proximate). The practice is as fraught with evidential difficulties for today's critics as for Jonson's contemporaries. Using the case of *Sejanus* as his '*exemplum*,' Richard Dutton cogently argues (following Philip Edwards) that if the play was indeed performed in 1603, it must very likely have been *before* James came to the throne, given the closing of the theatres for the rest of the year after Elizabeth's death to restrict political disorder and the spread of the plague. The play could not, then, be 'applied' to Ayers's more likely candidate, Ralegh, and the entire exercise is thrown into considerable doubt – unless we assume that it was the printing of the play in 1605, not its original production in 1603, that caused the uproar. See Dutton's *Mastering the Revels: The Regulation and Censorship of Renaissance Drama*, 10–14.

Still, given the tantalizing evidence we have, it is likely that *Sejanus* came in for some kind of contemporary analogical decoding, especially since, as Richard A. Burt points out in writing about *Julius Caesar*, 'Roman history was a discourse that one could not afford to ignore in the Renaissance. One had to make use of it' ('"A Dangerous Rome": Shakespeare's *Julius Caesar* and the Discursive Determinism of Cultural Politics,' 111. Burt concludes that this kind of interpretation should be based on the assumption that discourse determines politics rather than the other way around (as the new historicists believe) and that 'any such play [as *Julius Caesar* could be either] potentially orthodox or oppositional because of the discursive incongruence between the past and the present' (121).

16 James I, *The True Lawe of Free Monarchies: or the reciprock and mutuall duetie betwixt a free king, and his naturall subjectes* (Edinburgh, 1598), sigs. D4v–5.
17 Letter of 2 June 1607, reproduced in *Narrative and Dramatic Sources of Shakespeare*, ed. Geoffrey Bullough, 5:557.
18 I quote from Maurice Platnauer's translation of Claudian in the Loeb Clasical Library edition, 1:89 (lines 410–17).
19 HSS, 9:634.
20 See Christopher Ricks's account of these images in '*Sejanus* and Dismemberment.'
21 Gail Kern Paster, *The Idea of the City in the Age of Shakespeare*, 115.
22 Nancy J. Vickers, 'Diana Described: Scattered Woman and Scattered Rhyme,' rpt. in *Writing and Sexual Difference*, ed. Elizabeth Abel, 95–109.
23 For example, Leonard Barkan, in his wonderfully thorough study of the primary metaphor that I have been examining, *Nature's Work of Art: The Human Body as Image of the World*, argues that late in the play 'Tiberius has become confused and distracted, and the people do not know what he intends or what his orders are' (95). While his floundering interpreters are admittedly being driven to distraction by his prose, Tiberius's own position remains firm, and his political will is executed to the letter. Elsewhere Barkan claims that 'the metaphorical body of the emperor fails ultimately to hold the State together because his literal body has been enthralled to Sejanus' (92). As Tacitus makes clear, Tiberius had many more bodies to exploit sexually than Sejanus's; that body was wholly expendable, and the state did, in fact, hold together, at least for a while, after the events recorded in Jonson's play.

24 John Jowett makes much of the 'conflict between personal behaviour and ethical stance in a published work' which, he says Jonson must have been aware of in publishing *Sejanus*. 'The simplistic explanation,' according to Jowett, 'is that Jonson was moving from oppositional Catholic to court laureate, a process accelerated by his, or the general, reaction to the Gunpowder Plot. But Johnson [sic] did persevere in publishing *Sejanus*, and texts without any comparable sense of opposition or alienation may be found dating from 1603 (*The Entertainment at Althorp*) as well as 1605 (*The Masque of Blackness*). Jonson seems capable of assuming conflicting stances almost simultaneously, and his attempts to reconcile them are unconvincing.' See Jowett's '"Fall before this Booke": The 1605 Quarto of *Sejanus*,' 292. In *Licensed by Authority*, Richard Burt accounts for the 'deeply contradictory' relationship (175n10) of Jonson to the court and his patrons as a combination of his 'neurotic compromise[s]' (11) and the court's perennial inconsistencies in applying censorship standards (123).

On Jonson's poetry of praise and the patronage system see Robert C. Evans, *Ben Jonson and the Poetics of Patronage*. Evans builds on the important work of Richard Helgerson in *Self-Crowned Laureates: Spenser, Jonson, Milton, and the Literary System*. For an account of Jonson's life at court that stresses his audacity and the price he paid for it, see David Riggs, *Ben Jonson: A Life*, chapter 7. All of these critics have dealt with Jonson's desire to be accepted by both courtly and common audiences and with his spirited attacks on both (partly overlapping) audiences. None of their accounts, nor any I could offer, would make the contradictions go away. They are simply a feature of Jonson's life and times.

25 See the 'Apologeticall Dialogue' at the end of *Poetaster* (lines 222-8), where Jonson imagines with bitter satisfaction the dull audience of his comedies shrinking to just one judicious spectator at his proposed tragedy (HSS, 4:324).

26 'To the Readers' (lines 28-9). In fact, Jonson used Justus Lipsius's annotated edition of Tacitus, *Opera quae exstant* (Antwerp, 1600), drawing not only his own marginalia but also characters' speeches from Lipsius's apparatus. For example, Arruntius's comment on Cordus's futile self-defence during the trial scene in act III ('Freely, and nobly spoken' [III.461]) derives not from Tacitus but from a marginal rubric added by Lipsius ('*Libera & pulchra eius defensio*' [120]). I quote from the 1627 edition, which is identical to the one Jonson used in all important respects. For other examples of Jonson's scholarly raiding, see Daniel Boughner, 'Jonson's Use of Lipsius in *Sejanus*.' The most intelligent discussion of the marginated *Sejanus* that I have seen is Evelyn B. Tribble's in *Margins*

and Marginality, 146–57. The published text, she says, is 'literally surrounded by evidence of Jonson's insecurity about interpretation' (146). She concludes, 'The use of the plural authorities of the page is finally at odds with, although still embedded within, a unified book/self, which constructs a typographical unity for a diverse, contingent career' (157).

27 See Jonas Barish's edition of *Sejanus*, Introduction, 18, and Annabel Patterson, '"Roman-cast Similitude": Ben Jonson and the English Use of Roman History.' Patterson argues persuasively that Jonson in his marginal annotation 'deliberately invokes a model [i.e. Tacitus] whose reputation in England was already far from neutral, thanks to its vogue in the Essex circle' (385). She quotes Jonson's remark to Drummond that 'Tacitus ... wrott the secrets of the Council and Senate' (*Conversations*, line 146 [HSS, 1:136]). Jonson's habit of linking Tacitus with treachery and spying is further evident in his Epigram 92, 'The New Crie,' where Londoners obsessed with treachery and state spying 'carry in their pockets Tacitvs' (line 15) and in *Epicoene*, where the inept Sir John Daw protests, 'As I hope to finish Tacitvs, I intend no murder' (IV.v.50). On the Tacitean political philosophy in *Sejanus*, see also Peter Burke, 'Tacitism,' which argues for an Essex-*Sejanus* parallel, and K.C. Schellhase, *Tacitus in Renaissance Political Thought*, 159–61, which is sceptical that any such linkage would have been evident in the earliest years of the seventeenth century.

28 See Arthur F. Marotti, *John Donne, Coterie Poet*. Approaching texts somewhat differently at an earlier time in his career, Marotti found in *Sejanus* forms of self-conscious artistry that, in his view, destroy the play's tragic potential. See 'The Self-Reflexive Art of Ben Jonson's *Sejanus*.'

29 Giovanni Battista Manzini, *Politicall Observations upon the fall of Seianus*, trans. Sir T[homas] H[awkins] (London, 1634), 6. John Webster's Duchess of Malfi generalizes this trait to include all tyrants: 'a tyrant doubles with his words, / And fearfully equivocates' (I.ii.359-60). I quote from the Mermaid edition.

30 In this regard Jonson's play conforms to the pattern, noted by Catherine Belsey, of systematically denying a subject position to women in Renaissance drama. See Belsey's *The Subject of Tragedy: Identity and Difference in Renaissance Drama*. While other critics have demonstrated the limitations of Belsey's generalization where Shakespeare is concerned – notably Jean E. Howard and Marion F. O'Connor (in the Introduction to *Shakespeare Reproduced: The Text in History and Ideology*, 1–17) and Phyllis Rackin (in 'Genealogical Anxiety and Female Authority: The Return of the Repressed in Shakespeare's Histories') – Belsey's account of *un*voiced women admirably describes Jonsonian tragedy.

31 While Robert Ornstein believes that Fortune's wheel is rigged by Tiberius (*The Moral Vision of Jacobean Tragedy*, 96), Frederick Kiefer argues that 'if the play demonstrates anything it is that man lacks the wisdom and courage to deprive Fortune of her "deity"' (*Fortune and Elizabethan Tragedy*, 275).

Chapter Three

1 In *The Passions of the Minde in Generall* (London, 1604), Thomas Wright sets out a common contrast between Italians (whom he yokes with Spaniards) and Englishmen:

Some [nationalities] surpasse others in aptnes to deceyve, and in craftinesse to circumvent. And in this we may confese that Spaniards and Italians goe before vs, for commonly they can better conceale their owne Passions, and discover others, than we. ... [T]he Spaniard and the Italian demurreth much, and selleth his secrets and his friendship by drammes. ... [H]ee can observe his times better than we for his plots, and marke fitter occasions to effectuate his intent. ... In fine, he can dessemble better his owne passions, and vse himselfe therein more circumspectly, than we can doe. (sig. A5v)

Wright would have the morality of secrecy both ways, implicitly praising the English for their virtue of candour even as he is evidently praising the Catholic foreigners for their circumspection and effective sense of timing.

2 The letter is printed in HSS, 1:202. These events are discussed reliably by Mark Eccles, 'Jonson and the Spies'; speculatively by B.N. DeLuna, *Jonson's Romish Plot: A Study of 'Catiline' and Its Historical Context*; plausibly by James Tulip, 'Comedy as Equivocation: An Approach to the Reference of *Volpone*'; and biographically by David Riggs, *Ben Jonson: A Life*, 122–45. I find puzzling and unconvincing Riggs's identification of Jonson with both Volpone and his theatrical alter ego, Scoto of Mantua, the mountebank (137, 139). Jonson would (and did in the Epistle to *Volpone*) point to important distinctions between the licensed and unlicensed artificer. Much of this material was first brought to my attention by Grant Stanley Wilson when he was working on a master's thesis with me at the University of Saskatchewan. His carefully assembled research persuaded me that there is good reason to view Jonson's treatment of secrecy in *Volpone* as a scathing response to the Gunpowder Plot and also its counter-conspiratorial aftermath.

For evidence that Protestant England had already been actively and imaginatively countering Catholic spying on home soil for many years, see John Bossy's fascinating exposé of Giordano Bruno as a mole in chaplain's clothing in the French embassy in London during the early 1580s. Bruno's 007 methods included reporting to Walsingham, his 'control,' under the name of Henry Fagot in several hands and codes, including one message in which he incorporated into his native Italian errors consistent with a Spaniard trying to write the language. See *Giordano Bruno and the Embassy Affair*.

3 For a discussion of dating, see R.B. Parker's introduction to the Revels edition of *Volpone*, 6. On the staging and political possibilities of the tortoise device, see John Creaser, 'The Popularity of Jonson's Tortoise.'

4 Lacey Baldwin Smith, *Treason in Tudor England: Politics and Paranoia*, 141.

5 HSS, 1:220.

6 M. Thomas Hester comments extensively on this aspect of Donne's satires in *Kinde Pitty and Brave Scorn*.

7 Jonson very likely takes the image of the fake doctor with the ill-disguised ass's ears from Erasmus's *Praise of Folly*, at the point where Folly announces, 'I never wear disguises ... [and] I cannot be concealed even by those who most jealously arrogate to themselves the character and title of wisemen. ... However hard they try to hide it, the tips of their Midas-ears sooner or later slip out and betray them' (13). The ass-eared doctor is delightfully illustrated by Hans Holbein the Younger in the margin of Mycronius's copy of Johann Froben's 1515 edition published in Basel.

8 Robert Wiltenberg expresses a similar view, arguing that Mosca's 'main business is to separate each [of the gulls] from his true good (as he has Volpone) by inflating self-love and self-interest to the point that they rupture the already corroded bonds of affectionate reciprocity.' See *Ben Jonson and Self-Love: The Subtlest Maze of All*, 32.

9 In the eyes of respectable seventeenth-century Englishmen, modern fashions in dress and hair-style that blurred easy gender-distinction were as revolutionary and wicked as Guy Fawkes's plot. See, for example, the anonymous pamphlet, *Hic Mulier, or the Man-Woman, Being a Medicine to Cure the Coltish Desease of the Staggers in the Masculine-Feminine of Our Times. Exprest in a Briefe Declamation* (London, 1620), in which 'Masculine-women' are associated with 'Play-houses' and are said to be not so much 'halfe man, halfe woman' as 'all Diuell' (sigs. A3v-4).

10 In his essay 'Volpone as Antinous: Jonson and "Th' Overthrow of Stage-Playes,"' Joseph L. Simmons makes the important point that Jonson in many ways sympathized with the best puritan criticism of plays like Gager's. Volpone's stagy excesses may represent Jonson's critique of particular plays and players.

11 Leonard Dean wittily and accurately compares the situation to an operatic duet in which the soloists' grandly dramatic sentiments sail neatly over one another's heads. See 'Three Notes on Comic Morality: Celia, Bobadill, and Falstaff,' 264.
12 Jonathan Goldberg maintains that the myth of Venice preserved by republicanism is subverted by Volpone's absolutist desires, desires that are unwittingly parodied by Sir Politique (*James I and the Politics of Literature*, 72–80). He notes the keen interest in spying recorded in the ambassadorial letters written from Venice by Sir Henry Wotton in the years 1603–10, 1616–19, and 1621–3 (75).
13 Douglas Duncan makes this observation with considerable force in *Ben Jonson and the Lucianic Tradition*, 159.
14 Ibid.
15 Though his conclusions are very different from mine, Stephen J. Greenblatt has written one of the most stimulating essays on the play's ending that I know of. See 'The False Ending in *Volpone*.' Northrop Frye says in passing that the false fourth-act recognitions in *The New Inn* and *The Magnetic Lady* (to which I would add *Volpone*) correspond to the catastasis from Donatus's structural model of comedy. See *A Natural Perspective: The Development of Shakespearean Comedy and Romance*, 15.
16 *The Alchemist*, 'To the Reader,' line 6. This conception of a comic ending is parodied in *Volpone* as well when the Magnifico proposes that his dwarf and eunuch be summoned to announce a 'jig' at the latter end of his escape from the law (V.ii.59).
17 In 'The Suicide of Volpone,' Alexander Leggatt argues convincingly that, by fictionalizing his own death, the bored artist-trickster, requiring closure for his plays within the play, commits aesthetic suicide.
18 See Gail K. Paster, 'Ben Jonson's Comedy of Limitation,' on Jonson's technique of fixing characters psychologically within certain restrictive locales.
19 Mark Anderson argues that this desperate exploitation of the law is Jonson's ultimate satiric thrust at a system that has taken in everybody, from the gulls to the audience. See 'Structure and Response in *Volpone*.'
20 Duncan's *Ben Jonson and the Lucianic Tradition* frequently inclines to this view, as does John Sweeney's provocative, but in my view overstated essay, '*Volpone* and the Theater of Self-Interest' (also in his book entitled *Jonson and the Psychology of Public Theater*). I remain unconvinced that Jonson founded a 'theater' of any kind, and certainly not one that involves 'the final subversion of [its] moral significance' (240).
21 Pico della Mirandola, *Oration on the Dignity of Man*, as quoted by Alvin

Kernan in the introduction to his edition of *Volpone*, 14–15.
22 See *Epigrammes* CI. 'Inviting a Friend to Supper,' line 36, HSS 8:64–5. Pooly was a government spy present when Christopher Marlowe was murdered; Parrot, as the name implies, is an informer. Compare Jonson's Sir Pol.
23 See 'To Penshurst,' HSS 8:93–6, lines 36 and following.
24 *Hymenaei, or the Solemnities of a Masque and Barriers at a Marriage* (1606), HSS 8:209–41.

Chapter Four

1 Ejner Jensen records only six twentieth-century productions, all of them receiving truly dreadful reviews, the general tenor of which was that 'Jonson ... was distinctly for an age; or at least not for their [the critics'] age' (31). See *Ben Jonson's Comedies on the Modern Stage*, 30–5.
2 John Dryden, *The Essays of John Dryden*, 1:83; Ray L. Heffner, Jr, 'Unifying Symbols in the Comedy of Ben Jonson'; Jonas A. Barish, *Ben Jonson and the Language of Prose Comedy*, 142–86; William W.E. Slights, '*Epicoene* and the Prose Paradox.'
3 By her own account, for example, Karen Newman's 'reading of *Epicoene* willfully shifts its focus away from Morose and the gallants, away from Jonsonian satire and classical allusion, away from the exclusively literary, and gestures toward, in Althusser's terms, the production of a different theoretical *problematic*. On such a terrain of reading, it is not simply a question of *seeing* the woman, of putting "woman" into discursive circulation but of changing the terms of reading' (193). See her essay, 'City Talk: Women and Commodification,' rpt. in *Staging the Renaissance: Reinterpretations of Elizabethan and Jacobean Drama*, ed. David Scott Kastan and Peter Stallybrass, 181–95. This essay also appears as the final chapter of Newman's book, *Fashioning Femininity and English Renaissance Drama*.

Taking a slightly different tack, Lorraine Helms locates her reading of the play helpfully within the context of other theatrical representations of problematic gender issues in the period. See 'Roaring Girls and Silent Women: The Politics of Androgyny on the Jacobean Stage.'

For an excellent review of earlier feminist and materialist feminist work on the sex-gender system in the period see Jean E. Howard, 'Crossdressing, the Theatre, and Gender Struggle in Early Modern England,' 419n3 and 419–20n4. Howard discusses *Epicoene* succinctly and trenchantly on 429–30.
4 For a Lacanian analysis of the imperfections of self-representation see Joan Copjec, 'The Orthopsychic Subject: Film Theory and the Recep-

tion of Lacan.' 'Narcissism,' she concludes, 'seeks the self beyond the self-image, with which the subject constantly finds fault and in which it constantly fails to recognize itself' (70). Jonson's characters regularly fail to recognize anything of themselves in the images that they project in their attempts to mystify others.

5 Philip Mirabelli presents a somewhat strained argument that Truewit knew just what he was doing all along and that he emerges as the wise moral guide of the play. See 'Silence, Wit, and Wisdom in *The Silent Woman.*' I am more inclined to view Truewit as a slightly frantic improviser, clever but finally unable to master fully the social forces set loose in the play.

6 The poem in question is '*My Picture left in* Scotland,' from *Under-Woods* (HSS 8:149-50). The passages from *Conversations* are in HSS 1:139-41.

7 The conception of authorship implied here derives from Michel Foucault, 'What Is an Author?' in *Textual Strategies: Perspectives in Post-Structuralist Criticism*; rpt. in *The Foucault Reader*, ed. Paul Rabinow, 101-20.

8 This impertinent person seems to have been the Lady Arbella Stuart, cousin to the King. According to a coded communiqué from the Venetian ambassador in London dated 10 February 1610, she took offence at a passage from a stage comedy (probably *Epicoene* V.i.24) linking her to the *soi-disant* Prince of Moldavia, who had recently been in London and who subsequently spread rumours that he was engaged to be married to Lady Arbella. Her objections may explain the six-year delay in the play's publication, from its listing in the Stationer's Register to its appearance in the Jonson first folio. See Janet Clare, '*Art Made Tongue-Tied by Authority*': *Elizabethan and Jacobean Dramatic Censorship*, 168-70. Richard Dutton treats this material in his discussion of the boys' companies in *Mastering the Revels*, 188-9.

9 See Stanley Fish, *Self-Consuming Artifacts: The Experience of Seventeenth-Century Literature*, esp. 1-77. For an application of the concept to stage comedy of the English Renaissance, see Jonathan V. Crewe, 'God or the Good Physician: The Rational Playwright in *The Comedy of Errors.*' While Crewe finds Shakespeare hovering uncertainly between these two identities, I find that Jonson emerges as neither.

10 As in *Sejanus* (II. 1-138), face-painting is represented in *Epicoene* as shameful and unnatural. While in the earlier play it is conjoined with spying and treachery, in this one it is an individual vanity wholly dependent upon urban commerce.

11 See David Underdown, *Revel, Riot, and Rebellion: Popular Politics and Culture in England 1603-1660*, and his essay, 'The Taming of the Scold: The Enforcement of Patriarchal Authority in Early Modern England.' More

graphic evidence of public attempts to shame and silence women is presented by Lynda E. Boose in 'Scolding Brides and Bridling Scolds: Taming the Woman's Unruly Member.'

12 As David Underdown points out in *Revel, Riot, and Rebellion*, masterless women as well as men were perceived as threats to social stability not only because they might provide the devil with idle hands to do his work but, on the contrary, because their diligence and aggressiveness might improve their social status. He quotes *The Southampton Mayor's Book of 1606-1608* concerning women whose sole offence was to 'take chambers and so live by themselves masterless,' concluding that their conduct was 'serious because it ... defied conventional assumptions about women's dependence' (*Revel*, 36-7). A collective of such independent women – and book-readers into the bargain – must have presented an alarming prospect to London gallants like Truewit who relied heavily on the traditional prerogatives of patriarchy to keep themselves in the style to which they had become so thoroughly accustomed.

13 Alan Macfarlane makes clear in his study of the diary of the Essex clergyman Ralph Josselin that at least one forty-year-long marriage of the period was extraordinarily close and loving. See *The Family Life of Ralph Josselin*. Keith Wrightson adds more examples of close, private relationships, both marital and otherwise, in *English Society, 1580-1680*. Though companionate marriage was not so new a phenomenon in the seventeenth century as Lawrence Stone and others would have us believe, neither did a loving relationship preclude the necessity to negotiate and renegotiate patriarchal authority within marriages, as Susan Amussen amply demonstrates in 'Gender, Family and the Social Order, 1560-1725.' The more these negotiations were removed from public discourses such as the church homilies and carried out in the private spaces of domestic dwellings, the more there was perceived to be a need to reinforce the message of male authority and female subordination. This need was filled in part by women's manuals and public correction of private lapses from the patriarchal ideals. The relationship between increasingly inward experience and the refinement of enclosed architectural space is explored in Patricia Fumerton's *Cultural Aesthetics: Renaissance Literature and the Practice of Social Ornament*. As Lionel Trilling points out, the direction of the causal relationship between private space and private experience is difficult to determine: 'It is when he becomes an individual that a man lives more and more in private rooms; whether the privacy makes the individuality or the individuality requires the privacy the historians do not say.' See *Sincerity and Authenticity*, 24-5.

14 See, for example, Charles Estienne's *The Defense of Contraries*, trans. Anthony Munday (London, 1593). Estienne's paradoxes are translations, or rather, imitations of the widely known *Paradossi Cioe, Sententie fori del commun parere* of Ortensio Lando (Lyons, 1543; Venice, 1544).
15 Barbara Millard writes particularly well about the frantic attempts of the female characters to live up to the standard of beauty and behaviour set by the males. See her essay, '"An Acceptable Violence": Sexual Contest in Jonson's *Epicoene*.'
16 The ground-breaking book in this area is Eve Kosofsky Sedgwick's *Between Men: English Literature and Male Homosocial Desire*.
17 The term 'homosexual' being a much later coinage, Jonson had only such terms as 'engle,' 'catamite,' and 'sodomite.' He chose the most gentle of these. For information on Renaissance homoerotic activity and the differences in age, social position, and power between its participants, see Alan Bray, *Homosexuality in Renaissance England*. On the literary significance of homosexuality in the period see Simon Shepherd, 'Shakespeare's Private Drawer: Shakespeare and Homosexuality,' and Bruce R. Smith, *Homosexual Desire in Shakespeare's England: A Cultural Poetics*.
18 In Jonson's time, as in our own, homoeroticism was often constructed as a mysterious kind of sex-changing force. Under its influence, men were thought to be biologically and psychologically transformed into women. As Thomas Laqueur points out, such gender slippage in men was thought to result from 'excessive devotion to women.' See *Making Sex: Body and Gender from the Greeks to Freud*, 123. Theatrical cross-dressing was likewise said to 'effeminate' the minds of men. See Laura Levine, 'Men in Women's Clothing: Anti-Theatricality and Effeminization from 1579 to 1642.'

The medical and judicial implications of sexual indeterminacy, especially of 'intersex,' are considered at length in Julia Epstein's essay, 'Either/Or - Neither/Both: Sexual Ambiguity and the Ideology of Gender.' I am grateful to my colleague Raymond Stephanson for directing me to this article and suggesting useful ways to integrate Epstein's work with my own.
19 Jonas A. Barish, *Ben Jonson and the Language of Prose Comedy*, 177.
20 The quoted phrase is from Millard, '"An Acceptable Violence,"' 149. Also see *Epicoene*, ed. L.A. Beaurline, 117n. While jokes about castration run just beneath the surface of the entire sequence, the topic emerges most explicitly in an exchange between Dauphine and Morose, who wishes that he could reclaim the secret of his marriage from Cutbeard:

MOR. That I should bee seduc'd by so foolish a deuill, as a barber will make! ... Would I could redeeme it with the losse of an eye (nephew) a hand, or any other member.

DAV. Mary, god forbid, sir, that you should geld your selfe, to anger your wife. (IV.iv.3-11)

21 See the second chapter, '"A Martyr's Resolution": *Epicoene*,' in Donaldson's *The World Upside-Down: Comedy from Jonson to Fielding*, 24-45. A convenient update of the literature – from C.L. Barber and Robert Weimann to Michael Bristol and Peter Stallybrass – that establishes the importance of social ritual to the theatre of the period is the Introduction to *True Rites and Maimed Rites: Ritual and Anti-Ritual in Shakespeare and His Age*, ed. Linda Woodbridge and Edward Berry, 1-43.

22 See the analysis of comments about charivari made by Thomas Platter, a German visitor to England in 1599, in Susan Amussen, *An Ordered Society: Gender and Class in Early Modern England*, 49-50.

23 Cotgrave as quoted in François Laroque, *Shakespeare's Festive World: Elizabethan Seasonal Entertainment and the Professional Stage*, 288.

24 Underdown points specifically to 'a sort of under-class in [the pasture regions of England], hostile and resistant to Puritan reformation, and it was from this social level that skimmington performers were mainly drawn' (*Revel*, 103). Natalie Zemon Davis identifies the merry-makers in certain French rituals as primarily young men. See 'The Reasons of Misrule: Youth Groups and Charivaris in Sixteenth Century France.' In Jonson's London setting, the clamorous street musicians join with Truewit and his young, male co-conspirators to perform this part.

25 For a 'local' reading of *Coriolanus*, carried out in terms of the enclosure acts and the city liberties, see Leah S. Marcus, *Puzzling Shakespeare: Local Reading and Its Discontents*, 202-11. Marcus suggests (204) that the authorities had great difficulty holding in check not only rural but also urban economic unrest during this period.

26 Michael Bristol, 'Charivari and the Comedy of Abjection in *Othello*,' in *True Rites and Maimed Rites*, ed. Woodbridge and Berry, 84.

27 As Peter Stallybrass and Allon White argue in the Introduction to *The Politics and Poetics of Transgression*, it is dangerously misleading to essentialize the political functions of carnivalesque transgression (14-15).

28 D.A. Miller, 'Secret Subjects, Open Secrets,' 19.

29 In a paper entitled 'Masculine Silence: *Epicoene* and Jonsonian Stylistics,' delivered at the MLA convention in Toronto, December 1993, Douglas Lanier presented the view that Jonson's ideal of strong, male style is Dauphine, who blocks out the clamour to get the job of acquiring his inheritance done. As will become clear, I am less certain than Lanier that Jonson perfectly controls the poetics of silence in *Epicoene*.

30 A provocative account of male anxieties about controlling women's mouths in the period is Peter Stallybrass's 'Patriarchal Territories: The Body Enclosed.'
31 Starting from an enigmatic reference to the topos in Chapman, Raymond B. Waddington ably traces this persistent idea deep into classical antiquity. See 'The Iconography of Silence and Chapman's Hercules.'
32 For further variations on the theme see Huston D. Hallahan, 'Silence, Eloquence, and Chatter in Jonson's *Epicoene*.'
33 During this exchange, Clerimont slips in an odd and amusing exception to the catalogue of Morose's complaints: 'He would haue hang'd a Pewterers 'prentice once vpon a shroue-tuesdaies riot, for being o'that trade, when the rest were quit' (I.i.157-9). In this case Morose ironically vents his anger on the industrious apprentice who is plying his noisy trade instead of joining the holiday revellers, whom the killjoy would generally have been vilifying. François Laroque, incorrectly I think, cites the line as evidence of festive 'excesses that the townsfolk did not necessarily tolerate cheerfully' (*Shakespeare's Festive World*, 101).
34 Karen Newman, 'City Talk,' in *Staging the Renaissance*, ed. Kastan and Stallybrass, 186-7.
35 Lorraine Helms, 'Roaring Girls and Silent Women,' 67-8. Another important thing to remember about this particular theatrical venue is that Whitefriars was one of the 'liberties' that prized its own sometimes riotous freedom from regulation by either the City of London or the Crown. See Leah Marcus, *Puzzling Shakespeare*, 165-8.
36 The noted antitheatricalist William Prynne, in some ways an unlikely ally for Jonson, elaborates this fear in *Histrio-mastix* (1633):

> Men ... are unmanned on the Stage: all the honour and vigour of their sex is effeminated with the shame, the dishonesty of an unsinued body. He who is most womanish and best resembles the female sex, gives best content ... how a male might be effeminated into a female, how their sex might be changed by Art, that so the divell who defiles Gods workemanship, might be pleased by the offences of a depraved and effeminated body. (168-9)

This passage was brought to my attention by Jessica Slights, who has argued convincingly in her paper, 'The Shame of Unsinewed Bodies,' delivered at the Ohio Shakespeare Conference, March 1994, that representations of the Renaissance theatre as female derive from a virulent and persistent tradition of anti-feminist rhetoric. Jonson's representational rhetoric is certainly consistent with this view.
37 Francis Osborne, *The Secret History of the Court of James the First* (1658), 1:274-5.
38 In the first chapter of *Still Harping on Daughters: Women and Drama in the*

Age of Shakespeare, Lisa Jardine is prepared, in a way that I am not, to extend this type of argument to include the entire range of Elizabethan and Jacobean plays, whether or not they explicitly thematize sexual ambiguity.

39 By including both civil and ecclesiastical lawyers among his 'persons,' Truewit ensured a lively disputation because, as Leah Marcus points out in her discussion of *Measure for Measure* in *Puzzling Shakespeare*, there was 'no single Renaissance understanding of what constituted valid marriage – at least not in England' (172), and canon law concerning what constituted legal marriage had just been revised in 1604, following the Hampton Court Conference.

40 As Lorraine Helms shows, both 'myths' are revealed as male fantasies ('Roaring Girls,' 69).

41 On this matter I am forced to take issue with two first-rate readers of Jonson, Michael Shapiro and W. David Kay. In his essay, 'Audience v. Dramatist in Jonson's *Epicoene* and Other Plays of the Children's Troupes,' Shapiro argues that the 'three gallants constitute a small-scale model of an ideal aristocratic society, neither too detached from the world nor excessively involved in its vanities' (414). In 'Jonson's Urbane Gallants: Humanistic Contexts for *Epicoene*,' W. David Kay places the gallants within a tradition of Erasmian irony with which Jonson himself felt strong associations. While the values of humanist ironic detachment are important for Jonson, they prove slippery ones for him to embed in the popular drama. His 'normative' characters keep revealing themselves as self-indulgent emulators of the very behaviours they set out to ridicule.

42 Ian Donaldson, *The World Upside-Down*, 29.

Chapter Five

1 Differentiating criminal cozeners, vagabonds, papists, and other impostors from culturally legitimate, licensed theatrical impersonators (actors) in early modern England required the creation of what Richard Burt calls a semiotics of cozenage which relied on legal and economic sanctions – both permissive and punishing ones – to establish and maintain the distinction. See Burt's *Licensed by Authority: Ben Jonson and the Discourses of Censorship*, 86–92. I find Jonson playing with the looseness of this distinction to especially good comic purpose in *The Alchemist*.

2 Patricia Meyer Spacks does a careful job of tracing the gendering of this

much maligned form of communication in her book, *Gossip*.
3 In *Power on Display: The Politics of Shakespeare's Genres*, 40–71, Leonard Tennenhouse historicizes the subgenres of Renaissance drama, suggesting reasons for their growth and demise.
4 See William W.E. Slights, 'Unfashioning the Man of Mode: A Comic Countergenre in Marston, Jonson, and Middleton,' esp. 82–3, where I trace the emergence of this figure to John Marston's *The Dutch Courtesan*.
5 Such political meanings are not always so stable as Stephen Orgel believed at the time he wrote *The Jonsonian Masque*. For a more flexible approach to problems of referentiality within and around the masque form, see Leah S. Marcus, *The Politics of Mirth: Jonson, Herrick, Milton, Marvell, and the Defense of Old Holiday Pastimes*.
6 See Alvin Kernan's note on II.iii.208 in the Yale edition of *The Alchemist*, 213–14. Kernan's notes, with very few exceptions, are both accurate and helpful.
7 For instance, notice the title of Giovanni Battista Lambi's *The Revelation of the Secret Spirit. Declaring the Secret of Alchemie*, trans. R.N.E. Gent. (London, 1623). The term 'revelation' is, of course, biblically charged and shrewdly calculated in this context to sell secular – and not particularly original – books to the pious. In his article, 'Representing the Underworld: *The Alchemist*,' Jonathan Haynes makes the point that the amount of plagiarism among cony-catching pamphlets indicates that their authors were not especially concerned with keeping their exposés up to date. The point is set in the larger context of Jonson's realism in Haynes's book, *The Social Relations of Jonson's Theater*.
8 In a collection of essays entitled *Secrecy: A Cross-Cultural Perspective*, the sociologist Stanton K. Tefft uses conflict theory to argue that secrecy typically works to promote differentiation, exclusion, and the suppression of those power arrangements that lead to social change (49–63).
9 Paul Christianson, *Reformers and Babylon: English Apocalyptic Visions from the Reformation to the Eve of the Civil War*, 128–31. Christianson writes, '[Joseph] Mede's revival of millenarian thought fathered the Fifth Monarchists and Gerrard Winstanley. Like Brightman, the other great commentator of this period, he would have been shocked by many of the future manifestations produced by his interpretation of the Apocalypse. ... Once in print, the works of Mede – like those of Foxe and Brightman – became common property. Readers could and did interpret them as they wished, ignoring some parts and giving added emphasis to others' (129). The result was appropriation by the militant propagandists of the late 1630s and 1640s.

For another version of the relationship between alchemy and puritan

thought of the period see Robert M. Schuler, 'Some Spiritual Alchemies of Seventeenth-Century England,' esp. 303-8.
10 I suspect (though I can't prove) that Jonson was fascinated by the scholarly work being done by various puritan divines on ancient texts and regarded their work as more than trivial or mad. Broughton was notorious not only as polemical writer but as an indefatigable lecturer and preacher in London. There would have been ample opportunity for Jonson to hear him speak.
11 On alchemical explosions see, for instance, the *Canon Yeoman's Tale* in *The Works of Geoffrey Chaucer*, 217, lines 906-15.
12 Roger Bacon, *The Mirror of Alchimy* (1597), 15.
13 For two brief and very different sorties in Jonson's war with his audience, see the 'Apologeticall Dialogue' that concludes *Poetaster* and the address 'To the Reader' prefixed to *The Alchemist*. The entire campaign is surveyed by John Gordon Sweeney in *Jonson and the Psychology of the Public Theater*, 3-16 and by George E. Rowe in *Distinguishing Jonson: Imitation, Rivalry, and the Direction of a Dramatic Career*, 49-67.
14 Jonson produced several such book-launching poems (*envois*) and variations on the form, including 'Goe little Booke' (addressed to Lucy, Countess of Bedford, with a gift copy of *Cynthia's Revels*), 'To my Booke' (prefacing the *Epigrammes*), and 'Epigram, to my Book-seller' (an insulting piece enjoining his bookseller to act as his book's 'intelligencer' to spy out shallow, fashion-crazy would-be buyers of his volume of poems). A late example of the kind is Ezra Pound's 'Envoi (1919),' which begins, 'Go dumb-born book,' and alludes insistently to Edmund Waller's 'Go Lovely Rose.'
15 For an illuminating account of the circulation of manuscript verse 'as a kind of social currency' (12), see Arthur Marotti, *John Donne, Coterie Poet*, 3-24. Jonson was thought to be astoundingly audacious to publish a folio edition of his works in 1616.
16 Roger Bacon, 76, misnumbered as 40 in the Huntington Library copy.
17 See Thomas M. Greene, 'Resurrecting Rome: The Double Task of the Humanist Imagination.'
18 See Bacon's section on 'Subtiliation' in *The Mirror of Alchimy*, 39.
19 See *The Alchemist*, II.ii.63, and the note on the line in HSS, 10:74.
20 See, for example, Jonson's allusion at I.i.3-4 to a scatological story about Frederic Barbarossa, drawn from Rabelais's *Pantagruel* (book 4, chapter 45), in which prisoners seeking to have their lives spared were told to eat 'La Figue auecques les dens ... sans ayde de mains.' Subtle's insult to the supposed Spanish-speaking Surly, 'Would you have stoup'd a little, and kist our *anos*' (IV.iii.22), and his joke about Dapper

kissing the Fairy Queen's 'departing part' (V.iv.57) are just two instances of his insistence on Bakhtinian posteriority.
21 Wilson's essay originally appeared in *Triple Thinkers*, rev. ed., rpt. in *Ben Jonson: A Collection of Critical Essays*, ed. Jonas A. Barish, 60-74.
22 See Peter Womack, *Ben Jonson*, 117-18.
23 As Russ McDonald so aptly puts it, 'Each dreamer regards the "cunning man" as a source of secret knowledge, power, and change: "the tongues of carpes" and "camels heeles" are to Mammon what customers are to Drugger or knowledge of the duello is to Kastril.' See *Shakespeare and Jonson, Jonson and Shakespeare*, 106.
24 James Mason, publishing in the same year as Jonson's play, sees the potential humour in such mystical incantations: 'For whosoeuer shall looke into the dealings of those persons, which are accounted the onely cunning men in the world amongst us [e.g. the alchemists and other magus-figures], he shall see that they vse no outward meanes, but a sort of charmes: most of them so ridiculous and foolish, that a wise man must needes laugh at them, and euery one that hath but a sparke of religion, to loath & detest them.' See *The Anatomie of Sorcerie* (London, 1612).
25 It does not, however, go unnoticed by Robert Knoll in his *Ben Jonson's Plays: An Introduction*, appendix B, 198.
26 I quote from *The Geneva Bible: A Facsimile of the 1560 Edition*, intro. Lloyd E. Berry (Madison: University of Wisconsin Press, 1969).
27 William Blissett, 'The Venter Tripartite in *The Alchemist*.'
28 Jonas Barish provides an excellent account of Jonson's astounding range of specialized discourses in *Ben Jonson and the Language of Prose Comedy*.
29 See Edgar C. Knowlton, Jr, '"Kiss'd Our *Anos*" in Ben Jonson's *The Alchemist*.'
30 Alvin B. Kernan, *The Plot of Satire*.
31 Surly and Mammon represent the extremes of concealing and revealing secrets as outlined in Thomas Wright's *Passions of the Minde in Generall* (London, 1604):

> As some are so secret, that they neuer will open any thing, almost, touching their own affaires; so others contrarily are so simple and blabbish, that they discouer many of their conceits and matters, especially concerning themselues, to any man, almost at the first meeting. The former, commonly, are craftie, because friendship requireth some communication in secrets, principally, if he be an especiall friend: yet this offence may well be tolerated in this mischieuous world, and declining age, wherein profit is prized, and friendship dis-

pised; or at least, men loue men more for their owne interest, than for vertue. Therefore, if thou be wise, trust no man with that thou wouldest not haue publickely knowne, except he be a tried friend by long experience, yea, although he be thy friend. (119)

The opposition of profit prized and friendship despised speaks directly to Face's strategy of offering friendship and aid as an easy route to profit. In each case, what Wright calls the 'simple and blabbish' outstrips the 'craftie.'

32 See the note on IV.i.90 in HSS and also Charles Nicholl, *The Chemicall Theatre*, 19–22.
33 The most complete study of casuistry and the imaginative literature of the period is Camille Wells Slights, *The Casuistical Tradition in Shakespeare, Donne, Herbert, and Milton*. On the relationship of casuistry to the social codes and laws shortly after the age of Jonson see Margaret Sampson, 'Laxity and Liberty in Seventeenth-Century English Political Thought.'
34 Paul Goodman, *The Structure of Literature*, 82–103.
35 Keith Johnstone, *Impro: Improvisation and the Theatre*, 36.

Chapter Six

1 Jean de Marconville, *A Treatise of the Good and Evell Tounge. With the unstablenesse of the same, and also with the abuses thereof. With a discourse of the punishment which the Lord hath shewed on al those which through swearing and periuring themselues, haue broken Gods commandements: as by this Treatise most plainely appeareth.* (London, 1594), sigs. B3–4v.
2 HSS, 8:317–19, lines 280–6.
3 Michael Euchero concludes from his study of politics in *Catiline* that 'The tragedy of politics, in Jonson's view of it, derives from his disenchantment with the whole process of "Policy" or "Arte" which required that the state should survive, paradoxically, only by the travesty of the values by which, indeed, it ultimately hoped to survive.' See 'The Conscience of Politics and Jonson's *Catiline*,' 344.
4 Sallust, *The War with Catiline*, 51–3.
5 A perplexing question about the play is why Jonson chose to ignore Sallust's report of Caesar's excellent character (111–13) and instead to lend credence to what is usually reported as mere rumours of Caesar's involvement in Catiline's conspiracy. In his essay, '*Catiline* and the Nature of Jonson's Tragic Fable,' Joseph Allen Bryant, Jr, concludes that this emphasizes Cicero's political naïveté in brushing aside the threat posed by Caesar (272), while Robert Ornstein (*The Moral Vision of Jacobean Tragedy*, 100–2) argues that it reveals Cicero's Machiavellian shrewd-

ness in knowing when a contrary faction is too powerful to be openly identified and suppressed. I incline to Ornstein's view and also will argue that Jonson's handling of the continuing Caesar-Crassus conspiracy destabilizes the ending of Jonson's play.

6 Anne Barton, *Ben Jonson, Dramatist*, 163.
7 Jonson's attitude toward commoners is puzzling at best. David Norbrook argues that he was deeply suspicious of republicanism as not being sufficiently discriminating. See Norbrook's *Poetry and Politics in the English Renaissance*, 179-80. On the other hand, Bryant believes that Jonson's 'inclination toward what might be called classical republicanism is discernible in both his tragedies, but especially in *Catiline*' (273-4). Albert H. Tricomi shares this view in *Anticourt Drama in England, 1603-1642*, 73. Jonathan Goldberg's analysis of this issue in *Catiline* closely follows his interpretation of *Volpone* and *Sejanus* noted earlier: Cicero's absolutist government is just another version of Catiline's antirepublican conspiracy. See *James I and the Politics of Literature*, 193-203.
8 Lodowick Lloyd, *The Practice of Policy* (London, 1604), 38. Lloyd subsequently published two works that propose a link between Roman secrecy and events in Jacobean England. In *The Iubile of Britane* (London, 1607), he remarks on the Roman fascination with books 'full of mysticall Letters and secret signification' (8), and in *The Tragicomedie of Serpents* (London, 1607), he calls Robert Catesby, the convicted leader of the Gunpowder conspirators, 'a treacherous *Catelin*' (47). For a full working out of these links see B.N. DeLuna, *Jonson's Romish Plot: A Study of 'Catiline' and Its Historical Context*. This book is a rich mine of information, but in her effort to present an airtight case that *Catiline* is 'a classical parallelograph designed to "shadow forth" the most sensational "Romish" conspiracy of that or any other century: the still-controversial Gunpowder Plot of 1605' (32), DeLuna sometimes suffocates the political and dramatic vitality of Jonson's play with improbable seventeenth-century 'parallels.'
9 Eugene M. Waith, *The Herculean Hero in Marlowe, Chapman, Shakespeare and Dryden*. Compare the typically violent outburst of Cethegus against Cicero's stealing the starring role:
>   But your part
> Had not then beene so long, as now it is:
> I should haue quite defeated your oration;
> And slit that fine rhetoricall pipe of yours,
> I' the first *Scene*. (V.273-7)
10 Jonas Barish locates a more extended parody of *Catiline*, especially of Cicero's patriotic posturing and windy oratory, in the figure of Justice

Adam Overdo in *Bartholomew Fair*:
> Overdo's whole pose as savior of the state converts to burlesque what Jonson had just finished dramatizing with the most awful solemnity in *Catiline*. *Catiline* offers the spectacle of the authentic Cicero – or what Jonson took to be the authentic Cicero – endlessly orating against malefactors, tirelessly parading his patriotism, ceaselessly being acclaimed by the Senate for his zeal, ferreting out a plot against the state devised by a villain whose absolute blackness is not allowed a single mitigating trait. For Jonson to parody the admired Cicero in the crackbrained Overdo, and the conspiracy of Catiline in the 'enormities' of Bartholomew Fair, was to turn the tables on himself with a vengeance, to acknowledge the suspicion that Cicero was a canting prig and Catiline a preposterous bogey, to affirm once again the truthfulness of appearances, and so, in a sense, to heap ridicule on his own lifelong stance as watchdog of public morality.

See *Ben Jonson and the Language of Prose Comedy*, 213. Barish's rhetoric here is as fulsome and perfectly aimed as it nearly always is, though he fails to persuade Robert N. Watson (*Ben Jonson's Parodic Strategy: Literary Imperialism in the Comedies*, 259n49), whose notion of parody is rather narrowly focused on Jonson's appropriation of other authors' work.

11 James Mason, *The Anatomie of Sorcerie* (London, 1612), 75. Compare the definition of 'conjure' in John Bullokar, *An English Expositor* (London, 1616): 'To sweare or conspire together; to bind by oath, or vnder a great penalty.' See also Randle Cotgrave, *A Dictionarie of the French and English Tongues* (London, 1611): 'An adiuration, or coniuration; an earnest swearing vnto; also, th' exaction of an oath from others.'

12 Such fears had real grounds in the years immediately preceding the appearance of *Catiline*. For example, Robert Cecil was repeatedly accused of employing spies to harass English Catholics and of overplaying the plot to blow up Parliament in order to bring in stricter laws against them. In *An Answere to Certaine Scandalous Papers* (London, 1606), Cecil defends his 'endevours to countermine the secret mynes of Treason' (sig. D4v), severely scolding those who 'would condition' him 'to leave Plotting, as you tearme it, against Recusants' (sig. E). Jonson himself had long been part of this persecuted minority.

13 See my essay, 'Bodies of Text and Textualized Bodies in *Sejanus* and *Coriolanus*.'

14 See Ornstein's comment that Jonson 'allows Catiline to dominate only the first half of the tragedy; thereafter Catiline plays an increasingly minor role until he finally disappears in the fourth act. Only the first half of *Catiline* dramatizes the inner rot of conspiracy; the second half

portrays the patriotic struggle to preserve the state and introduces a second hero, the noble Consul Cicero' (*The Moral Vision*, 99).
15 Jongsook Lee, *Ben Jonson's Poesis: A Literary Dialectic of Ideal and History*, 31.
16 When Cicero resolves to let Catiline's ally, Caesar, go unpunished because it is 'an vnprofitable, dangerous act, / To stirre too many serpents vp at once' (IV. 528–9), he is in effect subscribing to the Machiavellian advice of the anonymous author of *The Cabinet-Council*: 'Whensoever a prince discovers a conspiracy, he must well consider the quality thereof, measuring the force of the conspirators with his own; and finding them many and mighty, the knowledge thereof is to be dissembled, until the prince's power be prepared to oppose them, otherwise he hazardeth his own security.' See *The Cabinet-Council: Containing the Chief Arts of Empire, and Mysteries of State; Discabineted in Political and Polemicall Aphorisms* in *The Works of Sir Walter Ralegh*, 8:100–1.
17 Annabel Patterson, 'Lyric and Society in Jonson's *Under-wood*,' 158.
18 G. A. Wilkes, editor of the modern-spelling Oxford edition of Jonson's plays, prints, 'To him that boards you next,' and glosses 'boards' as 'accosts,' alluding to *Twelfth Night*, I.iii.49–59. On Renaissance treatments of the open/closed body topos, see Peter Stallybrass, 'Patriarchal Territories: The Body Enclosed.' Stallybrass, pursuing the notion of transgression, has a great deal to say about unlicensed sexuality but does not share my emphasis on secrecy.

Chapter Seven

1 In the chorus following act II of *The Magnetic Lady*, Mr Probee chastises the snooping critic, Damplay, for asking whom the poet meant by a particular character: 'It is an insidious Question, Brother *Damplay*! Iniquity it selfe would not have urg'd it. It is picking the Lock of the Scene; not opening it the faire way with a Key' (lines 10–12). Though he never quite specifies just what he means by such a 'Key,' the ensuing critical discussion clearly implies that it would provide access only to the world of the theatre, not to the inner chambers of power. The general warning from *Bartholomew Fair* is explicitly repeated by Mr Probee: 'It is the solemne vice of interpretation, that deformes the figure of many a faire *Scene*, by drawing it awry' (lines 34–5).
2 Epistle to *Volpone*, lines 55–66. It appears that being in possession of a skeleton key that works on 'euery thing' isn't good enough. In *Volpone* and *The Alchemist* Jonson takes on, word for word, one such interpreter who claimed to hold the key to *all* the scriptures, namely Hugh Broughton.

3 Theodore B. Leinwand, *The City Staged: Jacobean City Comedy, 1603-1613*, 7 and 4.
4 On Jonson's habit of 'glancing' at contemporary events see Richard Dutton, *Ben Jonson: To the First Folio*, 133-55, as well as his *Mastering the Revels*.
5 *Bartholomew Faire, or variety of fancies* (London, 1641), 4 and 6 (misnumbered as 4). Frances Teague suggests that Jonson's play may have been familiar in 1641 through either its printed but not distributed edition of 1631 or its appearance in the 1641 folio. See *The Curious History of 'Bartholomew Fair,'* 53-4. Other descriptions of the fair are reviewed in Gamini Salgado, *The Elizabethan Underworld*, 65-78.
6 Jonson's tumultuous and deeply ambivalent relationship with his playhouse audiences is very well presented in George E. Rowe, Jr, 'Ben Jonson's Quarrel with His Audience and Its Renaissance Context,' and in John Gordon Sweeney, III, *Jonson and the Psychology of Public Theater*, 3-16. Richard Burt reviews the positions of Martin Butler, Kevin Sharpe, and Malcolm Smuts on the degree of heterogeneity in Jacobean and Caroline court audiences and argues that, at least later in his career, Jonson expressed no more hostility toward his audiences than did his rivals Philip Massinger, Thomas Carew, and William Davenant. See *Licensed by Authority*, 120-3.
7 For a stimulating discussion of the urinary construction of women in Jacobean plays, see Gail Kern Paster, 'Leaky Vessels: The Incontinent Women of City Comedy.' She is particularly perceptive about *Bartholomew Fair* (47-9).
8 As Katharine Eisaman Maus argues in her review of Robert N. Watson's *Ben Jonson's Parodic Strategy*, 'Jonsonian "reality" is always constructed in relation to prior texts, so that the correct distinction is not between "literature" and "life" but between good and bad methods and models for *imitation*.' I would add that this kind of intertextuality engages his audience in the effort to distinguish between good and bad methods of *interpretation*.
9 For a schematic account of the play's family groups and their disintegration see Richard Levin, 'The Structure of *Bartholomew Fair*.'
10 R.B. Parker, 'The Themes and Staging of *Bartholomew Fair*,' 299.
11 Newman says that soliloquies 'present a mind in conflict with itself by thematizing the theatrical conventions of dialogue.' See *Shakespeare's Rhetoric of Comic Character: Dramatic Convention in Classical and Renaissance Comedy*, 4.
12 One of the best brief histories of the cony-catching pamphlets and their literary uses is Jonathan Haynes, 'Representing the Underworld,' reproduced in his book, *The Social Relations of Jonson's Theater*, 99-118.

13 *The Life and Complete Works ... of Robert Greene*, 10:74.
14 See David McPherson, 'The Origins of Overdo: A Study in Jonsonian Invention.' Using information gleaned from the *Remembrancia preserved among the Archives of the City of London* (1878), McPherson corrects the misidentification originally made by C.S. Alden, the play's 1904 Yale editor. In doing so he calls attention to a variety of relevant contemporary texts that recommend and record state-spying.
15 George Whetstone, *A Mirour for Magestrates of Cyties* (London, 1584), sig. Aiiiv.
16 Gabriele Bernhard Jackson, *Vision and Judgment in Ben Jonson's Drama*.
17 The procedures for overseeing court performances are outlined by Richard Dutton in *Mastering the Revels*. These procedures were not, however, very systematically adhered to, and as Richard Burt maintains, the court and its representatives were far from coherent in offering a 'model of cultural legitimation' (*Licensed by Authority*, 123). Certainly it is the case that not all factions in Jonson's society subscribed to the authority of the Master of the Revels, which, for example, Zeal-of-the-Land Busy mocks with the phrase 'Master of the *Rebells*' [i.e. Satan] (V.v.19).
18 Particularly illuminating on the matter of warrants in the play are Ray L. Heffner, Jr, 'Unifying Symbols in the Comedy of Ben Jonson,' and Jackson I. Cope, '*Bartholomew Fair* as Blasphemy.'
19 Lester A. Beaurline argues imaginatively that the game of vapours is Jonson's travesty of formal Renaissance methods of disputation. See *Jonson and Elizabethan Comedy*, 217-30. Rosalind Miles helpfully distinguishes between a Jonsonian 'humour' (a 'psychological imbalance') and a 'vapour' ('an original sin in temperament'). See *Ben Jonson, His Craft and Art*, 190.
20 Parker, 'Themes and Staging,' 298-9, and Cope, '*Bartholomew Fair* as Blasphemy,' 142-6.
21 Theories of festivity and carnival in Renaissance drama have become widely known through C.L. Barber, *Shakespeare's Festive Comedy*; Mikhail Bakhtin, *Rabelais and His World*; Robert Weimann, *Shakespeare and the Popular Tradition in the Theater*; Michael Bristol, *Carnival and Theater: Plebeian Culture and the Structure of Authority in Renaissance England*; and François Laroque, *Shakespeare's Festive World*. For applications of these theories to *Bartholomew Fair* see, for example, Joel Kaplan, 'Dramatic and Moral Energy in Ben Jonson's *Bartholomew Fair*'; Jonathan Haynes, 'Festivity and the Dramatic Economy of Jonson's *Bartholomew Fair*,' rpt. in Haynes's *The Social Relations of Jonson's Theater*, 119-38; Michael Shapiro, 'The Casting of Flute: Planes of Illusion in *A Midsummer Night's Dream* and *Bartholomew Fair*'; and Leah S. Marcus, *The Politics of Mirth: Jonson, Herrick,*

Milton, Marvell, and the Defense of Old Holiday Pastimes, 38–63.
22 David Norbrook, *Poetry and Politics in the English Renaissance*, 183.
23 In his treatise, 'Of Hypocrisie,' Richard Greenham describes the first of these types as 'a perillous and close [hypocrite], wrapped vp round in a sheeps skin, that no man can spie him, but that eie that seeth all things' and the second as a man who, in himself, 'is delighted with faining any good, or intention of any euil.' He also caricatures the inept hypocrite who, like Busy, wraps himself 'in a sheeps skinne, but his eares hang out so long, that he is easily espied.' *The Workes of Richard Greenham*, revised by H[enry] H[olland] (London, 1605), 512.

   In a brief note entitled 'Hypocrites and Puppets in *Bartholomew Fair*,' Debora K. Shuger connects the puppets' Pauline confounding of Busy (Gal. 3:28; *Bartholomew Fair* V.v.104–5) with the 'central theme' of hypocrisy in the play. She concludes that 'The "message" then, of the play, is one of cosmic humility; the hypocrites must throw off their oversized masks and (like true Christians) sit down to dinner with thieves and publicans' (72–3). I have some reservations about whether such a Christian thematic is actually realized in the play.
24 Daniel Dyke, *The Mystery of Selfe-Deceiuing* (London, 1615), sig. A3r-v.
25 See Jonas Barish, *Ben Jonson and the Language of Prose Comedy*, 201–3 and Camille Wells Slights, *The Casuistical Tradition in Shakespeare, Donne, Herbert, and Milton*, 35–43.
26 John Selden, *Table-Talk* (1689), as quoted in HSS, 10:213.
27 Jonas Barish, *The Antitheatrical Prejudice*.
28 Patricia Fumerton, '"Secret" Arts: Elizabethan Miniatures and Sonnets,' 125. This material also appears in Fumerton's book, *Cultural Aesthetics: Renaissance Literature and the Practice of Social Ornament*.
29 Thomas Nashe's preface to *Syr P. S. his Astrophel and Stella* (London, 1591), sig. A3.
30 The play was performed at the Hope Theatre 31 October 1614 (Induction, line 68) by the Lady Elizabeth's Servants (Title-page, 1631 folio) and at court on 1 November. See Frederick G. Fleay's *A Biographical Chronicle of the English Drama (1559–1642)*, 1:376 and HSS, 2:131.
31 George E. Rowe, *Distinguishing Jonson: Imitation, Rivalry, and the Direction of a Dramatic Career*, 149–50. Rowe believes that Jonson, too, falls victim to his own 'relentless dismantling of difference' (154).
32 Robert Greene, *The Third Part of Conny-Catching* (1592), as excerpted in *Narrative and Dramatic Sources of Shakespeare*, ed. Geoffrey Bullough, 8:218.
33 C.H. Herford and Percy and Evelyn Simpson reject C.R. Baskerville's surmise that Jonson knew *Sir Thomas More*, a play in which nearly everyone *except* Jonson seems to have had a hand, preferring to argue instead

Notes to pages 166–77

that Jonson and the *More* authors drew on the same 'traditional story' (HSS, 10:167–9).

34 Richard Burt speaks of 'generic indefinition' (108) in the play because of the contradictions between its happy and its mercenary outcome, a contradiction paralleled in the play's theatrical politics by the licensing of entertainment forms that are radically anti-authoritarian. See Burt's *Licensed by Authority*, 100–9.

35 Jonson comments in Epigram 92, 'The New Crie,' that his ever-busy, over-ripe 'statemen' will 'talk yet' about the 'poulder-plot,' presumably well after the fact. As late as 1762 G.A. Stevens writes glowingly of 'Punch's whole play of the Gunpowder plot.' See HSS, 10:208. Jonson's response to the miraculous preservation of London in this crisis was not nearly so honorific. He seems to have viewed puppet motions as an appropriately bathetic legacy for the over-reaction of the nation to this particular conspiracy.

36 See Stephen Orgel, *The Illusion of Power: Political Theater in the English Renaissance* on sight-lines and the King's chair in masque performances. For a slightly different reading of Jonson's epilogue to *Bartholomew Fair*, one that stresses its kinship with Erasmus's *Praise of Folly*, see Douglas Duncan, *Ben Jonson and the Lucianic Tradition*, 212–13.

37 Busy denounces Leatherhead for being, 'all *license, euen licentiousnesse* it selfe' (V.v.16). In his book, *The Place of the Stage: License, Play, and Power in Renaissance England*, Steven Mullaney argues that the culture placed this drama beyond the bounds of all licence, in the Liberties of London, that marginal or liminal space that rendered tenuous any claim to official control. Richard Burt finds in Jonson's request for royal licence a thoroughly circular outcome: 'under the rubric of dramatic art, the king licenses the subversion of authority within the fair, and that subversion in turn issues in an invitation to James to reassert his political authority' (*Licensed by Authority*, 102).

38 Janet Clare, '*Art Made Tongue-Tied by Authority*,' 19.

39 Jonson calls the lawyer in *The Staple of News* 'Picklock.'

Conclusion

1 Steven Marcus, *The Other Victorians: A Study of Sexuality and Pornography in Mid-Nineteenth-Century England*.
2 Sissela Bok, *Secrets: On the Ethics of Concealment and Revelation*, 26.
3 See *Dio's Roman History*, 7:213.
4 Michel Foucault, 'Nietzsche, Genealogy, History,' 142.
5 Frank Kermode, *The Genesis of Secrecy: On the Interpretation of Narrative*, 144.

Works Cited

Abel, Elizabeth, ed. *Writing and Sexual Difference*. Chicago: University of Chicago Press, 1982.
Amussen, Susan. 'Gender, Family and Social Order, 1560-1725.' In *Order and Disorder in Early Modern England*. Ed. Anthony Fletcher and John Stevenson. Cambridge: Cambridge University Press, 1985. 196-217.
- *An Ordered Society: Gender and Class in Early Modern England*. Oxford: Basil Blackwell, 1988.
Anderson, Mark. 'Structure and Response in *Volpone*.' *Renaissance and Modern Studies*, 19 (1975): 47-71.
Anon. *Bartholomew Faire, or Variety of Fancies*. London, 1641.
- *The Cabinet-Council: Containing the Chief Arts of Empire, and Mysteries of State; Discabineted in Political and Polemicall Aphorisms*. In *The Works of Sir Walter Ralegh*. Oxford: Oxford University Press, 1829. 8 vols.
Archer, John Michael. *Sovereignty and Intelligence: Spying and Court Culture in English Renaissance Writing*. Stanford: Stanford University Press, 1993.
Ayers, Philip J. 'Jonson, Northampton, and the Treason in *Sejanus*.' *Modern Philology*, 80 (1983): 356-63.
Bacon, Roger. *The Mirror of Alchimy*. London, 1597.
Bakhtin, Mikhail. *Rabelais and His World*. Trans. Helene Iswolsky. Cambridge, Mass.: MIT Press, 1968.
Bancroft, Richard. *Dangerous Positions and Proceedings, published and practised within this iland of Brytaine*. London, 1593.
Barber, C.L. *Shakespeare's Festive Comedy*. Princeton: Princeton University Press, 1959.
Barish, Jonas A. *The Antitheatrical Prejudice*. Berkeley: University of California Press, 1981.
- *Ben Jonson and the Language of Prose Comedy*. Cambridge, Mass.: Harvard University Press, 1960.

- ed. *Ben Jonson: A Collection of Critical Essays.* Englewood Cliffs: Prentice-Hall, 1963.
Barkan, Leonard. *Nature's Work of Art: The Human Body as Image of the World.* New Haven: Yale University Press, 1975.
Barker, Francis. *The Tremulous Private Body: Essays on Subjection.* London: Methuen, 1984.
Barroll, Leeds. *Politics, Plague, and Shakespeare's Theater: The Stuart Years.* Ithaca: Cornell University Press, 1991.
Barton, Anne. *Ben Jonson, Dramatist.* Cambridge: Cambridge University Press, 1984.
Beaurline, Lester A. *Jonson and Elizabethan Comedy.* San Marino: Huntington Library Press, 1978.
Bellman, Beryl L. *The Language of Secrecy: Symbols and Metaphors in Poro Ritual.* New Brunswick: Rutgers University Press, 1984. Foreword by James Fernandez.
Belsey, Catherine. *The Subject of Tragedy: Identity and Difference in Renaissance Drama.* London: Methuen, 1985.
Bevington, David. *Medieval Drama.* Boston: Houghton Mifflin, 1975.
Blissett, William. 'The Venter Tripartite in *The Alchemist.*' *Studies in English Literature,* 8 (1968): 323-34.
Bok, Sissela. *Secrets: On the Ethics of Concealment and Revelation.* New York: Vintage Books, 1984.
Boose, Lynda E. 'Scolding Brides and Bridling Scolds: Taming the Woman's Unruly Member.' *Shakespeare Quarterly,* 42 (1991): 179-213.
Bossy, John. *Giordano Bruno and the Embassy Affair.* New Haven: Yale University Press, 1991.
Boughner, Daniel C. 'Jonson's Use of Lipsius in *Sejanus.*' *Modern Language Notes,* 73 (1958): 247-55.
Bray, Alan. *Homosexuality in Renaissance England.* London: Gay Men's Press, 1982.
Bristol, Michael D. *Carnival and Theater: Plebeian Culture and the Structure of Authority in Renaissance England.* London: Methuen, 1985.
- 'Charivari and the Comedy of Abjection in *Othello.*' In *True Rites and Maimed Rites.* Ed. Linda Woodbridge and Edward Berry. Urbana: University of Illinois Press, 1992. 75-97.
Bryant, Joseph Allen, Jr. '*Catiline* and the Nature of Jonson's Tragic Fable.' *PMLA,* 69 (1954): 265-77.
Bullokar, John. *An English Expositor.* London, 1616.
Bullough, Geoffrey, ed. *Narrative and Dramatic Sources of Shakespeare.* London: Routledge and Kegan Paul, 1957-75. 8 vols.
Burke, Peter. 'Tacitism.' In *Tacitus.* Ed. T.A. Dorey. London: Routledge and Kegan Paul, 1969. 149-71.
Burt, Richard A. '"A Dangerous Rome": Shakespeare's *Julius Caesar* and the

Discursive Determinism of Cultural Politics.' In *Contending Kingdoms: Historical, Psychological, and Feminist Approaches to the Literature of Sixteenth-Century England and France.* Ed. Marie-Rose Logan and Peter L. Rudnytsky. Ithaca: Cornell University Press, 1991. 109-27.
- *Licensed by Authority: Ben Jonson and the Discourses of Censorship.* Ithaca: Cornell University Press, 1993.
- '"Licensed by Authority": Ben Jonson and the Politics of the Early Stuart Theater.' *ELH*, 54 (1987): 529-60.
Cecil, Robert. *An Answere to Certaine Scandalous Papers.* London, 1606.
Chaucer, Geoffrey. *The Works of Geoffrey Chaucer.* Ed. F.N. Robinson. Boston: Houghton Mifflin, 1957.
Christianson, Paul. *Reformers and Babylon: English Apocalyptic Visions from the Reformation to the Eve of the Civil War.* Toronto: University of Toronto Press, 1978.
Clare, Janet. *'Art Made Tongue-Tied by Authority': Elizabethan and Jacobean Dramatic Censorship.* Manchester: Manchester University Press, 1990.
Claudianus, Claudius. *Claudian.* Trans. Maurice Platnauer. Loeb Classical Library. London: William Heinemann, 1922. 2 vols.
Cope, Jackson I. *'Bartholomew Fair as Blasphemy.' Renaissance Drama,* 8 (1965): 127-52.
Copjec, Joan. 'The Orthopsychic Subject: Film Theory and the Reception of Lacan.' *October,* 49 (1989): 53-71.
Cotgrave, Randle. *A Dictionarie of the French and English Tongues.* London, 1611.
Cowell, John. *The Interpreter, or Booke containing the signification of words.* London, 1607.
Creaser, John. 'The Popularity of Jonson's Tortoise.' *Review of English Studies,* 27 (1976): 38-46.
Crewe, Jonathan V. 'God or the Good Physician: The Rational Playwright in *The Comedy of Errors.*' *Genre,* 15 (1982): 203-23.
D'Acuto, Afinati. *The Dumbe Divine Speaker.* Trans. A[nthony] M[unday]. London, 1605.
Davis, Natalie Zemon. 'The Reasons of Misrule: Youth Groups and Charivaris in Sixteenth Century France.' *Past and Present,* 50 (1971): 41-75.
Dawson, Anthony. 'Giving the Finger: Puns and Transgression in *The Changeling.*' *Elizabethan Theatre* XII (1993). 93-112.
Dean, Leonard F. 'Three Notes on Comic Morality: Celia, Bobadill, and Falstaff.' *Studies in English Literature,* 16 (1976): 263-71.
Dekker, Thomas. *Dramatic Works.* Ed. Fredson Bowers. Cambridge: Cambridge University Press, 1953-61. 4 vols.
DeLuna, B.N. *Jonson's Romish Plot: A Study of 'Catiline' and Its Historical Context.* Oxford: Clarendon Press, 1967.
Derrida, Jacques. 'The Law of Genre.' *Glyph: Textual Studies,* 7 (1980): 202-32.

Dio Cassius. *Dio's Roman History*. Trans. Earnest Cary. Loeb Classical Library. London: William Heinemann, 1914–27. 9 vols.

Dollimore, Jonathan. *Radical Tragedy: Religion, Ideology and Power in the Drama of Shakespeare and His Contemporaries*. Chicago: University of Chicago Press, 1984.

Donaldson, Ian. *The World Upside-Down: Comedy from Jonson to Fielding*. Oxford: Clarendon Press, 1970.

Donne, John. *The Satires, Epigrams and Verse Letters*. Ed. W. Milgate. Oxford: Clarendon Press, 1967.

– *Selected Prose*. Ed. Helen Gardner and Timothy Healy. Oxford: Clarendon Press, 1967.

Dryden, John. *The Essays of John Dryden*. Ed. W.P. Ker. New York: Russell and Russell, 1961. 2 vols.

Duncan, Douglas. *Ben Jonson and the Lucianic Tradition*. Cambridge: Cambridge University Press, 1979.

Dutton, Richard. 'Ben Jonson and the Master of the Revels.' In *Theatre and Government under the Early Stuarts*. Ed. J.R. Mulryne and Margaret Shewring. Cambridge: Cambridge University Press, 1993. 57–86.

– *Ben Jonson: To the First Folio*. Cambridge: Cambridge University Press, 1983.

– *Mastering the Revels: The Regulation and Censorship of English Renaissance Drama*. Iowa City: University of Iowa Press, 1991.

Dyke, Daniel. *The Mystery of Selfe-Deceiuing*. London, 1615.

Eccles, Mark. 'Jonson and the Spies.' *Review of English Studies*, 13 (1937): 385–97.

Elton, G.R. *Policy and Police: The Enforcement of the Reformation in the Age of Thomas Cromwell*. Cambridge: Cambridge University Press, 1972.

Epstein, Julia. 'Either/Or – Neither/Both: Sexual Ambiguity and the Ideology of Gender.' *Genders*, 7 (1990): 99–142.

Erasmus, Desiderius. *Of the Yong Man and the Evill Disposed Woman*. Trans. Nicholas Leigh. London, 1568.

– *Moriae Encomium*. Basel, 1515.

– *The Praise of Folly*. Trans. Clarence H. Miller. New Haven: Yale University Press, 1979.

Estienne, Charles. *The Defense of Contraries*. Trans. Anthony Munday. London, 1593.

Euchero, Michael J.C. 'The Conscience of Politics and Jonson's *Catiline*.' *Studies in English Literature*, 6 (1966): 341–56.

Evans, Robert C. *Ben Jonson and the Poetics of Patronage*. Lewisburg: Bucknell University Press, 1989.

Finkelpearl, Philip J. '"The Comedians' Liberty": Censorship of the Jacobean Stage Reconsidered.' *English Literary Renaissance*, 16 (1986): 123–38.

Fish, Stanley. *Self-Consuming Artifacts: The Experience of Seventeenth-Century Literature*. Berkeley: University of California Press, 1972.

Fleay, Frederick G. *A Biographical Chronicle of the English Drama (1559-1642).* London, 1891. Rpt. New York: Burt Franklin, 1962. 2 vols.
Forset, Edward. *A Comparative Discourse of the Bodies Natural and Politique.* London, 1606.
Foucault, Michel. *Discipline and Punish: The Birth of the Prison.* Trans. Alan Sheridan. New York: Pantheon, 1977.
– *The Foucault Reader.* Ed. Paul Rabinow. New York: Pantheon Books, 1984.
– 'Nietzsche, Genealogy, History.' In *Language, Counter-Memory, Practice: Selected Essays and Interviews.* Ed. and trans. Donald F. Bouchard and Sherry Simon. Ithaca: Cornell University Press, 1977. 139-64.
– 'What Is an Author?' In *Textual Strategies: Perspectives in Post-Structuralist Criticism.* Ed. Josué V. Harari. Ithaca: Cornell University Press, 1979. 141-60.
French, Peter J. *John Dee: The World of an Elizabethan Magus.* London: Routledge and Kegan Paul, 1972.
Frye, Northrop. *A Natural Perspective: The Development of Shakespearean Comedy and Romance.* New York: Columbia University Press, 1965.
Fuller, Thomas. *The Holy State.* Cambridge, 1642.
Fumerton, Patricia. '"Secret" Arts: Elizabethan Miniatures and Sonnets.' In *Representing the English Renaissance.* Ed. Stephen Greenblatt. Berkeley: University of California Press, 1988. 93-133.
– *Cultural Aesthetics: Renaissance Literature and the Practice of Social Ornament.* Chicago: University of Chicago Press, 1991.
Geneva Bible: A Facsimile of the 1560 Edition. Introduction Lloyd E. Berry. Madison: University of Wisconsin Press, 1969.
Ginzburg, Carlo. 'High and Low: The Theme of Forbidden Knowledge in the Sixteenth and Seventeenth Centuries.' *Past and Present* 73 (1976): 28-41.
Girard, René. 'Myth and Ritual in Shakespeare: *A Midsummer Night's Dream.*' In *Textual Strategies: Perspectives in Post-Structuralist Criticism.* Ed. Josué V. Harari. Ithaca: Cornell University Press, 1977. 187-212.
Gohlke, Madelon. '"I wooed thee with my sword": Shakespeare's Tragic Paradigms.' In *The Woman's Part: Feminist Criticism of Shakespeare.* Ed. Carolyn Ruth Swift Lenz, Gayle Greene, and Carol Thomas Neely. Urbana: University of Illinois Press, 1980. 150-70.
Goldberg, Jonathan. *James I and the Politics of Literature: Jonson, Shakespeare, Donne, and Their Contemporaries.* Baltimore: Johns Hopkins University Press, 1983.
– 'Shakespearean Inscriptions: The Voicing of Power.' In *Shakespeare and the Question of Theory.* Ed. Patricia Parker and Geoffrey Hartman. New York: Methuen, 1985. 116-37.
Goodman, Paul. *The Structure of Literature.* Chicago: University of Chicago Press, 1954.

Gordon, D.J. 'Rolls and Mysteries' (1965). Rpt. in *The Renaissance Imagination*. Ed. Stephen Orgel. Berkeley: University of California Press, 1975. 3–23.

Greenblatt, Stephen J. 'The False Ending in *Volpone*.' *Journal of English and Germanic Philology*, 75 (1976): 90–104.

– *Shakespearean Negotiations: The Circulation of Social Energy in Renaissance England*. Berkeley: University of California Press, 1988.

Greene, Robert. *The Life and Complete Works ... of Robert Greene*. Ed. Alexander Grosart. Rpt. New York: Russell and Russell, 1964. 15 vols.

Greene, Thomas M. 'Ben Jonson and the Centered Self.' *Studies in English Literature*, 10 (1970): 325–48.

– 'Resurrecting Rome: The Double Task of the Humanist Imagination.' In *Rome in the Renaissance: The City and the Myth*. Ed. Paul A. Ramsey. Binghamton: Center for Medieval and Early Renaissance Studies, 1982. 41–54.

Greenham, Richard. *The Workes of Richard Greenham*. Revised by H[enry] H[olland]. London, 1605.

Hallahan, Huston D. 'Silence, Eloquence, and Chatter in Jonson's *Epicoene*.' *Huntington Library Quarterly*, 40 (1977): 117–27.

Haynes, Jonathan. 'Festivity and the Dramatic Economy of Ben Jonson's *Bartholomew Fair*.' *ELH*, 51 (1984): 645–68.

– 'Representing the Underworld: *The Alchemist*.' *Studies in Philology*, 86 (1989): 18–41.

– *The Social Relations of Jonson's Theater*. Cambridge: Cambridge University Press, 1992.

Hazlitt, William. *Lectures Chiefly on the Dramatic Literature of the Age of Elizabeth*. London: Stodart and Steuart, 1820.

Heffner, Ray L., Jr. 'Unifying Symbols in the Comedy of Ben Jonson.' In *English Stage Comedy*. Ed. W.K. Wimsatt. English Institute Essays, 1954. New York: Columbia University Press, 1955. 74–97.

Helgerson, Richard. *Self-Crowned Laureates: Spenser, Jonson, Milton, and the Literary System*. Berkeley: University of California Press, 1983.

Helms, Lorraine. 'Roaring Girls and Silent Women: The Politics of Androgyny on the Jacobean Stage.' In *Women in Theatre*. Themes in Drama III. Cambridge: Cambridge University Press, 1989. 59–73.

Herz, Neil. 'Dora's Secrets, Freud's Techniques.' *Diacritics*, 13 (1983): 65–80. Rpt. in *Contemporary Literary Criticism: Modernism through Poststructuralism*. Ed. Robert Davis. New York: Longman, 1986.

Hester, M. Thomas. *Kinde Pitty and Brave Scorn*. Durham: University of North Carolina Press, 1982.

Hic Mulier, or the Man-Woman, Being a Medicine to Cure the Coltish Desease of the Staggers in the Masculine-Feminine of Our Times. Exprest in a Briefe Declamation. London, 1620.

Howard, Jean E. 'Crossdressing, the Theatre, and Gender Struggle in Early Modern England.' *Shakespeare Quarterly*, 39 (1988): 418-40.
- and Marion O'Connor, eds. *Shakespeare Reproduced: The Text in History and Ideology.* New York: Routledge, 1987.
Hume, Martin. *Treason and Plot.* London: Eveleigh Nash, 1908.
Jackson, Gabriele Bernhard. *Vision and Judgment in Ben Jonson's Drama.* New Haven: Yale University Press, 1968.
James I. *The Political Works of James I.* Ed. Charles H. McIlwain. Cambridge, Mass.: Harvard University Press, 1918.
- *The True Lawe of Free Monarchies: or the reciprock and mutuall duetie betwixt a free king, and his naturall subjects.* Edinburgh, 1598.
Jardine, Lisa. *Still Harping on Daughters: Women and Drama in the Age of Shakespeare.* Sussex: Harvester Press, 1983.
Jensen, Ejner. *Ben Jonson's Comedies on the Modern Stage.* Ann Arbor: UMI Research Press, 1985.
Johnstone, Keith. *Impro: Improvisation and the Theatre.* New York: Theatre Arts Books, 1979.
Jonson, Ben. *The Alchemist.* Ed. Alvin B. Kernan. New Haven: Yale University Press, 1974.
- *Ben Jonson.* Ed. C.H. Herford and Percy and Evelyn Simpson. Oxford: Oxford University Press, 1925-52. 11 vols.
- *The Complete Plays of Ben Jonson.* Ed. G.A. Wilkes. Oxford: Oxford University Press, 1981-82. 3 vols.
- *Epicoene, or The Silent Woman.* Ed. L.A. Beaurline. Regents Renaissance Drama Series. Lincoln: University of Nebraska Press, 1966.
- *Sejanus.* Ed. Philip J. Ayers. The Revels Plays. Manchester: Manchester University Press, 1990.
- *Sejanus.* Ed. Jonas A. Barish. New Haven: Yale University Press, 1965.
- *Volpone.* Ed. Alvin B. Kernan. New Haven: Yale University Press, 1962.
- *Volpone.* Ed. R.B. Parker. The Revels Plays. Manchester: University of Manchester Press, 1983.
Jowett, John. '"Fall before this Booke": The 1605 Quarto of *Sejanus*.' *Text: Transactions of the Society for Textual Scholarship*, 4 (1988): 279-95.
Kaplan, Joel. 'Dramatic and Moral Energy in Ben Jonson's *Bartholomew Fair*.' *Renaissance Drama*, n.s. 3 (1970): 137-56.
Kastan, David Scott, and Peter Stallybrass, eds. *Staging the Renaissance: Reinterpretations of Elizabethan and Jacobean Drama.* New York: Routledge, 1991.
Kay, W. David. 'Jonson's Urbane Gallants: Humanistic Contexts for *Epicoene*.' *Huntington Library Quarterly*, 39 (1975-76): 251-66.
Kelso, Ruth. *Doctrine for the Lady of the Renaissance.* Urbana: University of Illinois Press, 1956.

Kermode, Frank. *The Genesis of Secrecy: On the Interpretation of Narrative.* Cambridge, Mass.: Harvard University Press, 1979.
Kernan, Alvin B. *The Plot of Satire.* New Haven: Yale University Press, 1965.
Kiefer, Frederick. *Fortune and Elizabethan Tragedy.* San Marino: Huntington Library, 1983.
Knights, L.C. *Drama and Society in the Age of Jonson.* 1937. Rpt. New York: W.W. Norton, 1968.
Knoll, Robert E. *Ben Jonson's Plays: An Introduction.* Lincoln: University of Nebraska Press, 1964.
Knowlton, Edgar C., Jr. '"Kiss'd Our *Anos*" in Ben Jonson's *The Alchemist.*' *Maledicta*, 8 (1984–5): 119–22.
Lambi, Giovanni Battista. *The Revelation of the Secret Spirit. Declaring the Secret of Alchemie.* Trans. R.N.E. Gent. London, 1623.
Lando, Ortensio. *Paradossi Cioe, Sententie fori del commun parere.* Lyons, 1543; Venice, 1544.
Lang, Andrew. *James VI and the Gowrie Mystery.* London: Longman, Green, 1902.
Lanier, Douglas. 'Masculine Silence: *Epicoene* and Jonsonian Stylistics.' Unpublished paper presented at the Modern Language Association of America Convention. Toronto, 1993.
Laqueur, Thomas. *Making Sex: Body and Gender from the Greeks to Freud.* Cambridge, Mass.: Harvard University Press, 1990.
Laroque, François. *Shakespeare's Festive World: Elizabethan Seasonal Entertainment and the Professional Stage.* Trans. Janet Lloyd. Cambridge: Cambridge University Press, 1991.
Lee, Jongsook. *Ben Jonson's Poesis: A Literary Dialectic of Ideal and History.* Charlottesville: University Press of Virginia, 1989.
Leggatt, Alexander. *Ben Jonson: His Vision and His Art.* London: Methuen, 1981.
– *Citizen Comedy in the Age of Shakespeare.* Toronto: University of Toronto Press, 1973.
– 'The Suicide of Volpone.' *University of Toronto Quarterly*, 39 (1969): 19–32.
Leigh, William. *Great Britains great deliverance from ... popish powder.* London, 1606.
Leinwand, Theodore B. *The City Staged: Jacobean City Comedy, 1603–1613.* Madison: University of Wisconsin Press, 1986.
Levin, Richard. 'The Structure of *Bartholomew Fair.*' *PMLA*, 80 (1965): 172–9.
Levine, Laura. 'Men in Women's Clothing: Anti-Theatricality and Effeminization from 1579 to 1642.' *Criticism*, 28 (1986): 121–43.
Lloyd, Lodowick. *The Iubile of Britane.* London, 1607.
– *The Practice of Policy.* London, 1604.
– *The Tragicomedie of Serpents.* London, 1607.
Macfarlane, Alan. *The Family Life of Ralph Josselin.* Cambridge: Cambridge University Press, 1970.

Manzini, Giovanni Battista. *Politicall Observations upon the fall of Seianus.* Trans. Sir T[homas] H[awkins]. London, 1634.
Marconville, Jean de. *A Treatise of the Good and Evell Tounge.* London, 1594.
Marcus, Leah S. *The Politics of Mirth: Jonson, Herrick, Milton, Marvell, and the Defense of Old Holiday Pastimes.* Chicago: University of Chicago Press, 1986.
- *Puzzling Shakespeare: Local Reading and Its Discontents.* Berkeley: University of California Press, 1988.
Marcus, Steven. *The Other Victorians: A Study of Sexuality and Pornography in Mid-Nineteenth-Century England.* New York: Basic Books, 1966.
Marotti, Arthur F. *John Donne, Coterie Poet.* Madison: University of Wisconsin Press, 1986.
- 'The Self-Reflexive Art of Ben Jonson's *Sejanus.*' *Texas Studies in Literature and Language,* 12 (1970): 197-220.
Mason, James. *The Anatomie of Sorcerie.* London, 1612.
Massinger, Philip. *The City Madam.* Ed. Cyrus Hoy. Regents Renaissance Drama Series. Lincoln: University of Nebraska Press, 1964.
Maus, Katharine Eisaman. *Ben Jonson and the Roman Frame of Mind.* Princeton: Princeton University Press, 1984.
- Review of Robert N. Watson, *Ben Jonson's Parodic Strategy. Renaissance Quarterly,* 41 (1988): 532-3.
McDonald, Russ. *Shakespeare and Jonson, Jonson and Shakespeare.* Lincoln: University of Nebraska Press, 1988.
McPherson, David. 'The Origins of Overdo: A Study in Jonsonian Invention.' *Modern Language Quarterly,* 37 (1976): 221-33.
Memorials of Affairs of State in the Reigns of Q. Elizabeth and K. James I. Ed. Edmund Sawyer. London, 1725. 3 vols.
Middleton, Thomas, and William Rowley. *The Changeling.* Ed. George Walton Williams. Regents Renaissance Drama Series. Lincoln: University of Nebraska Press, 1966.
Miles, Rosalind. *Ben Jonson, His Craft and Art.* London: Routledge, 1990.
Millard, Barbara. '"An Acceptable Violence": Sexual Contest in Jonson's *Epicoene.*' *Medieval and Renaissance Drama in England,* 1 (1984): 143-58.
Miller, D.A. 'Secret Subjects, Open Secrets.' *Dickens Studies Annual,* 14 (1985): 17-38.
Miller, Henry Knight. 'The Paradoxical Encomium with Special Reference to Its Vogue in England, 1600-1800.' *Modern Philology,* 53 (1956): 145-78.
Milton, John. *Complete Poems and Major Prose.* Ed. Merritt Y. Hughes. New York: Odyssey 1957.
Mirabelli, Philip. 'Silence, Wit, and Wisdom in *The Silent Woman.*' *Studies in English Literature,* 29 (1989): 307-36.

Montrose, Louis Adrian. '"Shaping Fantasies": Figurations of Gender and Power in Elizabethan Culture.' *Representations*, 2 (1983): 61-94.

Mooney, Michael E. *Shakespeare's Dramatic Transactions*. Durham: Duke University Press, 1990.

Mullaney, Steven. *The Place of the Stage: License, Play, and Power in Renaissance England*. Chicago: University of Chicago Press, 1988.

Nashe, Thomas, Preface to *Syr P.S. his Astrophel and Stella*. London, 1591.

Nelson, Alan H. 'Some Configurations of Staging in Medieval English Drama.' *Medieval English Drama: Essays Critical and Contextual*. Ed. Jerome Taylor and Alan H. Nelson. Chicago: University of Chicago Press, 1975. 116-47.

Newman, Karen. 'City Talk: Women and Commodification.' *ELH*, 57 (1989): 503-18.

– *Fashioning Femininity and English Renaissance Drama*. Chicago: University of Chicago Press, 1991.

– *Shakespeare's Rhetoric of Comic Character: Dramatic Convention and Renaissance Comedy*. London: Methuen, 1985.

Newton, Richard C. '"Ben./Jonson": The Poet in the Poems.' In *Two Renaissance Mythmakers: Christopher Marlowe and Ben Jonson*. Ed. Alvin Kernan. Selected Papers from the English Institute 1975-76. Baltimore: Johns Hopkins University Press, 1977. 165-95.

Nicholl, Charles. *The Chemicall Theatre*. London: Routledge and Kegan Paul, 1980.

Norbrook, David. *Poetry and Politics in the English Renaissance*. London: Routledge and Kegan Paul, 1984.

Orgel, Stephen. *The Illusion of Power: Political Theater in the English Renaissance*. Berkeley: University of California Press, 1975.

– *The Jonsonian Masque*. Cambridge, Mass.: Harvard University Press, 1965.

Ornstein, Robert. *The Moral Vision of Jacobean Tragedy*. Madison: University of Wisconsin Press, 1960.

Osborne, Francis. *The Secret History of the Court of James the First* (1658). Edinburgh: James Ballantyne and Co., 1811. 2 vols.

Parfitt, George. *Ben Jonson: Public Poet and Private Man*. New York: Barnes and Noble, 1976.

Parker, R.B. 'The Themes and Staging of *Bartholomew Fair*.' *University of Toronto Quarterly*, 39 (1970): 293-309.

Paster, Gail Kern. 'Ben Jonson's Comedy of Limitation.' *Studies in Philology*, 72 (1975): 51-71.

– *The Body Embarrassed: Drama and the Disciplines of Shame in Early Modern England*. Ithaca: Cornell University Press, 1993.

– *The Idea of the City in the Age of Shakespeare*. Athens: University of Georgia Press, 1985.

- 'Leaky Vessels: The Incontinent Women of City Comedy.' *Renaissance Drama*, 18 (1987): 43-65.
Patterson, Annabel. *Censorship and Interpretation: The Conditions of Writing and Reading in Early Modern England*. Madison: University of Wisconsin Press, 1984.
- 'Lyric and Society in Jonson's *Under-wood*.' In *Lyric Poetry: Beyond New Criticism*. Ed. Chaviva Hošek and Patricia Parker. Ithaca: Cornell University Press, 1985. 148-63.
- '"Roman-cast Similitude": Ben Jonson and the English Use of Roman History.' In *Rome in the Renaissance*. Ed. Paul A. Ramsey. Binghamton: Medieval and Renaissance Texts and Studies, 1982. 381-94.
Potter, Lois. *Secret Rites and Secret Writing: Royalist Literature, 1641-1660*. Cambridge: Cambridge University Press, 1989.
Pound, Ezra. *Collected Shorter Poems*. London: Faber and Faber, 1971.
Proceedings of Parliament 1610. Ed. Elizabeth Read Foster. New Haven: Yale University Press, 1966. 2 vols.
Prynne, William. *Histrio-mastix*. London, 1633.
Puttenham, George. *The Arte of English Poesie*. Ed. Gladys Doidge Willcock and Alice Walker. Cambridge: Cambridge University Press, 1936.
Rackin, Phyllis. 'Genealogical Anxiety and Female Authority: The Return of the Repressed in Shakespeare's Histories.' In *Contending Kingdoms: Historical, Psychological, and Feminist Approaches to the Literature of Sixteenth-Century England and France*. Ed. Marie-Rose Logan and Peter L. Rudnytsky. Detroit: Wayne State University Press, 1991. 323-45.
- *Stages of History: Shakespeare's English Chronicles*. Ithaca: Cornell University Press, 1990.
Read, Conyers. *Mr. Secretary Walsingham and the Policy of Queen Elizabeth*. Oxford: Clarendon Press, 1925. 3 vols.
Ricks, Christopher. '*Sejanus* and Dismemberment.' *Modern Language Notes*, 76 (1961): 301-8.
Riggs, David. *Ben Jonson: A Life*. Cambridge, Mass.: Harvard University Press, 1989.
Rose, Mark. *Shakespearean Design*. Cambridge, Mass.: Harvard University Press, 1972.
Rowe, George E. 'Ben Jonson's Quarrel with His Audience and Its Renaissance Context.' *Studies in Philology*, 81 (1984): 438-60.
- *Distinguishing Jonson: Imitation, Rivalry, and the Direction of a Dramatic Career*. Lincoln: University of Nebraska Press, 1988.
Ruthven, John. *The Earle of Gowries Conspiracie against the Kings Maiestie of Scotland*. London, 1600.
Salgado, Gamini. *The Elizabethan Underworld*. London: J.M. Dent and Sons, 1977.

Sallust. *The War with Catiline.* Trans. J.C. Rolfe. Loeb Classical Library. London: Heinemann, 1931.
Sampson, Margaret. 'Laxity and Liberty in Seventeenth-Century English Political Thought.' In *Conscience and Casuistry in Early Modern Europe.* Ed. Edmund Leites. Cambridge: Cambridge University Press, 1988. 72–118.
Schellhase, K.C. *Tacitus in Renaissance Political Thought.* Chicago: University of Chicago Press, 1976.
Schuler, Robert M. 'Some Spiritual Alchemies of Seventeenth-Century England.' *Journal of the History of Ideas,* 41 (1980): 293–318.
Scot, Reginald. *The Discoverie of Witchcraft.* London, 1584.
Sedgwick, Eve Kosofsky. *Between Men: English Literature and Male Homosocial Desire.* New York: Columbia University Press, 1985.
– 'Sexualism and the Citizen of the World: Wycherley, Sterne, and Male Homosocial Desire.' *Critical Inquiry,* 11 (1984): 226–45.
Shakespeare, William. *The Riverside Shakespeare.* Ed. G. Blakemore Evans, et al. Boston: Houghton Mifflin, 1974.
Shapiro, Michael. 'Audience v. Dramatist in Jonson's *Epicoene* and Other Plays of the Children's Troupes.' *English Literary Renaissance,* 3 (1973): 400–17.
– 'The Casting of Flute: Planes of Illusion in *A Midsummer Night's Dream* and *Bartholomew Fair.*' Forthcoming in *Elizabethan Theatre XIII* (1994): 1–29.
Shepherd, Simon. 'Shakespeare's Private Drawer: Shakespeare and Homosexuality.' In *The Shakespeare Myth.* Ed. Graham Holderness, et al. Manchester: Manchester University Press, 1988. 96–109.
Shuger, Debora K. 'Hypocrites and Puppets in *Bartholomew Fair.*' *Modern Philology,* 82 (1984): 70–3.
Simmons, Joseph L. 'Volpone as Antinous: Jonson and "Th' Overthrow of Stage-Playes."' *Modern Language Review,* 70 (1975): 13–19.
Simpson, Evelyn M. *A Study of the Prose Works of John Donne.* Oxford: Oxford University Press, 1948.
Slights, Camille Wells. *The Casuistical Tradition in Shakespeare, Donne, Herbert, and Milton.* Princeton: Princeton University Press, 1981.
Slights, Jessica. 'The Shame of Unsinewed Bodies.' Unpublished paper presented at the Ohio Shakespeare Conference. Cincinnati, 1994.
Slights, William W.E. 'Bodies of Text and Textualized Bodies in *Sejanus* and *Coriolanus.*' *Medieval and Renaissance Drama in England,* 5 (1990): 181–93.
– '*Epicoene* and the Prose Paradox.' *Philological Quarterly,* 49 (1970): 178–87.
– 'Unfashioning the Man of Mode: A Comic Countergenre in Marston, Jonson, and Middleton.' *Renaissance Drama,* 15 (1984): 69–91.
Smith, Bruce R. *Homosexual Desire in Shakespeare's England: A Cultural Poetics.* Chicago: University of Chicago Press, 1991.

Smith, Lacey Baldwin. *Treason in Tudor England: Politics and Paranoia.* Princeton: Princeton University Press, 1986.
Spacks, Patricia Meyer. *Gossip.* New York: Knopf, 1985.
Stallybrass, Peter. 'Patriarchal Territories: The Body Enclosed.' In *Rewriting the Renaissance: The Discourse of Sexual Difference in Early Modern Europe.* Ed. Margaret W. Ferguson, Maureen Quilligan, and Nancy J. Vickers. Chicago: University of Chicago Press, 1986. 123-42.
- and Allon White, eds. *The Politics and Poetics of Transgression.* Ithaca: Cornell University Press, 1986.
Sweeney, John Gordon, III. *Jonson and the Psychology of Public Theater.* Princeton: Princeton University Press, 1985.
- '*Volpone* and the Theater of Self-Interest.' *English Literary Renaissance,* 12 (1982): 220-41.
Tacitus. *Opera quae exstant.* Antwerp: Plantinian, 1600.
Teague, Frances. *The Curious History of 'Bartholomew Fair.'* Lewisburg: Bucknell University Press, 1985.
Tefft, Stanton K., ed. *Secrecy: A Cross-Cultural Perspective.* New York: Human Sciences Press, 1980.
Tennenhouse, Leonard. *Power on Display: The Politics of Shakespeare's Genres.* New York: Methuen, 1986.
Thomas, Keith. *Religion and the Decline of Magic.* New York: Charles Scribner's Sons, 1971.
Tillyard, E.M.W. *The Elizabethan World Picture.* London: Chatto and Windus, 1943.
Tribble, Evelyn B. *Margins and Marginality: The Printed Page in Early Modern England.* Charlottesville: University Press of Virginia, 1993.
Tricomi, Albert H. *Anticourt Drama in England, 1603-1642.* Charlottesville: University Press of Virginia, 1989.
Trilling, Lionel. *Sincerity and Authenticity.* Cambridge, Mass.: Harvard University Press, 1974.
Tulip, James. 'Comedy as Equivocation: An Approach to the Reference of *Volpone.*' *Southern Review* (Australia), 5 (1972): 91-101.
Underdown, David. *Revel, Riot, and Rebellion: Popular Politics and Culture in England 1603-1660.* Oxford: Clarendon Press, 1985.
- 'The Taming of the Scold: The Enforcement of Patriarchal Authority in Early Modern England.' In *Order and Disorder in Early Modern England.* Ed. Anthony Fletcher and John Stevenson. Cambridge: Cambridge University Press, 1985. 116-36.
Vickers, Nancy J. 'Diana Described: Scattered Woman and Scattered Rhyme.' *Critical Inquiry,* 8 (1981): 265-79.

Waddington, Raymond B. 'The Iconography of Silence and Chapman's Hercules.' *Journal of the Warburg and Courtauld Institutes*, 33 (1970): 248–63.
Waith, Eugene M. *The Herculean Hero in Marlowe, Chapman, Shakespeare and Dryden.* New York: Columbia University Press, 1962.
Watson, Robert N. *Ben Jonson's Parodic Strategy: Literary Imperialism in the Comedies.* Cambridge, Mass.: Harvard University Press, 1987.
Wayne, Don E. *Penshurst: Semiotics of Place and the Poetics of History.* Madison: University of Wisconsin Press, 1984.
Webster, John. *The Duchess of Malfi.* Ed. Elizabeth M. Brennan. New Mermaid Series. New York: Hill and Wang, 1966.
Weimann, Robert. *Shakespeare and the Popular Tradition in the Theater: Studies in the Social Dimension of Dramatic Form and Function.* Ed. Robert Schwartz. Baltimore: Johns Hopkins University Press, 1978.
Whetstone, George. *A Mirour for Magestrates of Cyties.* London, 1584.
Whigham, Frank. 'Sexual and Social Mobility in *The Duchess of Malfi.*' *PMLA*, 100 (1985): 167–86.
Whitney, Geoffrey. *A Choice of Emblemes.* Leiden, 1586.
Wilson, Edmund. 'Morose Ben Jonson.' In *The Triple Thinkers: Twelve Essays on Literary Subjects.* New York: Oxford University Press, 1949. 213–32.
Wiltenberg, Robert. *Ben Jonson and Self-Love: The Sublest Maze of All.* Columbia: University of Missouri Press, 1990.
Womack, Peter. *Ben Jonson.* Oxford: Basil Blackwell, 1986.
Woodbridge, Linda. *Women and the English Renaissance: Literature and the Nature of Womankind, 1540–1620.* Urbana: University of Illinois Press, 1984.
– and Edward Berry, eds. *True Rites and Maimed Rites: Ritual and Anti-Ritual in Shakespeare and His Age.* Urbana: University of Illinois Press, 1992.
Wright, Thomas. *The Passions of the Minde in Generall.* London, 1604.
Wrightson, Keith. *English Society, 1580–1680.* New Brunswick: Rutgers University Press, 1982.
Yates, Frances. 'The Hermetic Tradition in Renaissance Science.' In *Art, Science, and History in the Renaissance.* Ed. Charles S. Singleton. Baltimore: Johns Hopkins University Press, 1968. 255–74.

Index

Abel, Elizabeth: *Writing and Sexual Difference*, 188n22
Alchemist, The, 23, 29, 82, 110, 160, 170, 202n19; bodily functions in, 113; conspiracy in, 64, 105, 107, 124-7, 175; dedicated to Lady Mary Wroth, 106; disguise in, 120-1; humour in, 193n16; impersonation in, 200n1; interpretation and, 207n2; intrigue in, 12; parody of apocalypse in, 111; revelation of secrets in, 22, 107, 109-10; secrecy in, 7, 105, 107, 108, 109; significance of secrecy in, 173; status in, 124-6; 'To the Reader' in, 202n13; women in, 106
Alchemy: explosions and, 115, 202n11; Puritan thought and, 201-2n9; timing and, 123
Alcibiades, 44
Alden, C.S., 209n14
Althusser, Louis, 194n3
Ames, William, 158
Amussen, Susan: 'Gender, Family and the Social Order, 1560-1725,' 196n13; *An Ordered Society*, 198n22

Anderson, Mark: 'Structure and Response in *Volpone*,' 193n19
Arcana, 172, 173; *Dei*, 7, 97; *imperii*, 7, 9, 174, 176, 185n19; *naturae*, 7, 183n9
Archer, John Michael: *Sovereignty and Intelligence*, 179n2
Aristophanes, 135
Aristotle, 111
Ayers, Philip J.: 'Jonson, Northampton, and the Treason in *Sejanus*,' 187n15; edition of *Sejanus* by, 187n15

Bacon, Francis: dictum of, 118
Bacon, Roger, 202n16; *The Mirror of Alchemy*, 111, 202n12, 202n18; on alchemy, 111; on Hebrew, 113; on secrecy, 112
Bakhtin, Mikhail, 94, 155, 203n20; *Rabelais and His World*, 209n21
Bancroft, Archbishop Richard: *Daungerous Positions and Proceedings*, 33, 186n2
Barbarossa, Frederic, 202n20
Barber, C.L., 155, 166, 198n21; *Shakespeare's Festive Comedy*, 209n21
Barish, Jonas A., 48, 205-6n10; *The*

Antitheatrical Prejudice, 210n27; *Ben Jonson and the Language of Prose Comedy*, 194n2, 197n19, 203n28, 206n10, 210n25; *Ben Jonson: A Collection of Critical Essays*, 203n21; on *Epicoene*, 78; *Sejanus*, edition by, 190n27

Barkan, Leonard: *Nature's Work of Art*, 188n23

Barker, Francis, 42; *The Tremulous Private Body*, 187n11

Barroll, Leeds: *Politics, Plague, and Shakespeare's Theater*, 181n15

Bartholomew Fair, 75, 175, 206n10, 208n7, 209n20; authority in, 149, 155, 164; epilogue to, 168, 211n36; hypocrisy in, 210n23; intention of characters in, 166; interpretation and, 145, 146, 176, 207n1; intertextuality in, 152; intrigue in, 12; Jonson's intention in, 145, 147; language in, 176; misappropriation of texts in, 170; representaton of love in, 163; secrecy in, 63, 176

Bartholomew Faire, or variety of fancies, 147, 208n5

Barton, Anne: *Ben Jonson, Dramatist*, 182n19, 186n1, 205n6; on Jonson's early and mid-career plays, 12; on *Catiline*, 134; on *Sejanus*, 32

Baskerville, C.R., 210n33

Beaurline, Lester A.: *Epicoene*, edition of by, 197n20; *Jonson and Elizabethan Comedy*, 209n19

Bedford, Countess Lucy of, 202n14

Bellman, Beryl L.: *The Language of Secrecy*, 182n6

Belsey, Catherine: *The Subject of Tragedy*, 180n5, 190n30

Berry, Edward: *True Rites and Maimed Rites*, 198n21, 198n26

Berry, Lloyd: *The Geneva Bible: A Facsimile of the 1560 Edition*, 203n26

Bevington, David: *Medieval Drama*, 184n12

Biron, Duke de, 187n12

Blissett, William: on *The Alchemist*, 118; 'The Venter Tripartite in *The Alchemist*,' 203n27

Bodin, Jean, 44

Bok, Sissela, 31, 58, 173; *Secrets: On the Ethics of Concealment and Revelation*, 16, 182n5, 211n2

Boose, Lynda E.: 'Scolding Brides and Bridling Scolds,' 196n12

Bossy, John: *Giordano Bruno and the Embassy Affair*, 191–2n2

Boughner, Daniel: 'Jonson's Use of Lipsius in *Sejanus*,' 189n26

Bray, Alan: *Homosexuality in Renaissance England*, 197n17

Brightman, 201n9

Bristol, Michael, 94, 155, 198n21; *Carnival and Theater*, 180n5, 209n21; 'Charivari and the Comedy of Abjection in *Othello*,' 198n26

Broughton, Hugh: *A Concent of Scripture*, 110, 113; Jonson's awareness of, 111, 202n10, 207n2; *The Revelation of the Holy Apocalyps*, 110

Browning, Robert: 'My Last Duchess,' 83

Bruno, Giordano, 17, 191–2n2

Bryant, Joseph Allen, Jr: '*Catiline* and the Nature of Jonson's Tragic Fable,' 204n5; on Jonson's republicanism, 205n7

Buc, Sir George, 154

Buckingham: effeminacy of, 100

Bullokar, John: *An English Expositor*, 206n11
Bullough, Geoffrey: *Narrative and Dramatic Sources of Shakespeare*, 188n17, 210n32
Burke, Peter: 'Tacitism,' 190n27
Burt, Richard: censorship, views of, 10-11; discourse theory and, 183n10; impersonation, 200n1; '"A Dangerous Rome,"' 188n15; *Licensed by Authority*, 10, 180n3, 181n16, 183n10,189n24, 200n1, 208n6, 209n17, 211n34, 211n37; '"Licensed by Authority": Ben Jonson and the Politics of the Early Stuart Theater,' 180n3
Butler, Martin, 208n6

Cabinet-Council: Containing the Chief Arts of Empire, 207n16
Carew, Thomas, 208n6
Casuistry, 204n33
Catesby, Robert, 205n8
Catiline, His Conspiracy, 205-6n10, 206n12; audience hostility against, 10; authority, treatment of in, 142; closure in, 141; compared to *The Alchemist*, 138; compared to *Sejanus*, 141; conspiracy in, 64, 124, 131-4, 136-8, 141, 175-6, 204n5, 206n14; discovery in, 137; fear in, 140; female characters in, 186n6; intrigue in, 12, 137; Jonson's political understanding in, 132; language in, 139; misappropriation of texts in, 176; power through secrecy in, 141; privacy in, 138; secrecy in, 136, 137, 140, 175; sexuality in, 140, 143; spies in, 13; spying in, 136

Catullus, 70
Cecil, Robert, 62, 181n11, 187n12; *An Answer to Certaine Scandalous Papers*, 206n12
Censorship, 6, 10, 11, 18, 31, 112, 141, 142, 170, 171, 181n15, 181n17, 183n10; Jonson's opinion of, 35, 172
Chaplin, Charles, 125
Chapman, George, 6, 11, 13, 170, 181n18, 199n31
Charivari, 91, 93-5, 96, 175, 198n22, 198n24
Chaucer, Geoffrey: *Canon Yeoman's Tale*, 202n11
Christianson, Paul: *Reformers and Babylon*, 201n9
Clare, Janet: '*Art Made Tongue-Tied by Authority*,' 181n15, 195n8, 211n38; on interpretation and censorship, 169-70
Claudian, 45, 46
Closure, 25, 27, 38, 73, 141, 164, 168, 193n17
Coke, Sir Edward, 187n15
Concealment, 3, 4, 17, 18, 21, 23, 24, 25, 26, 29, 31, 32, 58, 88, 111, 169, 203n31; *see also* Revelation
Conrad, Joseph, 13-14
Conspiracies; 6, 164; Babington Conspiracy, 5; Gowrie Plot, 5, 179n2; Guise Plan, 5; Ridolfi Plot, 5; *see also* Gunpowder Plot
Conspiracy: discovery of, 60, 136-7, 207n16; effect on personality of, 65; Jacobean and Roman, links between, 205n8; language of, 120; purpose of, 66, 67; satire of by Jonson, 75; secrecy and, 4, 46, 143; status and, 124-7; timing and, 123; men-

tioned, 4, 5, 7, 13, 25, 63, 64, 65, 66, 69, 70, 72, 75, 120, 129, 131–4, 136–7, 141, 159, 173, 174; *see also under* play titles
Conversations, 11, 186n3, 186n5, 190n27
Cope, Jackson I., 155; 'Bartholomew Fair as Blasphemy,' 209n18, 209n20
Copjec, Joan: 'The Orthopsychic Subject: Film Theory and the Reception of Lacan,' 194–5n4
Cordus, 47
Coriolanus, 44
Cotgrave, Randall, 198n23; *Dictionarie of the French and English Tongues*, 91, 206n11
Cowell, John: *The Interpreter*, 181n11
Creaser, John: 'The Popularity of Jonson's Tortoise,' 192n3
Crewe, Jonathan V.: 'God or the Good Physician: The Rational Playwright in *The Comedy of Errors*,' 195n9
Cromwell, Thomas: spies and, 5
Cross-dressing, 79, 91, 99; effeminizing effect of, 197n18; wickedness of, 192n9
Cynthia's Revels, 10, 64, 70, 83, 202n14

D'Acuto, Afinati: *Il muto chè parla (The Dumbe Divine Speaker)*, 96
Davenant, William, 208n6
Davis, Natalie Zemon: 'The Reasons of Misrule: Youth Groups and Charivaris in Sixteenth Century France,' 198n24
Dawson, Anthony: 'Giving the Finger: Puns and Transgression in *The Changeling*,' 185n17

De Arcanis Naturae, see under Mizaldus, Antonius
Dean, Leonard: 'Three Notes on Comic Morality,' 193n11
Dee, John, 17
Dekker, Thomas, 8, 9, 11, 112, 181n12; *The Magnificent Entertainment Given to King James*, 8
DeLuna, Barbara: *Jonson's Romish Plot*, 187n15, 191n2, 205n8
Derrida, Jacques, 22; 'The Law of Genre,' 185n15
Devil Is an Asse, 146
Dickens, Charles, 30
Dio Cassius: *Dio's Roman History*, 40, 45, 186n9, 211n3
Discovery, theatrical, 75, 169
Disguise, 29, 31, 59, 65, 73, 81, 84, 91, 120, 121, 148, 153, 163, 164, 192n7
Dismemberment, 46; eroticism and, 47; *see also under Sejanus*
Dollimore, Jonathan: *Radical Tragedy*, 180n5
Donaldson, Ian: '"A Martyr's Resolution": *Epicoene*,' *The World Upside Down*, 91, 198n21, 200n42
Donne, John, 49, 63, 192n6; *Satyre IV*, 63, 72
Drummond, William, 11, 35, 81, 186n3, 190n27
Dryden, John, 78; *The Essays of John Dryden*, 194n2
Duncan, Douglas: *Ben Jonson and the Lucianic Tradition*, 193n13–n14, 193n20, 211n36
Dutton, Richard: censorship, views on, 11, 40, 90, 180n3; closing of theatres, 187n15; 'Ben Jonson and the Master of the Revels,' 180n3, 181n17; *Ben Jonson: To the First Folio*, 208n4; *Mastering the*

Index

Revels, 180n3, 188n15, 195n8, 208n4, 209n17
Dyke, Daniel: *The Mystery of Selfe-Deceiuing*, 156–7, 210n24

Eastward Ho, 10, 146, 181n18
Eavesdropping, 13, 18, 21, 28, 29, 80, 105, 152
Eccles, Mark: 'Jonson and the Spies,' 191n2
Edwardes, Richard: *Damon and Pithias*, 167
Edwards, Philip, 187n15
Effeminization, 26, 175, 182n4, 197n18, 199n36
Elizabeth I, 5, 12, 44, 62, 135, 162, 187n15
Elton, G.R.: on spies, 5; *Policy and Practice*, 179n1
Entertainment at Althorp, The, 189n24
Epicoene, or the Silent Woman, 4, 75, 112, 176, 190n27, 195n8; audience hostility against, 10; compared to *Volpone*, 78; conspiracy in, 55, 64, 94, 105, 174; critical evaluation of, 78; cross-dressing in, 99, 103;disguise and, 81, 91, 102; effeminacy in, 102, 103; gender-role reversal in, 89, 95; intrigue in, 12; male silence in, 198n29; performed at White-friars, 97, 99, 100, 101; representation of love in, 163; secrecy in, 77, 86, 90, 95, 100, 103, 104, 105, 107; self-revelation in, 80; shaming ritual in, 92; significance of secrecy in, 172, 173; vanity in, 195n10; women in, lack of power of, 55; women in, representation of, 98–99, 194n3, 197n15

Epigrammes, 194n22, 202n14
Epstein, Julia: 'Either/Or-Neither/Both: Sexual Ambiguity and the Ideology of Gender,' 197n18
Erasmus, Desiderius: *Of the Yong Man and the Evill Disposed Woman*, 183–4n11; *Praise of Folly*, 192n7, 211n36
Espionage, 16, 131, 143; *see also* Spying
Estienne, Charles: *The Defense of Contraries*, 197n14
Euchero, Michael: 'The Conscience of Politics in *Catiline*,' 204n3
Evans, Robert C.: *Ben Jonson and the Poetics of Patronage*, 189n24
Every Man In His Humour, 63, 83, 150, 176
Every Man Out of His Humour, 76

Fawkes, Guy, 60, 192n9
FBI, 171
Feminist critics: Jonson and, 83
Fernandez, James: in *The Language of Secrecy*, 17, 182n6, 183n8; on secrecy, 17, 18
Fifth Monarchists, 110, 201n9
Finkelpearl, Philip J.: '"The Comedians' Liberty": Censorship of the Jacobean Stage Reconsidered,' 180n3
Fish, Stanley, 75, 82; *Self-Consuming Artifacts*, 195n9
Fleay, Frederick G.: *A Biographical Chronicle of the English Drama (1559–1642)*, 210n30
Forrest, The, 170
Forset, Edward, 44; *A Comparative Discourse of the Bodies Natural and Politique*, 187n13
Foucault, Michel, 14, 54, 177,

183n10; *Discipline and Punish*, 41, 186n10 ; 'Nietzsche, Genealogy, History,' 182n21, 211n4; 'The Spectacle of the Scaffold,' 186n10; *Textual Strategies*, 195n7; 'What Is an Author?,' 195n7
Foxe, John, 201n9
François Ier, 44
French, Peter: *John Dee: The World of an Elizabethan Magus*, 183n9
Freud, Sigmund, 22
Froben, Johann, 192n7
Frye, Northrop: *A Natural Perspective*, 193n15
Fuller, Thomas: *The Holy State*, 185n19
Fumerton, Patricia, 163; *Cultural Aesthetics*, 196n13, 210n28; '"Secret" Arts: Elizabethan Miniatures and Sonnets,' 210n28

Gager, William, 192n10; *Ulysses Redux*, 68
Geneva Bible, see under Berry, Lloyd
Gent, R.N.E., 201n7
Gibbon, 46
Ginzburg, Carlo: 'High and Low,' 181n9
Globe Theatre, 29
Gohlke, Madelon: '"I wooed thee with my sword,"' 182n4; on male fear of effeminization, 26, 182n4
Goldberg, Jonathan, 9, 26; *James I and the Politics of Literature*, 181n13, 186n4, 186n6, 193n12, 205n7; 'Shakespearean Inscriptions,' 185n20
Goodman, Paul: on *The Alchemist*, 124; *The Structure of Literature*, 204n34

Gordon, D.J., 9; 'Rolls and Mysteries,' 181n13
Gossip: secrecy and, 184n11; women and, 184n11; *see also* Spacks, Patricia Meyer
Greenblatt, Stephen: 'The False Ending in *Volpone*,' 193n15; on secrecy and power, 183n10; 'Shakespeare and the Exorcists,' 182n2; *Shakespearean Negotiations*, 180n5, 182n2
Greene, Robert, 164–5; *The Life and Complete Works ... of Robert Greene*, 209n13; *Second Part of Conny-Catching*, 153; *The Third Part of Conny-Catching*, 210n32
Greene, Thomas M., 30; 'Resurrecting Rome,' 202n17
Greenham, Richard: 'Of Hypocrisie,' 210n23; *The Workes of Richard Greenham*, 210n23
Guiccardini, Francesco, 44
Gulls, 170, 193n19; conspiracy and, 4, 67, 115, 116, 126; self-love and, 192n8
Gunpowder Plot, 5, 22, 58, 60, 61, 62, 76, 167, 180n2, 189n24, 191n2, 205n8, 211n35; *see also* Conspiracies

Hallahan, Huston D.: 'Silence, Eloquence, and Chatter in Jonson's *Epicoene*,' 199n32
Harsnett, Samuel: *Declaration of Egregious Popish Impostures*, 182n2
Hawkins, Sir Thomas, 190n29
Hayes, Sir Thomas, 153
Haynes, Jonathan: 'Festivity and the Dramatic Economy of Jonson's *Bartholomew Fair*,' 209n21; 'Representing the Underworld:

Index

The Alchemist,' 201n7; The Social Relations of Jonson's Theater, 201n7, 208n12, 209n21
Hazlitt, William: Lectures Chiefly on the Dramatic Literature of the Age of Elizabeth, 187n14; on Sejanus, 44
Heffner, Ray L., 78; 'Unifying Symbols in the Comedy of Ben Jonson,' 194n2, 209n18
Helgerson, Richard: Self-Crowned Laureates, 189n24
Helms, Lorraine: 'Roaring Girls and Silent Women,' 194n3, 199n35, 200n40
Herbert, George, 172
Herford, C.H., 46, 182n18, 210n33; see also HSS (Ben Jonson)
Hermeneutic(s), 112, 114, 142, 177
Hermeticism, 7, 17
Hester, M. Thomas: Kinde Pitty and Brave Scorn, 192n6
Hic Mulier, or the Man-Woman, 192n9
Hitchcock, Alfred, 82
Hobbes, Thomas, 44
Holbein, Hans (The Younger), 192n7
Holland, Henry, 210n23
Hooker, Richard, 44
Hope Theatre, 210n30
Horace: Ars Poetica, 132
Howard, Jean E.: 'Crossdressing, the Theatre, and Gender Struggle in Early Modern England,' 194n3; Shakespeare Reproduced, 190n30
HSS (Ben Jonson, Herford and Simpson, eds.), 180n4, 180n6, 182n18, 186n3, 186n5, 188n19, 189n25, 190n27, 192n5, 194n22, 194n23, 195n6, 202n19, 210n26
Hughes, Merritt Y., 184n14

Hume, Martin: Treason and Plot, 179n2
Hymenaei, 76, 194n24
Hypocrisy, 156, 157, 158, 210n23

Inspector General, The, 125
Interpretation, 4, 39, 40, 146–8, 207n1, 207n2, 208n8; Jonson's satire of, 7
Isle of Dogs, The, 146

Jackson, Gabriele Bernhard: on interpretation in Jonson, 154; Vision and Judgment in Ben Jonson's Drama, 209n16
James VI and I, 12, 61, 77, 100, 112, 135, 168, 181n11; absolutism of, 186n4, 187n15; Basilikon Doron, 8, 181n10; body-state metaphor and, 45; compared to Tiberius, 5; state secrets and, 41, 186n4; The True Lawe of Free Monarchies, 188n16
Jardine, Lisa: Still Harping on Daughters, 199–200n38
Jensen, Ejner: Ben Jonson's Comedies on the Modern Stage, 194n1
Johnstone, Keith: Impro: Improvisation and the Theatre, 124–5, 204n35
Jones, Inigo, 108
Jonson, Ben: attitude toward commoners of, 205n7; audacity of, 189n24, 202n15; authorial personae of, 82; authorial intention, problematizing of, 154; comical satires of, 12; complete works, publication of, 6; disintegration of self in, 30; envois by, 202n14; 'Epigram, to my Book-seller,' 202n14; fear of harassment of, 49; fear of interpretation,

190n26; 'Goe Little Booke,' 202n14; Gunpowder Plot, response to, 211n35; imprisonment of, 5, 63; late period of career of, 208n6; masculinity of, 107; middle period of career, *see* separate entry, below; nastiness of characters of, 173; on Hebrew, supposed secrets of, 113; opinion of by others, 9; opinion of censorship of, 11; opinion of power of, 7, 9; opinion of secrecy of, 112, 172; patronage and, 189n24; plays of, *see under* play titles; plots of, 3, 4, 12, 177; political dynamics in, 4; privacy of, 22; puritans and, 5, 6, 117, 156, 177, 202n10; realism of, 201n7; request for royal licence by, 211n37; Roman Catholicism and, 5, 6, 22, 60, 75–6, 180n4, 189n24, 206n12; satire of, characteristics, 128, 150, 154, 193n19; secrecy and, 4, 8, 9, 10, 13, 14, 22, 172, 177; silence in, 97; societal change, views on, 13; spying and, 5, 190n27; summoned before Privy Council, 44; suspicion of purity of, 156; tragedies of, characteristics, 128; treatment of audience by, 202n13, 208n6
Jonson, Ben: middle period of career of, 3, 32, 181n15; middle plays of, authority in, 128; conspiracy in, 63; exploitation in, 173; misinterpretation of texts in, 176
Josselin, Ralph, 196n13
Jowett, John: '"Fall before this Booke": the 1605 Quarto of *Sejanus*,' 189n24

Kaplan, Joel: 'Dramatic and Moral Energy in Ben Jonson's *Bartholomew Fair*,' 209n21
Kastan, David Scott: *Staging the Renaissance*, 194n3, 199n34
Kay, W. David: 'Jonson's Urbane Gallants,' 200n41
Kelley, Edward, 122–3
Kent, Earl of, 45
Kermode, Frank, 177; *The Genesis of Secrecy*, 31, 170, 185n25, 211n5
Kernan, Alvin B., 193–4n21; on *The Alchemist*, 109, 121, 201n6; *The Plot of Satire*, 203n30
Kiefer, Frederick: *Fortune and Elizabethan Tragedy*, 191n31
Knoll, Robert: *Ben Jonson's Plays: An Introduction*, 203n25
Knowlton, Edgar C., Jr: '"Kiss'd Our *Anos*" in Ben Jonson's *The Alchemist*,' 203n29

Lacan, Jacques, 194n4
Lady Elizabeth's Servants, 210n30
Lambi, Giovanni Battista: *The Revelation of the Secret Spirit*, 201n7
Lando, Ortensio: *Paradossi Cioe, Sententie fori del commun parere*, 197n14
Lang, Andrew: *James VI and the Gowrie Mystery*, 180n2
Lanier, Douglas: 'Masculine Silence: *Epicoene* and Jonsonian Stylistics,' 198n29
Laqueur, Thomas: *Making Sex: Body and Gender from the Greeks to Freud*, 197n18
Laroque, François: *Shakespeare's Festive World*, 198n23, 199n33, 209n21
Lee, Jongsook: *Ben Jonson's Poesis*, 186n7, 207n15

Leggatt, Alexander: 'The Suicide of Volpone,' 193n17
Leigh, William: *Great Britains great deliverance from ... popish powder*, 62
Leinwand, Theodore B., 147; *The City Staged: Jacobean City Comedy, 1603-1613*, 208n3
Levaillant, Nigel, 58, 59
Levin, Richard: 'The Structure of Bartholomew Fair,' 208n9
Levine, Laura: 'Men in Women's Clothing,' 197n18
Lipsius, Justus, 189n26
Lloyd, Lodowick: *The Iubile of Britane*, 205n8; *The Practice of Policy*, 205n8; *The Tragicomedie of Serpents*, 205n8

MacFarlane, Alan: *The Family Life of Ralph Josselin*, 196n13
Machiavelli, Niccolò, 44
Magnetic Lady, The, 193n15, 207n1
Malleus maleficarum, 15, 16, 182n2
Manzini, Giovanni Battista, 49; *Politicall Observations upon the fall of Seianus*, 190n29
Marconville, Jean de: *Treatise of the Good and Evell Tounge*, 130, 204n1
Marcus, Leah S.: on secrecy and power, 183n10; *The Politics of Mirth*, 180n3, 201n5, 209n21; *Puzzling Shakespeare*, 198n25, 199n35, 200n39
Marcus, Steven: *The Other Victorians*, 171, 211n1
Marlowe, Christopher, 6, 139, 170, 194n22; *Hero and Leander*, 167
Marotti, Arthur F.: *John Donne, Coterie Poet*, 190n28, 202n15; 'The Self-Reflexive Art of Ben Jonson's *Sejanus*,' 190n28

Marston, John, 13, 35, 181n18; *The Dutch Courtesan*, 201n4
Mason, James, 138; *The Anatomie of Sorcerie*, 203n24, 206n11
Masque of Blackness, The, 189n24
Massinger, Philip, 208n6; *The City Madam*, secrecy in, 20
Maus, Katharine Eisaman, 208n8
McDonald, Russ: *Shakespeare and Jonson, Jonson and Shakespeare*, 203n23
McPherson, David: 'The Origins of Overdo: A Study in Jonsonian Invention,' 209n14
Mede, Joseph, 201n9
Memorials of Affairs of State in the reigns of Q. Elizabeth and K. James I, 187n12
Mercury Vindicated from the Alchemists at Court, 7
Middleton, Thomas (Mayor of London), 153, 170
Middleton, Thomas (poet/playwright), 172; *The Changeling*, 21, 23, 24, 57, 184n13; disguise and, 81, 153; Jonson influence on, 13; marginality of, 48
Midlands Revolt (1607), 45
Miles, Rosalind: *Ben Jonson, His Craft and Art*, 209n19
Millard, Barbara: '"An Acceptable Violence": Sexual Contest in Jonson's *Epicoene*,' 197n15, 197n20
Miller, D.A., 30, 95; 'Secret Subjects, Open Secrets,' 185n24, 198n28
Milton, John, 153; *Complete Poems and Major Prose*, 184n14; *Samson Agonistes*, 184n14
Mirabelli, Philip: 'Silence, Wit, and

Wisdom in *The Silent Woman*,' 195n5
Mirandola, Pico della: *Oration and the Dignity of Man*, 193n21
Mizaldus, Antonius: *De Arcanis Naturae (Secrets in Nature)*, 24
Moldavia, Prince of, 195n8
Montrose, Louis, 183n10
Mooney, Michael E.: *Shakespeare's Dramatic Transactions*, 184n12
More, Sir Thomas, 165
Mullaney, Steven: *The Place of the Stage*, 211n37
Munday, Anthony (A.M.), see D'Acuto, Afinati; Etienne, Charles
Mystification of language, 119, 120, 121

Nashe, Thomas, 163; *Syr P.S. his Astrophel and Stella*, preface by, 210n29
Nazi Germany: secret codes and, 171
Nelson, Alan: *Medieval English Drama*, 184n12; 'Some Configurations of Staging in Medieval English Drama,' 184n12
New Inn, The, 193n15
Newman, Karen, 98, 150-1, 194n2; 'City Talk: Women and Commodification,' 194n3, 199n34; *Fashioning Femininity and English Renaissance Drama*, 194n3; *Shakespeare's Rhetoric of Comic Character*, 208n11
Newton, Richard C.: '"Ben./Jonson": The Poet in the Poems,' 180n8
Nicholl, Charles: *The Chemicall Theatre*, 204n32
Noah (Wakefield), 184n12

Norbrook, David, 156; *Poetry and Politics in the English Renaissance*, 205n7, 210n22
Northampton, 187n15
Northumberland, Earl of, 44
O'Connor, Marion F.: *Shakespeare Reproduced*, 190n30
'On the Famous Voyage,' 114
Orgel, Stephen, 9, 183n10; *The Illusion of Power*, 181n13, 211n36; *The Jonsonian Masque*, 181n13, 201n5; *The Renaissance Imagination*, 181n13
Ornstein, Robert: *The Moral Vision of Jacobean Tragedy*, 191n31, 204-5n5, 206-7n14
Osborne, Francis: *Secret History of the Court of James the First*, 100, 199n37
Ovid, 7, 70
Oxford Playhouse, 58

Paranoia, 61, 62, 172
Parker, R.B., 149, 155, 192n3; 'The Themes and Staging of *Bartholomew Fair*,' 208n10, 209n20
Paster, Gail Kern, 46; 'Ben Jonson's Comedy of Limitation,' 193n18; *The Body Embarrassed*, 182n7; *The Idea of the City in the Age of Shakespeare*, 188n21; 'Leaky Vessels,' 182n7, 208n7
Patriarchy, 196n12, 196n13
Patronage, 6, 141
Patterson, Annabel, 48, 141; *Censorship and Interpretation*, 9-10; 'Lyric and Society in Jonson's *Under-wood*,' 207n17; '"Romancast Similitude,"' 190n27
Paul, Lissa, 184n11
Perkins, William, 158
Persius, *Satire 1*, 150
Petrarch: *Rime sparse*, 47

Index

Phoenix Theatre, 21
Pico, 75
Pinter, Harold, 96
Platnauer, Maurice, 188n18
Platter, Thomas, 198n22
Plutarch: *Life of Marcus Brutus*, 25
Poetaster, 64, 70, 198n25; 'Apologeticall Dialogue' in, 202n13; censorship of 11
Pooly, 194n22
Poro (African tribe): secrecy among, 17, 18
Potter, Lois, 10; *Secret Rites and Secret Writing*, 181n14
Pound, Ezra: 'Envoi (1919),' 202n14
Prostitutes, 166, 167
Prynne, William: *Histrio-mastix*, 199n36
Puritans, 155, 168, 176, 198n24; alchemy and, 201–2n9; casuistry of, 158; conscience of, 123–4; disdain for civil authority of, 118; dramatic criticism by, 192n10; Jonson's opinion of, 156; Jonson's ridicule of, 117; language of, 128; ritual and, 157; secrecy and, 33; sexuality and, 159; spiritual economy of, 119; textual interpretation by, 8, 161

Rabelais, François: *Pantagruel*, 202n20
Rabinow, Paul: *The Foucault Reader*, 195n7
Rackin, Phyllis: 'Genealogical Anxiety and Female Authority,' 185n23, 190n30; *Stages of History*, 185n23
Ralegh, Sir Walter, 187n15
Read, Conyers: *Mr. Secretary Walsingham and the Policy of Queen Elizabeth*, 179n2
Remembrancia preserved among the Archives of the City of London, 209n14
Revelation (biblical text), 118; parody of, 161
Revelation, 3, 4, 17, 18, 21, 23, 24, 25, 26, 27, 29, 30, 31, 32, 58, 73, 75, 75, 81, 84, 88, 99, 108, 111, 120, 123, 143, 163, 168, 169, 177, 201n7, 203n31; *see also* Concealment
Richard II, 44
Ricks, Christopher: '*Sejanus* and Dismemberment,' 188n20
Riggs, David: *Ben Jonson: A Life*, 180n4, 189n24, 191n2
Roman Catholics: circumspection of, 191n1; spying against, 206n12; spying by, 191n2; witch hunting by, 15
Roman Catholicism, 62, 63, 84, 110, 117; Jonson and, *see under* Jonson; textual interpretation and, 8
Rose, Mark: *Shakespearean Design*, 185n18
Rowe, George E., 39; 'Ben Jonson's Quarrel with His Audience and Its Renaissance Context,' 208n6; *Distinguishing Jonson*, 180n8, 186n8, 202n13, 210n31
Rowley, William, 24, 184n13
Royal Court Theatre, 124
Rudolph II, Emperor, 123
Rufinus, 45
Ruthven, John: *The Earle of Gowries Conspiracie against the Kings Maiestie of Scotland*, 179

Salgado, Gamini: *The Elizabethan Underworld*, 208n5
Salisbury Court Theatre, 21
Salisbury, Earl of, 60
Sallust: *The Conspiracy of Catiline*, 132; source for *Catiline*, 152; *The War with Catiline*, 204n4
Sampson, Margaret: 'Laxity and Liberty in Seventeenth-Century English Political Thought,' 204n33
Schellhase, K.C.: *Tacitus in Renaissance Political Thought*, 190n27
Schuler, Robert M.: 'Some Spiritual Alchemies of Seventeenth-Century England,' 202n9
Scot, Reginald: *Discoverie of Witchcraft*, 15, 16, 182n1, 182n2
Secrecy, 38, 71, 114; audience comprehension and, 112-13; cultural fetish of, 14; definitions of, 3, 59, 183n8; different nationalities and, 191n1; effect of in Renaissance dramaturgy, 31; effect of on society, 56, 75, 201n8; hermeneutic of, 112, 177; impotence and, 16; interpretation of, 31; languages of, 19; limited effect of in Jonson, 173; New Historicists on power of, 183n10; power of, 16, 106, 107, 128; psychological need for, 10; revelation and, 11, 24, 107; role-playing and, 65; romantic poetics of, 162; sexuality and, 16, 23, 83, 87, 207n18; silence and, 96; source of social control of, 104; suitability of in drama, 90; techniques of in Jonson, 174; verbal, 22; visual, 22; witchraft and, 15, 182n3; *see also under* Jonson's play titles

Secret(s), 4, 12, 13-14; extracting of, 185n22; extremes of, 203-4n31; functions of, 27; gender and, 85; impossibility of keeping, 185n21; inexpressible, 186n4; of power, 108, 183n10; of state, 41, 44, 61, 130; significance of to culture, 171; types of, 18, 19
Secrets in Nature, see under Mizaldus, Antonius
Sedgwick, Eve Kosofsky: *Between Men: English Literature and Male Homosocial Desire*, 197n16; on women in Jonson, 86-7
Sejanus, His Fall, 6, 32, 129, 180n7, 189n24, 195n10; audience hostility against, 10; body-state metaphor in, 44-5; censorship and, 48; conspiracy in, 19, 32, 33, 34, 50, 55, 64, 124; derivation of story of, 45; decoding of, 188n15; dismemberment in, 42-3, 47, 50; Earl of Essex represented in, 187n15; female characters in, 51-5, 186n6; importance of, 12; interpreters of, 146; intrigue in, 12; language in, 176; male power in, 50, 51, 53; marginated, 189n26; power in, 174; secrecy in, 32, 36, 37, 50, 57, 107; significance of secrecy in, 172, 173; spies in, 13, 33, 35, 50; treason in suppressed, 77
Selden, John: *Table-Talk*, 160-1, 210n26
Sexuality, 69, 70, 100, 140, 143, 162, 200n38; charivari and, 94; economy of, 160; homosexuality, 197n17; secrecy and, 29, 37, 86, 87, 207n18; witchcraft and, 15, 16

Index

Shakespeare, William, 11, 23, 29, 30, 48, 80, 96, 172, 195n9; disguise and, 81; interpretation accepted by, 148; Jonson's influence on, 13; Ovid-based comedies of, 7; representation of women in, 26, 190n30; secrecy and, 14, 25, 173

Shakespeare, plays of: *All's Well That Ends Well*, secrets in, 27; *Coriolanus*, 92, 198n25; *Cymbeline*, 21; *Hamlet*, 23; *Julius Caesar*, 25, 188n15; *King Lear*, 184n11; *Macbeth*, 25, 86; *Measure for Measure*, 153, 200n39; *The Merry Wives of Windsor*, 21; *Much Ado about Nothing*, secrets in, 27–8; *Richard II*, 185n18; secrecy, concealment in, 28; *Richard III*, secrecy in, 20; *Romeo and Juliet*, revelation in, 27; *The Taming of The Shrew*, 101; *The Tempest*, secrets in, 28; silence and, 97; *Titus Andronicus*, 138, 185n21; *Twelfth Night*, 89, 207n18; *The Winter's Tale*, 165

Shapiro, Michael: 'Audience v. Dramatist in Jonson's *Epicoene* ... ,' 200n41; 'The Casting of Flute,' 209n21

Sharpe, Kevin, 208n6

Shepherd, Simon: 'Shakespeare's Private Drawer: Shakespeare and Homosexuality,' 197n17

Shrewsbury, Earl of, 45

Shuger, Debora K.: 'Hypocrites and Puppets in *Bartholomew Fair*,' 210n23

Sidney, Sir Philip, 163

Sidney family, 76

Simmons, Joseph L.: 'Volpone as Antinous: Jonson and "Th'Overthrow of Stage-Playes,"' 192n10

Simpson, Evelyn, 46, 210n33; *see also* HSS (*Ben Jonson*)

Simpson, Percy, 46, 181n18, 210n33; *see also* HSS (*Ben Jonson*)

Sir Thomas More, 210–11n33

Slaughter of the Innocents (Fleury), 184n12

Slights, Camille Wells: *The Casuistical Tradition in Shakespeare, Donne, Herbert, and Milton*, 204n33, 210n25

Slights, Jessica: 'The Shame of Unsinewed Bodies,' 199n36

Slights, William W.E.: 'Bodies of Text and Textualized Bodies in *Sejanus* and *Coriolanus*,' 206n13; '*Epicoene* and the Prose Paradox,' 194n2; 'Unfashioning the Man of Mode,' 201n4

Smith, Bruce R.: *Homosexual Desire in Shakespeare's England*, 197n17

Smith, Lacey Baldwin: on paranoia, 61; *Treason in Tudor England*, 179n2, 192n4

Smuts, Malcolm, 208n6

Soliloquy, 63, 153, 159; function of in drama, 13; in *Bartholomew Fair*, 150–2; Jonson's and Shakespeare's contrasted, 150–1; secrecy and, 24, 31, 37

Somerset, effeminacy of, 100

Southampton Mayor's Book of 1606–1608, The, 196n12

Spacks, Patricia Meyer: *Gossip*, 184n11, 200–1n2

Spenser, Edmund, 70

Spies, 132, 143, 176; audience as, 105; Cromwell's use of, 5; state, 48, 209n14; ubiquity of, 186n4

Spying, 21, 69, 72, 105, 121, 126, 136, 141, 152, 153, 155
Stallybrass, Peter, 198n21; 'Patriarchal Territories: The Body Enclosed,' 199n30, 207n18; *The Politics and Poetics of Transgression*, 198n27; *Staging the Renaissance*, 194n3, 199n34
Staple of News, The, 211n39
Stephanson, Raymond, 197n18
Stevens, G.A., 211n35
Stone, Lawrence, 196n13
Stuart, Lady Arbella, 195n8
Stuart, Sir Francis, 97
Sweeney, John Gordon, 22; *Jonson and the Psychology of the Public Theater*, 185n16, 193n20, 202n13, 208n6; 'Volpone and the Theater of Self-Interest,' 193n20

Tacitus, *Annals*, 45; Jonson on, 190n27; *Opera quae exstant*, 189n26; source for *Sejanus*, 152
Teague, Frances: *The Curious History of 'Bartholomew Fair*,' 208n5
Tefft, Stanton, 22, 183n10; *Secrecy: A Cross-Cultural Perspective*, 183n8, 185n24, 201n8
Tennenhouse, Leonard, 183n10; *Power on Display*, 201n3
Thomas, Keith, 16; *Religion and the Decline of Magic*, 182n3
Tillyard, E.M.W.: *The Elizabethan World Picture*, 180n5
Timber or Discoveries, 64, 118, 170
Topcliffe, Richard, 5
Tourneur, Cyril, 185n21
Tribble, Evelyn B.: *Margins and Marginality*, 189-90n26
Tricomi, Albert H.: *Anticourt Drama in England, 1603-1642*, 180n3, 180n6, 187n15, 205n7
Trilling, Lionel: *Sincerity and Authenticity*, 196n13
Tulip, James: 'Comedy as Equivocation: An Approach to the Reference of *Volpone*,' 191n2

Underdown, David, 84, 198n24; *Revel, Riot, and Rebellion*, 195n11, 196n12; 'The Taming of the Scold,' 195n11

Vickers, Nancy J., 47; 'Diana Described: Scattered Woman and Scattered Rhyme,' 188n22
Volpone, or The Fox, 7, 22, 23, 89, 110, 176; conspiracy in, 55, 57, 59, 63, 64, 67, 68, 69, 70, 74, 107, 175, 180n2; disguise in, 192n7; humour in, 77, 193n16; interpretation and, 207n2; intrigue in, 12; Jonson's self-censorship and, 48; secrecy and, 63, 74, 76, 191n2; secrecy and power in, 57, 107; significance of secrecy-revelation in, 172; spying in, 5, 13, 68; structure of, 193n15; women in, limited power of, 55

Waddington, Raymond B.: 'The Iconography of Silence in Chapman's Hercules,' 199n31
Waith, Eugene, M.: *The Herculean Hero in Marlowe, Chapman, Shakespeare and Dryden*, 205n9
Waller, Edmund: 'Go Lovely Rose,' 202n14
Walsingham, Sir Francis: spies and, 5, 179, 192n2

Watson, Robert N.: *Ben Jonson's Parodic Strategy*, 206n10, 208n8
Wayne, Don E., 183n10
Webster, John, 13, 182n20, 190n29; *The Duchess of Malfi*, secrecy in, 13; *The White Devil*, secrecy in, 20
Weimann, Robert, 155, 198n21; *Shakespeare and the Popular Tradition in the Theater*, 184n12, 209n21
Whetstone, George: *A Mirour for Magestrates of Cyties*, 153-4, 209n15
Whigham, Frank, 20-21; 'Sexual and Social Mobility in *The Duchess of Malfi*,' 183n11
White, Allon: *The Politics and Poetics of Transgression*, 198n27
Whitefriars, 97, 99, 100, 101, 175, 199n35
Whitney, Geoffrey: in *A Choice of Emblemes*, 183n7
Wilde, Oscar, 15, 18
Wilkes, G.A., 207n18
Williams, George Walton, 184n13
Wilson, Edmund: 'Morose Ben Jonson,' 113-14; *The Triple Thinkers*, 203n21
Wilson, Grant Stanley, 191n2

Wiltenburg, Robert: *Ben Jonson and Self-Love*, 192n8
Winstanley, Gerrard, 201n9
Winwood, Ralph, 187n12
Witchcraft, fear of, 15; *see also under* Secrecy, Sexuality
Womack, Peter: *Ben Jonson*, 203n22
Women: conspiracy and, 131, 174; demonization of, 86; disguise and, 174; function of in Jonson, 87; independence of, 196n12; marginalization of, 186n6; power of, 22; secrecy and, 18, 83, 84, 174; silence and, 95-6, 174; silencing of, 54, 196n11, 199n30; speech among, 84
Woodbridge, Linda: *True Rites and Maimed Rites*, 198n21, 198n26
Wotton, Sir Henry, 193n12
Wright, Thomas, 203-4n31; *The Passions of the Minde in Generall*, 191n1
Wrightson, Keith: *English Society, 1580-1680*, 196n13

Yates, Frances: 'The Hermetic Tradition in Renaissance Science,' 183n9
Yeats, W.B., 46